DO NOT REMOVE
CARDS FROM POCKET

The Cure for Death by Lightning

The Cure for
Death by Lightning

Gail Anderson-Dargatz

A MARC JAFFE BOOK
Houghton Mifflin Company
BOSTON   NEW YORK   1996

For information about this and other Houghton Mifflin
trade and reference books and multimedia products, visit The
Bookstore at Houghton Mifflin on the World Wide Web at
http://www.hmco.com/trade/.

Library of Congress Cataloging-in-Publication Data

Anderson-Dargatz, Gail,
    The cure for death by lightning / Gail Anderson-Dargatz.
    p. cm.
    "A Marc Jaffe book."
    ISBN 0-395-77184-6
    I. Title.
    PR9199.3.A49C87 1996
    813'.54—dc20   95-4881   CIP

Book design by Anne Chalmers

Printed in the United States of America

QUM 10 9 8 7 6 5 4 3 2 1

Two stories taken from earlier versions of this novel were pre-
viously published. "The Girl with the Bell Necklace" won first
prize in the 1993 Canadian Broadcasting Corporation's literary
competition and was subsequently dramatized for "The Arts
Tonight," a CBC radio program, and published in the antholo-
gy Frictions II, edited by Rhea Tregebov. "When One Coyote
Howls" was published in the Malahat Review, volume 104.

FOR FRANCES HICKLING

ACKNOWLEDGMENTS

Many people offered encouragement, suggestions, and practical help as I wrote this book. I thank Jack Hodgins, Denise Bukowski, Floyd Anderson-Dargatz, Bill Chalmers, Allen Looy, and Dagmar Round. I especially thank Irene Anderson and Eric Anderson for answering my many questions, and the First Nations Canadians and pioneer women, including my own grandmother, Elizabeth Ann Humphrey, whose recipes and remedies inspired those found in this book.

The Cure for Death by Lightning

THE CURE for death by lightning was handwritten in thick, messy blue ink in my mother's scrapbook, under the recipe for my father's favorite oatcakes:

Dunk the dead by lightning in a cold water bath for two hours and if still dead, add vinegar and soak for an hour more.

Beside this, some time later, my mother had written *Ha! Ha!* in black ink. The same page contained a tortoiseshell butterfly, pressed flat beside the cure for death so the wings left smudges of burgundy and blue on the back of the previous page. The bottom of one wing was torn away. My mother said that she'd caught the butterfly and pressed it between the pages of her scrapbook because of this torn wing. "Wonderful," she told me. "That it could still fly. It's a reminder to keep going."

The scrapbook sat on my mother's rocking chair next to the black kitchen stove and was hers just as the rocking chair was hers. I didn't sit in her chair or touch her scrapbook, at least not when she was in the room. My mother knew where to find a particular recipe or remedy by the page it was written on, because every page was different. She compiled the scrapbook during the Depression and into the Second World War when paper was at first expensive and then impossible to buy, so she copied her recipes on the backs of letters, scraps of wallpaper, bags, and brown wrapping, and on paper she made herself from the pulp of vegetables and flowers. The cover was red, one of the few bits of red my father allowed in the house, cut from the cardboard of a box of crackers. The book was swollen from years of entries. Pages were dusted with flour, stained with spots of tea, and warped from moisture. Each page had its own scent: almond extract or vanilla, butter or flour, the petals of the rose it was made from, or my mother's perfume, Lily of the Valley.

My mother didn't keep the book as a diary. If she kept a diary at all, I never found it. But she wrote brief thoughts along the margins or at the bottom of a page, as footnotes to the recipes and remedies, the cartoons and clippings — footnotes to the events of the day. She was always adding a new page, and it didn't matter how many times I stole the scrapbook from her chair and pilfered my few minutes with it, there was always some new entry or something I'd missed.

I still have my mother's scrapbook. It sits inside the trunk that was her hope chest. I sometimes take out the scrapbook and sit with it at my kitchen table, by the stove that is electric and white. Even now I find new entries in the scrapbook, things I've never seen before, as if my mother still sits each morning before I wake and copies a recipe, or adds a new page made from the pulp of scarlet flax.

My name is Beth Weeks. My story takes place in the midst of the Second World War, the year I turned fifteen, the year the world fell apart and began to come together again. Much of it will be hard to believe, I know. But the evidence for everything I'm about to tell you is there, in the pages of my mother's scrapbook, in the clippings describing the bear attacks and the Swede's barn fire and the children gone missing on the reserve, in the recipe for pound cake I made the night they took my father away, and in the funeral notices of my classmate Sarah Kemp and the others. The scrapbook was my mother's way of setting down the days so they wouldn't be forgotten. This story is my way. No one can tell me these events didn't happen, or that it was all a girl's fantasy. The reminders are there, in that scrapbook, and I remember them all.

1

WHEN IT CAME LOOKING for me I was in the hollow stump by Turtle Creek at the spot where the deep pool was hidden by low hanging bushes, where the fishing was the very best and only my brother and I figured we knew of it. Now, in spring, the stump blossomed purple and yellow violets so profusely that it became something holy and worth pondering. Come fall, the stump was flagrantly, shamefully red in a coat of dying leaves from the surrounding trees. This was my stump, where I stored my few illicit treasures: the lipstick my mother smuggled home for me in a bag of rice; the scrap of red velvet that Bertha Moses tucked in my pocket as she left the house on the day of my fifteenth birthday; the violet perfume I received as my gift at the Christmas pageant the year before; and the bottle of clear nail polish my father threw into the manure pile after he caught me using it behind the house, the bottle I had salvaged, washed, and spirited away.

I was in there, hiding, my knees up to my nose, listening to the sound of it rushing, crashing through the bush, coming for me. A cobweb stretched over my face, an ant roamed over the valleys in my skirt, spiders invaded my hair, and an itch started on my nose and traveled to my arm, but I stayed still. I closed my eyes and willed it away, and after a while the sound of crashing did move off. It became nothing but wind playing tricks on me, a deer I scared up with my own fear.

I waited, listening, until my leg cramped up, then climbed from the stump and wiped off my skirt. The weight of my body had pushed the perfume bottle and lipstick into the earth. I brushed off the scrap of velvet, smoothed it across my face, and rubbed it down the inside of my bare leg. I imagined I was touched that way, by a city man — no farmer's hands were like velvet — a man who worked in an office with clean papers, whose polished heels clicked along the pavement, and whose hands never dug into manure.

I opened the bottle of violets and sniffed them, took off my rubber boots and socks and touched a little perfume to the cracked soles of my feet where my father wouldn't have a chance to smell anything sweet after I'd done with chores. I rolled up my sleeves and applied a blush of red lipstick to the inside crook of my arm, then kissed those secret lips. I leaned against the stump with my skirt hiked up and my bare legs open like a whore and wished for nylons and red shoes, a pretty dress for dancing. Once the weather warmed up I went around barelegged most of the time. Now, with the war on, silk, like all good things, was rationed and wouldn't be wasted on a girl my age. Nylons were expensive and hard to get. Even my mother didn't own a pair of nylons. I looked out over the creek at the sun shining off the sprouting leaves and breathed in the too sweet scent of my feet. The perfume had gone a little bad, maybe, from all that time in the stump, but it was my perfume on my feet and my father didn't know a thing about it. After a while I hid away my little bottles and the red velvet as soft as a city man's skin, washed the perfume from my hands in the water, and followed the creek home.

Turtle Creek was a shallow, fast-moving stream, except for the pool at the hollow stump, and was filled with large smooth stones that I could skip across without getting my feet wet. Where it wound through our property, the stream was overhung with hemlock, alder, and pussy willow, and framed with watercress and forget-me-not. Violets and wild strawberries were slow-moving scavengers licking up everything dead along the creek shore: fallen trees, the mess of dead leaves turning to dirt, and the heap that, the summer before, had been a dead squirrel possessed by squirming white maggots.

I heard it again in the bush, where the path split from the creek and headed back to the farm. I held my breath and listened. It could be anything: a man like the ones my mother's friend Mrs. Bell warned of, who would catch a girl in the bush and do unspeakable things to her.

Or a bear gone crazy, like the bear that had killed Sarah Kemp just that week, or like the one that attacked our sheep camp in June of the year before.

It was after that bear attack that my father sold the sheep and went into dairy cows. We had spent the late spring and much of the summer living out of a tent on Adams Plateau or Queest Mountain, herding sheep from one grazing area to the next. We all slept together — my mother, father, Daniel, and myself — in a big stiff canvas tent, on bedrolls of canvas over balsam fir boughs. The tent, our clothes, and our hair were fragrant with balsam for the whole summer. The night the grizzly attacked our camp, the dogs woke us, and we left the tent together as a continuous black shadow. We were already dressed because on the mountain we slept in the clothes we spent our days in. Each of us, except my mother, had a gun in hand. It was a clear night with a quarter moon that reflected off the backs of the sheep.

The sheep were running. In their midst a great bear rose up on its hind legs, roaring and swatting. The sheepdogs were on him, but the bear paid them little mind. As my father aimed his rifle and tried to call back the dogs, the grizzly wrapped his huge jaws around the head of a full-grown ewe and shook her from side to side as a coyote shakes his prey. My father fired, and fired again, missing both times. The grizzly dropped the ewe and charged, first at the dogs and then at us.

"Oh Jesus," said my father. "Get down! Get down!"

My mother and father and Dan flung themselves to the ground, but I lost my head and ran back towards the tent and the great black shape chased me, snuffing and rank. I tripped and fell. My brother and father fired in the air, afraid of aiming in the dark and hitting me, but out of panic I aimed from the ground, where I had fallen, and fired at the bear. It was foolish because the little rifle I had would only annoy a monster that size. Yet I know I hit the bear because he howled, horribly, and ran off into the bush behind the tent, pursued by the dogs.

My father was the first to reach me. He fell to his knees beside me and took my shoulders up in his arms and all but shook me in panic. "You all right?" he said. "You all right?"

"I got him," I said.

"Sure you got him," he said.

My father left me to my mother's care and called off the dogs and told Dan and me to stay put with Mum and to keep a sharp eye out. He marched through the white ghosts in the bedding ground and into black.

Dan and I fiddled with our guns as we waited, turning and aiming at every rustle we heard in the bush.

"That was stupid," said Dan. "We would have had it."

"I got it," I said. "I know I did."

"With that gun, all it's got is a scratch."

"Well, if I had a better rifle, that bear would be dead."

"You can't hit nothing."

"Enough," said my mother. "Stay sharp."

One shot sounded that made us all stand taller. Then my father came back the way he'd left, across the bedding grounds behind the tent, a black shadow against all those white sheep. My mother lifted the lantern to him. He was shaking and covered in bits of undergrowth and had strange clawlike scratches down each side of his face. Against the darkness his eyes looked big and crazy before he held his hand up against the light.

My mother lowered the lantern. "John, what's happened?" she said.

My father didn't acknowledge her, didn't answer. He stumbled around in front of the tent for a time, and I watched him at it, growing scared. Dan took him by the arm and tried to get him to sit down on a stump, but he pulled away.

"Did you get him?" Dan said.

"I don't know," said my father. "So dark. Something came after me. I shot it. I think I shot it."

We watched for the grizzly all that night, but he didn't return. The next day Dan and my father tracked the bear's trail of blood for three miles to a patch of thick bush before giving up. There were too many stories of bears ambushing hunters for them to push farther. We never found the body of the bear, but then we never would. Bears bury their dead, just as they bury their kill.

The grizzly attack on our camp shook us all. My mother wouldn't let us out of her sight. My brother woke shouting. My father went silent and moody and sat around the camp with his gun over his knees eating whole legs of lamb, whole pots of stew, at a time. We watched him eat, amazed. A week after the grizzly attack, my father drove his entire flock of Corriedales to Salmon Arm, loaded them on a freight for Vancouver, and sold the dogs to a sheep trader named Currie. A month later my father went back to Currie and bought a handful of knot-headed, fence-breaking, black-faced Suffolk from him because he couldn't think well of himself without sheep and because they were going for next to nothing. When he bought ten Jersey cows from Ferguson to begin his dairy, he put an end to those glorious summers we spent wandering the mountains and began, wholeheartedly, his career of unhappiness.

I was fourteen last summer when the bear attacked, and so a lifetime of those summers on Adam's Plateau, Hunter's Range, and Queest had firmly fixed the need in my body to wander. Although I now hiked only within the hilly range that encompassed Turtle Valley, and though I now took my gun almost every time I left the house, I still had reason to fear, even here, by Turtle Creek. Sarah Kemp, who'd been killed by a bear that week, was a girl my age. I'd be going to her funeral in a day. So it was that with every rustle in the undergrowth my body tensed, with every crack in the bush I listened. But this time, this time, the sound of something following became a shushing through the grass, my fear at play. I let out my breath and kept on my way, back home.

The sky over the farm was ablaze with birds. Seagulls and crows jabbered and cawed over the barn, the manure pile, the stack of lumber and fence posts, and the heap of rocks that marked the graves of the homesteaders' children. Starlings chattered on the poplar that grew through the front end of my father's old Ford truck. Barn swallows darted between the handful of ewes in the orchard pasture that bordered on the Swede's property, and over the lake of violet flax past the house. They looped up and formed a circle in the sky for an instant, before diving down for insects between the bodies of the sheep. Swallows zoomed over the heads of my father, my brother, and our hired men, Dennis and Filthy Billy, as they coiled alfalfa hay into haycocks, by hand, with pitchforks. The starlings in the poplar flew up in a great breath, then landed on the roof of the house, enraging the rooster into crowing, and sending the little black lizards that lived around the yard scuttling into hiding. The chatter of birds was deafening, and because of them, I knew we had guests.

2

BERTHA MOSES and her daughters and her daughters' daughters were standing or sitting around the kitchen table drinking coffee left from breakfast. One of the daughters was ladling hot water from the reservoir on the cast-iron stove into the coffeepot. I'd polished the woodstove with stove black the day before to protect it from rusting, and it shone as black as the daughters' hair. I backed out the screen door and searched around the yard for my mother. When I found her in the barn, shoveling out the stalls, I called, "Mrs. Moses and her family are here," and went back to the house to set out more cups and spoons, cream, precious sugar, and a plate of oatcakes. Bertha Moses and her family were walking from the reserve into town — when they went to town they often stopped at our house on their way.

My mother entered the kitchen wiping her hands on her skirt. She wore her milking clothes, a brown housedress and gum boots, and her long, long hair was tucked away in a blue kerchief, so you'd think she had no hair at all. She smelled sour from the dairy.

"Bertha," she said. "Good to see you."

Bertha Moses dressed altogether differently from my mother. She had salt-and-pepper hair done up in a single braid that lay down the back of her red dress, and her sleeves were scandalously rolled to the elbow. She wore black stockings and moccasins decorated with porcupine quills and embroidery, strings and strings of brightly colored beads, and even now — out visiting — a pink apron filled with tobacco and papers and matches, bits of fabric, threads and beads, and a few dirty, crumpled dollar notes.

Nevertheless Bertha and my mother had a good deal in common. My mother had driven an ambulance and nursed during the First World War, and, until my father's jealous rages had flared up over the last year, she'd been called on by white farmers in the valley to nurse away simple ailments. Bertha was a midwife for women on the reserve and for white women too, farmwomen who lived in the valley. Bertha had known me before I'd known myself. She'd attended my mother at my birth, a potentially difficult birth because my mother was forty. Bertha wasn't that much older, but the deference her daughters treated her with and the authority she carried in her walk made her seem much older. She had lost her status as a Treaty Indian at fourteen when she'd married an elderly white man named Watson who owned a farm next to the Turtle Creek Reserve. She had three daughters by him. After Watson died of simple old age and was buried in the reserve graveyard when Bertha wasn't yet twenty, Bertha married an Indian man who'd taken the white name Moses. They lived on the Watson property, Bertha's property. A year into their marriage, Moses shot himself accidentally as he climbed over a fence with a gun, and died a half mile from home of blood loss, but not before he'd fathered a son Bertha would name Henry.

Now Henry, too, was dead and Bertha had no husband and no son. Her house was a house of women. One of the daughters' daughters was pregnant, another had webbed fingers, and some of the younger girls had blue or green eyes inherited from white fathers, farmhands likely. Each girl's hair was black, oiled with bear grease so it shone, and tied back with all manner of barrettes and ribbons. The daughter with webbed fingers wore a bolero jacket and skirt skillfully fashioned from an edge-to-edge coat. The sewing was Bertha's handiwork; with the war on and fabric hard to come by, Bertha was making a good living remaking new ladies' garments from old. Someone wore violet-scented talc. One of the daughters' daughters wore boys' jeans and a western shirt that stretched a little at the buttons across her breasts. She was my age and she wore lipstick and a necklace of bells strung together. I coveted that necklace. She saw me looking at it and jingled it, and the room filled with tinkling notes that lit up everyone's face. She lifted the necklace a little so light reflected from the bells onto my own face. I squinted and grinned at her. The room grew womanly.

"He any better?" said Bertha.

"No," said my mother.

They were speaking of my father, of course, as they always did now, on these visits. A head injury from the Great War had left my father sensitive to sound and bright lights and he had sometimes been irritable and demanding. But I had never really feared him, not until the bear attacked the camp the spring before. Now I feared his temper in public. I feared finding myself alone with him.

In the spring of 1941, not a month after the bear attacked our camp, my father had waltzed into the general store and punched Morley Boulee, the teacher's husband. The Fergusons, who had sold us our dairy herd, were close friends of Morley Boulee, and a week after my father hit Boulee, Mrs. Ferguson had caught me on the street in front of Bouchard and Belcham's general store and told me I had no right to hold my head up and walk that cocky, not with a father like the one I had, no right at all. I had watched her lips telling me what my father had done. She had one crooked bottom tooth, so tea-stained that it appeared, at first, to be gold.

"All Morley Boulee did was tip his hat to your mother, tip his hat! A neighborly thing! And your father yelled at your mother, right there, in the store, how she'd been flirting with him, seeing him on the sly. Morley Boulee, we're talking here! What would he want with a farmer's wife when he's got the schoolteacher? Morley stepped in, to defend your mother. He had to! And your father knocked him over, sent the stocking rack flying! What kind of father you got? Don't you hold your head up to me! Hoarders!"

When my father knocked over Morley Boulee and the rack of silk stockings, he'd knocked over our good name. In the year that followed, things went from bad to worse. Now the only visitors we got were the gloomy Mrs. Bell and Bertha Moses and her family.

My mother poured Bertha and herself more coffee and handed me the pot. I went around to the other women to top up their cups.

"I've been thinking maybe his blood's weak," said Bertha. "That's why he eats so much."

"Oh, I don't think he's anemic," said my mother. "That would make him tired, not like he is. He doesn't stop. He doesn't sleep through the night anymore. He only takes naps. I don't know what it is. For all the food he eats he doesn't gain weight."

My mother stood and offered the plate of cakes around. The daughter with the webbed fingers held her hand up to the window and watched the strange shadow it left on the floor. She saw me staring and tucked both hands into the pockets of her dress.

Bertha contemplated her coffee cup for a time and then asked my mother, "You going to the Kemp girl's funeral?"

"I guess the whole town will be going. A terrible thing. It's no way for a girl to die."

Bertha Moses nodded slowly for a long time. Fear slipped up on me briefly, even though I knew Morley Boulee, the man my father had punched, had shot the crazy bear who was supposed to have done the killing.

The girl with the necklace put her hand to her mouth as if she wanted to say something, but she kept quiet. I took the coffeepot around again, then set it back down on the stove and watched through the window as the Swede and his team of horses thundered down Blood Road. He was near the swamps at the far end of the fields and was heading towards us, chased by a red tide of dust. The Swede, a man named Johansson, drove a fine buggy with a fold-down top and a curved front pulled by a smart sorrel he called Old Mare, though she had wings on her hooves. Johansson was a short round-faced man with a red complexion, a white bristly mustache, and eyes so blue you had to look at him twice to believe the color. He kept the fact that he was almost completely bald under a wide-brimmed, greasy felt hat that he almost never took off, even in my mother's presence. The Swede had a son named Jack, a skinny, skittish man with his father's brilliant blue eyes. Everyone knew Jack was half-crazy, bushed. Jack had taken to living all by himself in a squatter's cabin on Bald Mountain after an argument with his father, and some time later the Indians began calling him Coyote Jack. He had a way of sliding in and out of shadows, disappearing and reappearing just like a coyote.

The conversation stopped for a moment as everyone in the kitchen listened to the Swede and his horses thunder by.

"The government's talking about rounding up the wild horses," said

Bertha. "They're going to slaughter them, send the meat over to the war. They're talking about giving farmers on the reserve money to round them up."

On weekends when I wasn't working on the farm, and sometimes after school, I hiked up to the top of Bald Mountain, where Blood Road pushed up into a blind hill before washing down into the next valley, and watched the horses graze the flat lands of the reserve below. The plain was named for them, Horse Meadows. Sometimes I clapped and the wind carried the sound down onto the plain. The wild horses took off in a group, swooping across the prairie exactly like a flock of birds taking off into the air. The horses belonged to no one and wintered as the deer did, on what they could find; they often ate off the stores of farmers' hay. Several families on the reserve made their living by capturing the wild horses, fattening them up, breaking them, and selling them.

"I think it's a foolish idea," said Bertha Moses. "Once those horses are gone, then what?"

"There's all those people starving in Europe," said my mother. "They must be fed."

"There's people starving right here," said Bertha Moses. She tapped the table with her finger. My mother said nothing and we spent a long silence listening to the crowing rooster, the cackling chickens, and the songs of many birds. The women shuffled and looked around and the room began to feel cramped. The woodstove became too hot, and my mother's prize Hosier cupboard towered over the kitchen table and the women standing around it. I leaned against this cupboard because Bertha's family had taken up every chair and stood around the room besides. No one else in the valley had anything like my mother's cupboard. It had a built-in flour container with a sifter, a pull-out cutting board and shelf, a sugar bin, a porcelain counter, and drawers above and below for pots and tins and foodstuffs. The very top shelf was stocked with the remedies for illness: honey and horehound candy wrapped in cheesecloth and tucked in a Nabob tea tin, a can of hot dry mustard ready to mix with flour and water for the chest of whoever got the cough this year, likely all of us; a pile of life-preserving flannel with which to apply the mustard paste and goose grease; black currant jam to make tea for colds; brown sugar to sprinkle over hot coals and then hold under boils, and cedar slivers, to break the infection; soda to mix with water, for stomach ailments.

The silence stretched on, filled with the complaints of chickens. I played with the little bird on the lid of the sugar bowl on the counter. My mother's best teaspoons were fastened on clips that ringed the bowl. Our everyday teaspoons were scattered over the white oilcloth on the table, leaving brown pools where the women of Bertha's household had placed them after stirring their coffee.

The girl with the bell necklace looked at me, then smiled at the floor. She drew circles on the floor with her bare feet. I grew shy and looked out the kitchen window at the woodshed and the blue lake of flowering flax. Beyond the flax, in the field of alfalfa, the three figures of my brother Dan, Dennis, and Filthy Billy labored away, shimmering in the heat. I strained to see my father and when I couldn't I grew uneasy.

I pushed myself away from the cupboard and filled a plate with the last of the oatcakes as my mother told the story of how my father tried to fool the hired help, Dennis and Filthy Billy, who were both Bertha's grandsons. My father hired older Indian boys who ran away from the residential school. He said he was doing them a favor, but the truth of it was that almost all the young men in the valley, white or Indian, had enlisted and those who hadn't had taken factory jobs in the cities. Now, with the war on, there was no shortage of jobs. The only men left were the native boys who hadn't yet enlisted or the old bachelors who couldn't be worked hard. Even before the war, my father hired Indian boys because they worked for cheap and didn't talk back unless they got drunk. If they got drunk, my father fired them.

"John brought home a porcupine yesterday," my mother told Bertha. "He skinned it, cleaned it, and said, 'It's chicken.' I said, 'That's not chicken.' He said, 'I said it's chicken, so it's chicken.' I said, 'Fine, it's chicken,' and cooked it as if it were chicken. Dennis and Filthy Billy come in for dinner, and John says, 'Maudie cooked chicken for dinner.' Everyone helps themselves, and then Dennis whispers, 'Porcie,' and Filthy Billy whispers, 'Porcie.'"

Everyone laughed because they knew what my father had become. The laughter became huge and shook the house and hid the sound of my father's boots on the porch. The screen door slammed shut and my father was there in the kitchen, a giant over us, dressed in the denim pants and jacket that were his field clothes, and his puttees from the Great War. His boots smelled bad, of dog shit.

"What's this about?" said my father. "What are you laughing at?" There was a pause. One of Bertha's daughters said, "Nothing."

My father pushed me out of his way and stood over Bertha Moses. Bertha became an old woman in my father's shadow. He sucked the air from her cheeks and made her eyes dull. "You told Dennis not to work," he said.

My mother said, "John," but he just stood there with his hands on his hips and his feet planted as if nothing could move him. Bertha Moses looked at my mother, then up at my father, and we all listened for a while to the noisy birds. Then Bertha stood and her daughters stood behind her. The sound of their chairs scraping against the floor drowned the birdsong and made my father appear smaller, as if he were an ordinary man. He held his forehead at the sound, flinched at it. The women's combined shadows pushed my father's shadow against the wall.

"I said he deserves more for the work he does," said Bertha. "I said he doesn't have to work into the night."

"You don't know nothing," said my father.

"There's a war on," said Bertha. "Dennis doesn't have to work for you. Billy neither."

"They'll get no better work."

"You hire our boys because they don't know how to ask for what they're worth," she said. "You treat them as if they were slaves."

"Shut up."

"They're not slaves."

"Get out of my house!" said my father.

The women moved forward and surrounded him. Bertha Moses's shadow gripped my father's shadow around the throat, forcing blood into his face. He began to shake and his face grew redder and redder until I thought he might explode. He stepped back through the women and pushed open the screen door.

"You get out of here," he said, and fled from the house.

My mother looked at her shoes. Bertha sighed.

"We should be going," said Bertha Moses.

"Yes," said one of the daughters, and the women made the motions of leaving.

"It was good to have you," said my mother.

The daughters and the daughters' daughters filed out the door, and the girl with the bells smiled and jingled her necklace as she went by. Each of her eyes was a different color, one blue and one green. She was a half-breed, then. Bertha stayed behind.

"Come again," said my mother. "Please. He won't remember. He gets angry and it washes away."

She tapped her forehead in the place where there was steel, not bone, in my father's forehead, where a scar marked his injury from the Great War. During that war my father had been running through a graveyard when the shells hit and buried him alive among the corpses. A second round of shells hit, at once unburying him and saving his life, and wounding him with shrapnel. Bertha knew this story, as everyone did.

"No," said Bertha. "I don't think it's that. I think what's got hold of Coyote Jack's got hold of your John."

When my mother laughed and looked puzzled, Bertha Moses took my mother's hand in both of her own. She glanced at her daughters waiting by the flower bed and lowered her voice. "John didn't turn until that bear attacked. You said so yourself. Something got him in the bush. You be careful. You and the girl."

But then she smiled, as if it were all a joke, and winked at me so her face crinkled up to nothing. She took a pinch of tobacco from a pouch in her apron pocket and rolled a skinny cigarette as she walked down the path to where the women waited. One of the daughters, a woman with a large strawberry birthmark on her cheek, lit a match on the side of her shoe and held it up to Bertha's cigarette. I followed the women a little way down Blood Road; the birds followed them too, attracted to their glittering jewelry and bright ribbons. Purple swallows zoomed around them. Bertha Moses and her daughters and her daughters' daughters sang hymns of praise all the way into town.

I STOKED the fire in the kitchen stove, cleared the cups from the table, and scrubbed the sticky spots of evil on the oilcloth where Bertha Moses and her daughters had left their coffee spoons. Mrs. Bell said all dirt was evil, and it was a Christian woman's duty to scrub away evil and never turn her back on it. Evil was what made you sick. Evil was what crept into your night dreams and made a sinner of you. A dirty house was an evil house, and a woman must guard against the evil men brought into the house on their boots. Mrs. Bell was the one town visitor we got those days, so what did I know? I scrubbed the evil from the oilcloth and from beneath the water tub in which we washed dishes; dusted it from the kitchen chairs, the gun cupboard, the parlor table, and from the family photographs sitting on the buffet; and swept it from the floor under the coat hooks where my father left his boots.

There were no photographs on the buffet of my brother and me, only pictures of my mother's family and the one photograph of my mother and father, taken on the day of their engagement. I knew little of my father's history, other than that his mother had died giving birth to him and that he had worked from the time he was ten until he was fifteen leading the pack ponies down into the black mouth of the mine. The ponies knew enough to come back up by themselves, hauling rock, but needed convincing to go back down again. There was a photograph of my mother with her parents, taken during the Great War. My mother wore a nurse's uniform and stood very tall over her own tiny mother. My grandmother was dressed in dark and lacy Victorian garb and looked very old and tired, but my grandfather, an engineer, looked quite dapper. He was smiling and had his hand around my mother's waist. Neither my grandmother nor my mother was smiling. About the time my mother became a woman, my grandmother took sick with an unexplained series of niggling illnesses, stomach complaints and headaches, weakness and malaise. My mother became the woman of the house then, making the meals and tending her mother and looking after her two younger sisters. As my grandmother became increasingly bedridden, my mother also became her father's escort to plays and concerts. She became his favorite of the three daughters. He bought her silk stockings, boxes of candy, and called her dear. There were two photographs of my mother's sisters: Aunt Lou, who sent Christmas packages each year from England, and Aunt Amy, who lived with her pastor husband in Australia. I had never met either of them, and my grandparents were long dead. When the great fire of polio still raged over Australia, my mother carried Aunt Amy's letters into the house in the manner I'd seen her carry out dead rats. She put the letters in the roasting pan and into the hot oven for a time, not so long that the letters burned, but long enough to kill the polio spirit that might have lived in them. When we were very young children, it was my mother's worst fear that she might put Dan or me to bed healthy only to have one of us awaken with a useless arm or leg that we could no more command than we could command a chair to dance. Infantile paralysis was what they called it then, and next to nothing could be done for it, though people believed in all manner of cures. The things you could believe then . . . that heating up a letter from the bottom of the world would stop a deadly bug from entering your house. If you could believe that, you could believe in ghosts. My mother did that too.

That other photo on the buffet, the one of my mother and father, was the one I dusted longer and gazed into with a kind of wonderment because all my history and all my future were captured in that moment. My mother was dressed in the drab nurse's outfit she wore to drive the horse-drawn ambulances during the war. My father wore his army uniform and the same puttees he now wound around his legs to do farm chores. In the photograph, his head was still bandaged. They had met when my mother drove my father from one London hospital to another. How my mother came to visit him as he lay for months in that hospital, I never knew. As the eldest daughter, my mother had nursed my ailing grandmother right up until the week of her own wedding, so perhaps she was at her strongest, at her most sure serving sickness. Later I would come to believe that she was.

I put down the photograph of my mother and father, went back into the kitchen, and took up my mother's scrapbook. There was a new page in it, made from brown wrapping, onto which she had glued Sarah Kemp's funeral notice from that week's newspaper. Beside the notice, my mother had added a story warning of bear attacks and an increase in livestock loss to coyotes. Next to this my mother had written my name, "Beth," in bold lettering, followed by an exclamation mark.

I slapped the scrapbook shut, convinced that my mother knew I peeked at it and that she was trying to lecture me in this sneaky way about walking alone in the bush. I placed the scrapbook as it had been, sitting on the rocker, and guiltily, angrily, I wiped down the oilcloth on the kitchen table all over again and washed all the spoons and cups.

Bertha's visit had set the day back; she'd come at a time when there were chores to be done and, as if she didn't know it, she and her family had waltzed themselves into the house, drunk our coffee, and wasted the time away with talk. Now chores weren't done and supper would be late and there'd be hell to pay when my father came in from the fields. Earlier, before I had started to clean up, my mother had grumbled all these things under her breath to her own mother, who'd been dead twenty years but was still watching over her, as she caught up a chicken in the coop, then killed it, cleaned it, and sat it in a bucket of cold water in the pantry. Then she'd saddled up the little mare, Cherry, and taken her up to the benchland to bring down the cows while I'd cleaned house. There'd been a coyote in the chicken house; coyote tracks and bloodied feathers were all over. The chickens were panicked, chasing each other in circles as if one of them had a worm. The rooster didn't have any rooster left in him. Most times he leapt up and showed his spurs to any passing shadow, but now he hid in a corner, nursing a wing. Lord knows how a coyote got in the coop, but he did, and how many he got was anybody's guess; there's no counting in a coop full of chickens.

My mother had carried the chicken, our supper, by its feet and wing tips so it would calm down before she reached the chopping block behind the house. A chicken that flaps its wings flaps itself into panic, and there's nothing as frustrating as trying to kill a panicked chicken. Mum took up the ax, laid the chicken's head over the edge of the chopping block, and eased the chicken back until its neck was stretched out. She slammed the ax through the chicken's neck into the chopping block, and flung the chicken's body onto the grass in front of the root cellar so it wouldn't flap itself into the mud. The chicken body danced a circle in the grass, spewing blood every which way, and fell on its back. The air left its lungs in a squawk, and the head still lying on the block opened and closed its beak as if trying to claim the noise. I watched the chicken head, waiting to see the point of death, something I was never certain of.

Mum was a master at the art of cleaning a chicken, and if you don't think it's an art, you watch, you just watch Mum heating up the kettle until it's good and hot but not boiling, and pouring the water into a bucket and dunking the chicken into it to loosen the feathers, but only for a few seconds. If the water boils, it burns the chicken skin. If you leave the chicken in the hot water too long, the skin tears when you pull off the feathers. The art is in the motion of it, in taking the bird by the legs and plunging it in the hot water without burning yourself; in swirling the bird around in the bucket, as if cleaning the bucket with the feathers; in grabbing the bird's flight feathers and letting it drop, all in one motion, so the bird's means of escape come off in your hands.

My mother hung the bird on the wash line by one foot, where, earlier in the day, she had hung our underwear out to dry inside pillowcases so they would neither entice nor offend a man who might come into our yard. Her hands flew over that bird, plucking the downy feathers and pin feathers until you'd think it was naked, but it wasn't, not quite. For the chicken's final humiliation, Mum lit a torch of rolled brown paper wrapping from the perpetual fire in the kitchen stove and ran it along the chicken, burning off the fine hairs that remained without burning the skin, heating the loose skin so that even now, in death, it drew back in horror and puckered tight. She pinched the flesh at the wishbone and cut out the crop, then cut the naked bird down by bending and cutting off its feet. The chicken was nothing now but meat. To clean out its insides, she took the bird into the house, laid it on the cutting board, and, with a knife that she sharpened right then and there, she sliced the bird from breast tip to pope's nose. This is the feel of the inside of a creature that was alive just a half hour ago: hot and wet, jelly and snakes, soothing for achy human hands. Cleaning a chicken wouldn't be anything but scrubbing out a particularly messy pot of noodles, if it weren't for the smell. The smell is what stirs the nausea, but the blood lust too. That lust crawls up the back of your neck and plants itself on you, an old beast excited by the smell of warm blood, the smell of coming-on-sick time and warm liver, of something hungry.

Once the cleaning was done, my mother rinsed off the chicken, dropped it in a bucket of the coldest water available, and allowed the chicken to stiffen in the pantry off the kitchen because a chicken that isn't left to die properly isn't worth eating; it's as tough as an old laying hen and has no flavor.

When I'd swept and washed all the evil from the house, I picked the sweet young peas from the garden and sat on the porch and shelled them, popping the end off the pod and running my thumb down the row of peas to loosen them. Peas on the vine are designed to fool you. Go down a row of peas once and you won't see a pod. Go down a second time and pea pods appear out of nowhere. Go down a third time, and still more appear, where there were none, as if looking for them creates them. I filled a white ceramic bowl with the sweet green peas I'd imagined into existence and picked a few leaves of mint to boil them with.

Dennis and Filthy Billy came into the house, took their boots off at the door, and sat down at the kitchen table. I didn't look at them, didn't even say hi, and kept my head on what I was doing. I washed my hands in the bowl on the bench by the door, made tea the way my father forbade, from the hot water in the stove reservoir, and put tea and cream and cups down in front of the men. I started cutting up the chicken for frying because that chicken was as stiff as it was going to get that night.

Dennis was also a grandson to Bertha Moses. He was just filling out, cocky as only a man of eighteen can be, and Indian all over. As most young Indian men did then, he wore a cowboy hat, a red plaid flannel shirt, jeans, and cowboy boots, and I suppose like all the young men left on the reserve he hoped to ride the rodeo circuit once the war was over and life could go on. The Indian boys too young to enlist still rode the wild horses for the empty stands at the reserve corral, though there was no one to watch or coach them but the old women and tired young mothers whose men were so far away they could no longer imagine their faces.

Dennis sat with his hands behind his head and watched as I tossed chicken pieces in flour and fried them in the big cast-iron spider pan. His watching made me conscious of how my skirt pulled across my bottom, how my breasts shifted under my blouse. He made me think of my own body and I didn't know what to make of that.

"Chicken again tonight?" said Dennis. "That was good chicken we had last night, eh, Billy?"

I looked up and he winked at me.

"(Shit) I took some of them (fuck) chicken quills home for (shit) Granny's moccasins," said Billy.

Dennis stood up and leaned against the cupboard beside me.

"You going to be my girlfriend?" he said.

I looked past him, past the screen door, out to the barn.

"He's still in the field checking the corn," said Dennis.

I went back to the business of frying chicken.

"How come you're not going to be my girlfriend?" he said.

I gave him a mean look.

"No, really," he said. "You could be my girlfriend."

"You got hands like sandpaper," I said.

Filthy Billy wheezed out a laugh that, for the moment, overpowered the swearing. Unlike Dennis or Dan or any farmhand we'd ever had working for us, Billy cleaned his nails and shaved daily. He wasn't as Indian as Dennis was. He had fairer skin and odd blue-brown eyes. He and Dennis shared Bertha Moses as a grandmother, but Billy's mother was a German woman who'd married Billy's father, Henry Moses, during the Great War. When the German woman came back with Henry to the reserve as a war bride, she panicked at the squalor and their marriage quickly fell apart. She'd worked as a cleaning woman in town until she'd raised the money to leave on a train, but not before she gave birth to Billy. She left him with his father, Henry Moses, on a cold day before Christmas when Billy wasn't a year old. But just as his father had, Henry Moses took his own life, on purpose or by accident. He got drunk on beet wine and fell onto a broken wine bottle and died from lack of blood or too much cold. The Swede found Henry's body in the snow-covered pasture across Turtle Creek, where we grew our timothy hay. Johansson had followed a trail of beet wine spilled in the snow, thinking it was blood and thinking it might be from a deer shot but not dead, or from something else he could cook for supper. He followed the beet wine to the body of Billy's father and to the deeper stains in the snow that were blood, true blood.

"I thought some animal had come eat him," the Swede said when he pulled out this story. "Blood all over and there were coyote tracks all around the body, great circles of tracks. I must have chased the coyotes off with my coming. Off in the bush I could hear them, snuffing and yipping around. Then one howls, and you know how they are. One coyote howling sounds like a bunch of them howling, like a chorus of them."

After the Swede found the body, Bertha Moses raised her grandson, Billy, along with the other casualties of domestic war on the reserve. Billy got the name Filthy because he didn't own his voice. It made him say words no one liked, and the best Filthy Billy could do was make the renegade words come out in a whisper. He ate with us, but rarely said a word during the meal, and when he was done eating, he ran out the door and all the way to the cabin, yelling the words he'd been holding back.

This night he had to hold in those words while my father and brother took off their boots and cleaned their hands in the tub on the bench by the door, while my mother went into the bedroom and changed her sour milk clothes for a clean blue skirt and white blouse, while she brushed her long hair and wound it into a fresh bun, while my brother harassed me, stealing bits of chicken, tugging at my apron strings, while I set a jug of water at my father's place, and put the cooked peas sweating butter, the biscuits, and the fried chicken on the table before him. Billy held his breath and waited with his eyes closed, and his face red. When I set down the chicken, he grabbed a leg bone, my father's favorite, and a couple of buns, and ran out the door, knocking over his chair on the way. My father winced at the sound, held the scar on his head, and yelled at my brother, "Pick that goddamned thing up!" But it was Dennis who picked up the chair and put it right, and I watched him doing it, watched the bones in his big hands. Nobody talked for a long time after that. We listened instead to Billy hooting swear words at the owls.

"Crazy man," said my father. Dennis looked over at my brother and grinned, and Dan grinned back at him. My brother was still in his field denims, and he'd rolled his shirtsleeves to his elbows, exposing his arms, but my father said nothing about it that night. Daniel was a big man, nineteen already, the image of my father (though my father now denied him during arguments, said he was a cuckolded son, no son of his), but with my mother's sweet smile of apology always on his face, even when he tormented my father by not giving in. He had my father's broad, heavy jaw and big features and my father's hands, hands too huge to be believed, made that way by a lifetime of work. For the two years he'd been out of school, Dan had worked full-time on the farm with my father. He was the only farmer's son in the valley who hadn't joined up.

"I don't want that squaw here again," said my father.

"You like Bertha," said Mum.

"I don't like nobody who tells me how to run my farm."

Dennis and Dan exchanged a look and then went back to cleaning their plates with their bread.

"Goddamned Swede tried digging in the fence again," said my father. "You see that?"

My brother grunted.

"We'll fix him," said my father. "Tonight, you hear?"

Dan went on eating, and my mother played nervously with the rim of her plate. Dennis ate with his face close to his plate and looked from me to my father, from my father to me. I pulled my sweater over my breasts and buttoned it.

"Is your suit clean for the funeral?" said my mother.

"Sure," said Dan.

"You spilled food on it at the church supper."

"I wiped it off. It's clean enough."

"And you've got your blue dress," said my mother. "You should set your hair tonight."

"Yes," I said.

"You still have your boots on," she said.

"My feet are cold."

"I brushed down the black suit and put the button back on the white shirt," said my mother.

My father grunted and kept eating. We ate in silence for a while. Past the barn, Filthy Billy swore at the sheep, God, the Devil, and the stars. Bells on the lead cow and sheep rang out as they ran to escape his profane march through their pastures. My father piled yet another helping of chicken and peas on his plate.

"Good chicken," said Dennis. "Almost as good as last night's."

My brother laughed. My father looked up at my brother and at Dennis and went back to refilling his plate.

"You going to the funeral, Dennis?" my mother asked.

"I didn't know her, only to see her," said Dennis.

"Terrible thing," said my mother. "I'm glad they got the bear before it could get anyone else. That could have been you, Beth, if that grizzly reached you last spring. We were so lucky."

"I heard Sarah was all scrapped apart," said my brother. "Her stomach all eaten up."

"Enough," said my mother.

"Bears go for your head first," said Dennis, and his eyes lit up. "They try to rip your head off. Nothing like this one. That must've been one crazy bear."

I put my fork down and pushed my plate away and Dennis grinned at that. Dan leaned across the table and pointed his fork at me.

"They said she was pulled apart from the crotch up," said my brother. "And the tops of her legs were just gone. Nothing. That's what would've happened to you, if that bear got you last spring. They say her breasts were eaten off."

"Shut your filthy mouth," said my father. He pointed his finger at my brother until Dan gave in and looked at his plate. My father went back to eating.

"I heard the bear walked right up to Morley Boulee," said Dennis. "Walked right up like a tame bear and Morley Boulee shot him dead, like it was nothing."

I looked over at my father to see if he'd react to Mr. Boulee's name, but he didn't say anything.

"I killed a bear with a .22 once," said Dennis. "The trick is to get real close, then throw your arms up, like you're challenging the bear. When the bear stands up, on its hind legs, and growls at you, when its mouth is open, that's when you shoot it, through the mouth!"

"What a bunch of baloney," said Dan.

"That's an old Indian way," said Dennis. "Taught to me by my grandfather."

"That's bullshit, is what that is!" said Dan.

"Enough!" said my mother.

Dennis grinned. "Yeah, well, it's a good story, anyway."

"Can you believe it?" said my brother. "Her breasts eaten off!"

"Keep your mouth shut," said my father. "Keep your goddamned mouth shut."

We didn't talk anymore about Sarah Kemp, or anything else. My brother's talk left me without appetite. I played with my peas, arranging them in circles. My mother stood up and began clearing away dishes and I helped. Dennis stood up too and carried his plate and cup to the washtub.

"You don't have to," said my mother.

"Sure I do," he said, and he kissed my mother on the cheek.

My mother and I took a quick look over at the table to see if my father was watching, but he was still hunched over his plate, serving up another spoonful of peas. My brother had leaned back in his chair with his hands behind his head. His eyes were closed. I turned back to my mother and the dishes. Dennis tousled my hair and left the kitchen. Shortly after, Dan jumped up, took the .22 down from the wall rack, and left the kitchen without saying a word to anyone.

"Where are you going?" said my father, but all he got for an answer was the screen door slapping shut. I looked out the kitchen window and saw Dan striding up the driveway towards Blood Road with the gun bouncing in his hand. He was a black silhouette against the sunlit lake of flax.

I cleared the rest of the dishes from the table and dipped out some water for washing from the reservoir on the stove. My mother sat at the kitchen table cutting something from a magazine and gluing it to the page where the tortoiseshell butterfly fluttered over the oatcake recipe. I ignored what she was doing so she wouldn't get the idea that I had any interest at all in her musty old scrapbook, and so she wouldn't put warning notes in there for me to find. My father wound the gramophone in the parlor, put on Enrico Caruso, and sat in the thick chair that was his alone.

My mother tapped the recipe. "We're out of oatcakes," she said. "I served the last of them to Bertha. One more thing to do." She sat there for a time, looking tired, feeling the corner of the page made from blue striped wallpaper and staring at the recipe as if wishing would make the oatcakes appear. My mother's recipe was easy, really. It called for:

a quarter pound of butter
a quarter pound of sugar
three tablespoons of golden treacle
one teaspoon of almond extract
and half a pound of oats

I call it my mother's recipe, though she may have copied it from somewhere; she was always copying down a recipe. But this one was not cut from a magazine, or copied from the newspaper, as she did, by rubbing wax paper over newsprint to collect the words and then rubbing the wax paper on a page of the scrapbook, transferring all those little black newsprint letters. This recipe was in her handwriting: *"Melt butter, sugar, and treacle, and add essence. Take off the fire, add oats. Mix well, pour into a greased baking dish, and bake in an oven with a moderate fire for half an hour. Let cool. Cut into squares."*

"Add essence." By this she meant "add almond extract," but when she made oatcakes she did add essence, her own essence. When I made oatcakes, they didn't taste anything like my mother's, though I followed my mother's recipe to the letter. They tasted good enough, but they tasted of my essence, not my mother's. There are no two cooks that can make the same dish; you'll find that essence in one and not the other. Or the essence in each is just different. I don't know. But you'll know the essence of a good cook when you find it in a dish. You'll just know. It was there in my mother's cooking. My father knew it. He'd eat the oatcakes my mother made, but not the oatcakes I made.

My mother began mixing the oatcakes as I finished up the dishes. I went into my bedroom, passing by my father and the voice of Enrico Caruso, who had the power to make my father cry. My father jerked awake as I walked by and wiped the moisture from his eyes.

The window of my room looked directly over the garden, farmyard, and barn. I had no curtains and very little furnishing: a chair in the corner opposite my bed, a vanity my father made for me from orange crates, hooks on the wall in the corner next to the window, on which my dresses hung, and below this a basket that Bertha Moses had made and sold some years before to my mother. The basket held my socks and sweaters, the underwear my mother made for me from soft sugar sacks, and my few pairs of stockings. In the summer I went barelegged, but in the winter I wore itchy wool stockings, or stockings made of cotton or lisle. I wished for silk stockings or, better yet, the new nylon stockings. My Aunt Lou in Britain all but begged my mother to send her a pair of nylons — a woman couldn't get a pair of them at all over there unless she had a doughboy, an American soldier, for a boyfriend — but my father said no to that, and no to a pair for my mother. They were too expensive, and nylon was better used in the war effort, to build aircraft and weapons. So I wouldn't be seeing a pair of nylons for a very long time.

Over the chair hung a pair of my brother's old denim pants, a pair he'd long ago outgrown. I put these on under my skirt, chose a sweater, and inspected my hair in the hand mirror on my vanity. This much my father had allowed, even given to me: the hand mirror, brush, and comb that came as a set and a packet of Jo-Cur, a powder I mixed with water to form a jelly that I combed through my hair before setting it in rags, as I would do before bed this night. I had a bottle of hand lotion that my mother made herself from six ounces of mutton tallow that she strained and cooled until it thickened and mixed with three ounces of glycerine and a few drops of oil of geranium and then whisked with an egg beater into a soft cream.

I owned no jewelry, no make-up my father knew about, or fragrances, except the secret bottle of violet perfume in the hollow stump. I had no pictures on the walls, not even a calendar. My bedclothes were flannel sheets, two gray camp blankets, and a blue quilt my mother had made during the Depression from the printed fabric of old dresses and flour sacks. The only decoration in my room was the circle of blue forget-me-nots painted on the brown metal headboard of my bed, and the two ceramic dolls, past Christmas presents, that sat on my vanity.

I didn't think of myself as pretty, though now I look at the pictures of myself in my mother's scrapbook and see that I was. I shared my father's large-boned features, but I had blond hair that I wore past my shoulders and rolled at my temples in the style of the times, fine full lips, and blue eyes. I was a big girl, muscular from milking, riding horses, and doing farm chores, with the ruddy complexion that comes from fresh air, sun, and plenty of good food. But that wasn't the beauty of the time; then a woman was beautiful if she was fragile and had smooth, manicured hands that didn't grow callused or red from work. The magazines I read said it was a woman's duty to maintain her beauty for the war effort. But how could I have skin "caressingly smooth" when I needed the calluses to milk cows and shovel manure? How could I have bright lips when my father forbade lipstick? And who was there to look beautiful for? All the young men were gone, to the training camps, or overseas, or working in factories, and if there were a young man around, my father wouldn't let me near him. Hired men were different, of course. A girl didn't mess with a hired man.

When I left my room, my father sat with his head against the back of his chair, still listening to Caruso. He watched me as I walked through the parlor and into the kitchen. My mother was readying the kitchen for the night, covering the window with heavy wool blankets. Even there, in Turtle Valley, we were under blackout.

"Where are you going?" said my mother.

"For a walk," I said.

"This time of day? It's almost dark."

I ignored my mother and left the house. When I swung around the barn and headed for the creek through the sheep pasture, the lead sheep ran up to me, her bell ringing, and sniffed my hands; lambs trotted up, then bounced back under the cherry trees when I turned to them. Our fruit trees grew there, in the sheep pasture. Cherry, plum, apple, and pear trees flourished from the creek end of the pasture to the house. The pasture itself was held in check by the Swede's magical fence, which was constructed from living trees and bramble. The sheep had just been turned back into this meadow and the grass was still long. I waded through it, intending to follow Turtle Creek up to the benchland and back, when suddenly it was there, at the far end of the pasture near the house, something cutting a path through the orchard grass. I walked backwards a little way to see if it followed and it did; the swath through the grass turned and kept coming at me. I didn't stop to find out what it was. I ran, heading towards the hired hands' cabin, and jumped the pasture fence. The thing in the grass kept coming, so I ran up to the cabin and reached it out of breath and terrified.

Dennis answered the door. "Well," he said. "My girlfriend's here. You want to come in?"

I looked back at the swath in the orchard grass running parallel to the path I'd made. The second path stopped at the fence. Mine went on, flattening a trail through the grass all the way to the cabin.

"You okay?" said Dennis.

I nodded without looking him in the eye. Behind Dennis, Filthy Billy sat on his bunk tying a piece of binder twine around his pant leg.

"What's he doing?" I said.

Filthy Billy looked up, grinned, swore, apologized, and went back to his pant leg.

"He's getting ready for bed," said Dennis. "He saw a black lizard today, when we were working. You know, those little guys, about this long."

Dennis held his thumb and index finger about three inches apart. I nodded and looked back at the field. There was only one path now, the one I had made, as if nothing at all had been following me. I'd been chased by wind and stories of Sarah Kemp.

"That's so the lizard doesn't get up his pants and eat his heart," said Dennis. "You see one of those lizards, it'll follow you, and when you're asleep it'll go up your pants and eat your heart."

"I see those lizards all the time," I said. "They're everywhere. Never ate my heart."

"Guess those lizards don't like white meat," said Dennis.

Filthy Billy wheezed out a laugh.

"Your heart's up here," I said. "Why doesn't he tie his shirtsleeves shut if he's so worried?"

"The lizard enters your body someplace else," said Dennis, and he grinned at me wickedly.

I grew shy and watched as Filthy Billy tied the other pant leg tight around his ankle until Dennis pointed at the campfire a few yards behind the cabin. Filthy Billy and Dennis had set up a circle of stones in which they sometimes broke the blackout and lit fires. I'd watched the fire from my bedroom window at night and heard their laughter.

Around the fire they'd placed several logs for sitting, and about a cord of carefully stacked firewood stood between two paper birch nearby. The cabin was at the far edge of the flax field from the house, set up against the bush, and the yard around the cabin was no yard at all, just the crazy mix of growth found at any field edge: young pine, aspen and brambles, milkweed and purple-headed thistles, wild strawberry and lamb's-quarters. The hearth in the circle of stones still smoked.

"Billy built a fire and jumped over it," said Dennis. "To confuse the lizard, so he'd follow Billy into the fire and get burnt up."

I laughed.

"You don't believe me?" said Dennis. "I'll show you!"

He took my hand and that sent my heart rocking and knocked thoughts of Sarah Kemp flat. My hand became a huge thing inside his; I knew every tingle, every squeeze, and was aware of little else. He walked me to the forest edge, squatted in the grass, and pulled me down next to him. He still held my hand, cupped it, in fact, in both his hands. I leaned into him because I could do nothing else, and breathed in the sweetness of his sweat. Then I caught a whiff of the sour smell, from milking, on myself. It embarrassed me and brought me back to myself; I began to fear my father.

Dennis pointed out a thing on the ground. It was a forked stick jammed into the earth. Tied between the tines, pieces of grass cradled something I was unsure of at first.

"That's one of them lizards," said Dennis. "That's one I caught. Billy's too scared to go after them. You go after them and tie them up like this, then they can't come and eat your heart."

Held above the moisture of the ground, the lizard hadn't rotted, but mummified. Dennis stood and held out his hand and helped me up. "Anyway," he said. "Did you want something?"

I looked at my feet, and then at the remnants of the fire. I shook my head.

"Just come for a visit, eh?" said Dennis.

I shrugged and immediately regretted it. Mrs. Bell said shrugging looked slovenly. Dennis watched for a time as I looked down at my feet, embarrassed by my sour milk clothes and my weak attempts at vanity, the perfume on my feet, the lipstick in the crook of my arm. I couldn't think of a thing to say. He patted me on the shoulder as my brother might and that hurt worse than any spoken rejection. Nevertheless he said, "You just come over any time, any time."

I walked home through the twilight and the field of violet flax, feeling the tiny blue flowers with the palms of my hands, no longer chased by bloody images of Sarah Kemp, but by a blood heat of another kind, one I didn't have words for yet, but one that had everything to do with Dennis.

As I passed the barn, my father stepped out of the dark, scaring my heart into my throat. He pushed me up against the barn wall and pressed his weight against me. "You don't ever go to that cabin," he said. "Hear me?"

His fried-chicken breath in my face and the dog shit still on his boots made me think of the chicken killing that day, and with that came, clear and unwelcome, a picture of Sarah Kemp's face, blood-smeared and chewed. I looked up at the stars past my father's shoulder and willed myself there. My mother called from the house, "John, cocoa's ready!" and my father let go, looked me down for a time, and then strode around the barn and across the yard to the house. After a little while I straightened my blouse and followed him.

4

MY FATHER woke my brother in the middle of the night before Sarah Kemp's funeral and together they went out, once again, to cut down the Swede's living fence. The dispute between my father and the Swede had begun that spring with a notion that took hold of my father and wouldn't let go: he believed he owned a piece of land on the Swede's side of the fence. Long before my father bought the farm, the Swede had built a fence of living trees, in the style of his homeland, on what my father was now convinced was our property. My father had in fact bought the farm from the Swede's in-laws.

Johansson was fond of telling how he'd bought a ticket on the *Titanic* and missed the boat because he got drunk the night before at his sister's wedding. He took another, less ill-fated boat to the New World, and, after shifting around the continent working where he could find jobs, he took on the homestead in Turtle Valley next to another Swede by the name of Olsen, whose bad luck was legendary. Olsen had married a Turtle Creek Indian woman named Mary and had had eight children by her, but each and every one of the children had died. Everyone seemed to have a story about it. I'd heard from Lily Bell, Mrs. Bell's silly daughter, that the children had come down with an illness that took their minds, and made them see things that weren't there, before it took their bodies. Dennis had told Dan and me that the homesteader's children had been attacked, one by one, by a bear or a cougar, something that had left the children half-eaten in any case. I thought these were just stories, and the children had died of childhood diseases. All the children were buried on what was now our property, off beside the barn.

By the time Johansson had moved to Turtle Valley, the only child left to the Olsens was Caroline, a sweet, frightened half-breed Johansson married when she was sixteen and he was twenty-seven. Caroline died a year later of consumption, three months after giving birth to a son the Swede named Jack, because he liked the sound of it. After Olsen died, his widow took up with an Indian fellow, moved back to the reserve, and put the farm up for sale. That was when my father purchased the farm. He added on to the house, and put up a new barn, picked rocks from the field and piled them to hide the graves of the homesteader's children and to rid himself of their bad luck.

My father swore that the titles office clearly showed the land on which the Swede had built his fence was now ours, although he brought home no proof of it, and that spring after he sold the flock was the first we'd heard of it. The piece of land in dispute was one mile long and one foot wide.

He and the Swede had never argued the point; they had never even discussed it. Every few nights my father went out and took down a section of the Swede's living fence and put up his own barbed wire. Every few days I'd find the Swede had undone my father's work and tried to replant the section of his strange fence where he figured it should be.

The night before Sarah Kemp's funeral, my brother and father dressed to cut down the Swede's fence under the weight of my mother's protestations. My mother stood in the doorway of the bedroom she and my father shared, and amplified my father's foolishness so God could hear she had no part in it.

"At least talk to the man," she said. "You haven't talked to the man. Maybe he'll sell the land. Look at you! Building fences in the middle of the night!"

I shuffled into the corner of the parlor and leaned against the dish cupboard, in the dark, so they wouldn't see me. My door opened on the parlor, as did all the rooms of the house: my parents' bedroom, my brother's, and the door to the kitchen. From my bedroom door I could see into the kitchen and straight across to my parents' room. The house had once been the Olsens' cabin, onto which my father had added our bedrooms and the kitchen; the parlor was the only original room. Sometimes when the house was quiet at night, or when I walked past the rock pile by the barn that marked the Olsens' graves, I imagined I heard their footsteps, the noise of their play, or the sound of a child crying. There was no upstairs and only one doorway out of the house, the one in the kitchen, though each room had a window. We all had to pass through the parlor and then through the kitchen to leave the house. The parlor was dark, though my mother had boarded up the log and chink walls and covered the boards with wallpaper. The floors of all the rooms were of the same dark unfinished wood that my father had laid when he built onto the house.

My mother followed my father through the parlor and into the kitchen. Her hair fell to her hips, the buttons on her nightgown were done up her neck, and her sleeves were pulled down to her wrists. She hugged herself. My father carried a kerosene lamp, but he stumbled into chairs and tables anyway, thrown by my mother's complaints. My father looked like a hunkered monster; my mother's face was that of a ghost.

"Don't do this," said my mother. "Please."

My father set the lamp on the kitchen table and put on his boots.

"Let me talk to him," she said. "It's all a mistake, I'm sure of it."

When he didn't reply, my mother lifted the lamp to the corners of the kitchen to hunt out spiders. She found one, lifted the lamp higher, and the spider became drunk on the fumes of the lamp. It dropped into the flame and sizzled briefly before turning to smoke. My brother came into the kitchen and slid on his boots without tying them. My father got up, took down a gun from the wall rack, and pulled the lamp from my mother.

"You don't need a gun," she said. "Why are you taking a gun?"

"I may need it," said my father.

When my mother tried to block their exit through the kitchen door, my father tightened his lips and pushed past her. Dan scratched his hair into a haystack and rubbed the day-old beard growing on his big jaw. He smiled a sweet apology at Mum, but he went with my father.

"He's got every right to shoot you," my mother shouted after them. "Every right."

She banged around in the dark kitchen for a time, stoking up the fire in the stove. She would keep it burning even through the brightest heat of the coming summer and would go on stoking it all fall and all winter and into next spring.

"He hasn't got the sense God gave a goose," she said out loud. Then she mumbled, as she tended the fire, so the words only sometimes drifted up to be heard.

"Hell to pay," she said, and the words faded again. Then "Fool" and "Wasn't I right?" She looked up briefly, as if listening to someone talking, and said, "No, no, I can't do that," and went back to poking at the fire.

I knew who she was talking to. She had told me once, as we baked bread together. The day she told me, her hair had been pinned up into an unruly knot, and her hands were so muscled from milking and kneading bread that they made me think of knotted wood. Her face was red from the heat and work. She had mumbled under her breath as she kneaded the dough, as if I wasn't right there, trying to knead the dough in unison with her. My hands ached from the labor.

I said, "Who are you talking to all the time?"

She stopped kneading and looked up at me a little dazed, as if surprised to see me in the kitchen with her. "Oh," she said. "Oh, well, that's my mother."

"What do you tell her?"

"Things. About the day," she said.

"Does she answer?"

"Oh, well," said my mother. "If I said yes, you'd think me crazy."

"No, not crazy," I said.

"I think she's here with us," my mother had said. "Sometimes I think that."

My mother chilled me when she talked to my dead grandmother. This night, as she finished stoking up the fire and took her place in her rocking chair, hugging her scrapbook, I hid myself deep in my bed and eventually slept. I dreamed of the triple-seater outhouse at school and in my dream, Goat, the doctor's idiot son, sat on the roof with his back to me. The outhouse was filthy with excrement and bits of dirty magazine pages, and I was so disgusted I woke up. For a moment I thought I had wet the bed. Then the fuzziness of sleep left me and I realized how badly I had to pee.

Each of us had our own pail, not the pretty chamber pots the catalogues sold to slip under the bed; our chamber pails were large and made of white enamel with a black rim around the top and a white lid. I used mine instead of the outhouse most nights, and then emptied the night soil into the manure pile in the morning. My father and brother stepped onto the porch in the middle of the night and peed into my mother's flower patch, though she called them dogs for it. The outhouse sat to the side of the barn, close to the fence surrounding the sheep pasture and orchard. Over its history the outhouse had been moved several times and had been knocked over by neighbor boys on several Halloweens. It now leaned towards the barn and groaned when anyone stepped into it. There was no toilet paper, only magazines and catalogues to wipe with. There were always spiderwebs over the toilet seat and, above all else, the outhouse stank. Flies buzzed around your head, mosquitoes bit your behind, your ankles, your arms, the back of your neck. When I was very young Dan told me things lived down that hole, huge hairy things. So I didn't sit, I barely hovered. The fear of those unnamed, unseen things in the outhouse was still with me, at night, when reason flew away. Now I squatted over the chamber pail in my bedroom, trying to avoid making contact with the rim because it was so cold. When I got back into bed, it was a long time before I warmed up enough to fall asleep again.

When light started up the sky, I dressed listening to the snoring of my brother and my father, and the clear high whistle of my mother's sleep. I put on the blue dress I'd wear to the funeral later in the day, and pulled the rags from my hair but left the curls in disarray; there was no use combing them yet. I intended to start milking early on this day of Sarah Kemp's funeral, but when I went out to bring the cows into the barnyard, I found that my father and Dan had left the gate to the sheep pasture open in the night. The cows were down near the creek, more curious than hungry, sniffing at the damage my father had inflicted on the Swede's fence. On the other side of the fence, Johansson's goat stood guard, lip-curling and sniffing the air.

The Swede himself lived in a cabin the size of our parlor, the size of the cabin that my father had built for our hired hands. The Swede didn't have an outhouse behind his cabin, as everyone else in the valley did. He built his outhouse right over the creek, so his refuse was flushed away by the water downstream to the reserve. People living on the reserve used water from that creek as drinking water, and the

Swede knew it, but he also knew they wouldn't complain. He kept a small weedy garden that Mrs. Bell despised him for, and a bunch of scraggly chickens that he fed in summer by stringing fish above the coop. The chickens didn't eat the fish, they couldn't reach them, but flies laid eggs on the fish and their maggots, wriggling, dropped to the ground. The chickens ate the maggots.

In fall the Swede hunted on my father's property for deer without my father's permission. He owned a three-legged Lab that shat freely all over the yard around his house and would have come into our yard, but my father fired the shotgun at him, always missing. The dog was yellow and yellow-eyed. It sometimes ran as if it had four legs, as if it still had the ghost leg that had been caught in a coyote trap. It was because of this, my father said, that he always missed the dog. Both the Swede and the dog smelled like fish.

The Swede had built his fences with living trees for fence posts; he had planted young poplars between mature trees, and bent and wove them into crossbars that he held in place with vines of honeysuckle. Because honeysuckle never dies, the vines flourished, winding themselves farther around the living fence posts and crossbars, year after year, building an impenetrable hedge that came into leaf and blossomed from May to October.

Near the creek, my father and brother had cut down a section of the Swede's fence and piled it neatly on our side of the property. In its place, my father had put up ten feet of barbed wire and post fence, but he'd stepped it one foot into what the Swede claimed as his property. He had left the roll of barbed wire at the point where the two fences met, so he and Dan could pick up where they left off another night. The going would be slow because my father and brother used a crosscut saw, in the dark, and the Swede's fence had become a tangled forest over the years. Whenever he took down my father's barbed wire fence, he'd plant fast-growing poplars, back where he figured the fence should be. But the trees drooped sadly and never had the chance to set their roots. My father and brother simply pulled them up by hand. I picked up a bit of the Swede's fence, a thin poplar branch so grown past the honeysuckle's confines that it looped into itself like a curl of my hair.

I moved the cows through the sheep pasture and into the barnyard, locked the gate, and went into the barn. I gave up trying to do the chores alone, and instead went looking for cats. The barn cats were wild. They screeched and clawed at me if I was unlucky enough to catch one. But the very young kittens, the ones with eyes not yet opened, hadn't seen enough to run scared. The mother cats hid their kittens in the dark, miniature alleyways between stacks of hay in the barn loft. I hid them from my father and the old white tom and his appetites. He'd eat his own offspring if he found them early enough, bloody enough, or else he'd lick them clean and carry them away to some nest like a mother cat. He was unnatural, turning like that.

The morning of Sarah Kemp's funeral I came across the old white tom in the corner of an empty calf stall clutching two kittens under his back legs. He humped against the head of the kittens, as if mating a female. I threw a pebble at the tom and missed. He looked at me, tucked the kittens tighter against his body and humped again. I threw another rock, then a stick. The tom finally ran off and the kittens scattered.

I climbed the ladder to the hayloft. When I found a nest of kittens tucked in a hole in the hay, I pulled one from the nest and sat with it in my lap, a kitten so tiny and soft, its bones so close to the surface, its heartbeat so quick, it was a wonder it didn't die of heartbreak. I clenched my teeth in the love of it, its utter dependency.

My father called my name and entered the barn, walking down the alleyway, looking from side to side. I became very still. He called my name again, then listened and looked up for a long time at the place where I hid. I swallowed and held my breath and thought of how I might escape if he began climbing the ladder. That ladder was the only way down. Finally my mother called him and he left the barn. When the screen door to the house slammed shut, I breathed out and fell back into the loose hay.

My mother came into the barn carrying the milk buckets, and I climbed down and opened the gate to let the first four cows into the barn.

"You shouldn't be wearing your good dress for milking," she said.

"I'll be careful."

"More kittens?"

"There's a calico," I said. "Don't tell Dad."

We pulled the empty stumping powder boxes up to the cows and milked with sleep still on us and the faces of our dreams still around us. We were milking Jerseys, and Jersey cows are the most jittery, the easiest to scare, but also the most gentle when treated right. With chocolate brown eyes and sweet long lashes, they're the beauty cows. The irony is that the Jersey bull is the meanest bull you'll ever find.

Whatever you take into milking is amplified by the act of milking. If you begin milking angry, the cow will feel it, stiffen, and kick; or she might not let her milk down for you, and your anger will only get bigger. If you go into milking with sleep still on you, then milking is a meditation; the cow feels your sleepiness and is calmed by it; you feel the muscles in her big side relax, and she lets her milk down. Then the rhythm of the milking takes over: the steady shush-shush of the milk into the bucket, the rocking of your body as you squeeze one teat, then the other, one teat, then the other.

Everyone who milks has her own way and her own rhythm. At home I could tell who was milking just by listening to the rhythm of the squirt into the galvanized steel pails. My father's rhythm was too fast, without a steadiness to it; he rarely milked the cows because when he did, they kicked him. I'd seen him go sprawling across the barn floor and the box on which he sat go flying. It's no small wonder he got kicked because he yanked on the cow's teats as if they were ropes on a church bellpull. There were unbelievably long spaces between the squirts in my brother's milking; he milked one cow in the time it took my mother to milk three, so he didn't milk much. Mostly it was my mother and I, milking to the rhythms of our own heartbeats, so close sometimes that the milk squirted into the pails in unison, like an iambic drumbeat. My mother sang quietly, and we milked with our heads against the warm flanks of our cows. They knew us enough to trust us. When we opened the doors to them, the cows came in by themselves, always in the same order, the lead cow with the bell first, and found their own stalls, always the same. Cows are creatures of habit and get agitated by anything new — a new box in the barn, a different smell on our clothes, even milking at a different time — so we tried to wear the same clothes each day, and milk at the same time, quietly and evenly.

We set each full bucket of milk aside with a cover because even the smallest fleck of manure tainted the milk. When we were done milking,

I lowered one pail into the well so that the base was just touching water, to keep the milk cool for our own use. My mother and I then carried the remaining buckets into the house. My job was to work the cream separator in the pantry while my mother washed up and made breakfast. I pinned cheesecloth to the separator bowl with wooden clothespins and strained the milk through it, adding more as the level went down. Then I turned the separator handle, and turned it and turned it. The handle had a bell on it that dinged as it went around, then changed to a different tone, and finally stopped when it was time to let the milk and cream out. I'll always remember the sound of the separator — whir, ding, click, whir, ding, click — faster and faster as I turned until the bell stopped ringing and I opened the tap on the bottom of the bowl and let the skim milk run into a bucket below, and let the cream flow into a second smaller pot. I did this over and over again, until all the milk was separated.

I carried the skim milk and cream outside, poured the cream into the shipping can we stored in the well, and fed the buckets of skim milk to the few calves we kept in the heifer pasture. The calves lifted their noses and bunted the buckets, as they would their mothers, to let their mother's milk down, and then stepped awkwardly away with foam all over their faces. The calves were heifers, our next generation of milk cows. They learned to drink from a bucket quickly, but their instinct to suckle was so strong they sucked one another's faces, joining in odd slobbering kisses. They came up to me from behind and bunted me, thinking I was their mother, and even then tried to suck my clothing. I slapped them away, but a week-old calf is a big strong creature, if clumsy, and many times, as they did this morning, they chased me from the heifer pasture.

When I returned to the house, my brother and father were at the kitchen table with their boots on. I poured them coffee and helped my mother serve their bowls of porridge and plates of eggs and sausage. I ate quickly, then took the separator bowl, spouts, discs, rubber ring, and float off the separator to wash them, and wiped out the machine. While I was cleaning, a man and his wife came to the door. The man had a red face and a loud voice. When my mother opened the door he stepped right in without waiting to be asked. The woman hung behind. She wore a gray dress with buttons all the way up her neck. They looked rumpled and hot, as if they'd walked a long way already that morning.

I disliked salesmen. Because we lived so close to the road and appeared to be the last house before the reserve (the Swede's house was set far back in the woods), they always stopped by selling horse collars and harnesses, cistern pumps, gang plows, cream separators, poorly made accordions and other instruments, sewing machines, brushes, and patent medicines — all the things we could get in the Eaton's catalogue if we really needed them.

"We've come to talk about the state of the world today," said the man.

My father looked up from the breakfast table. "What do you want?" he said.

The man walked right up to the kitchen table. The woman stayed by the door, fiddling with her purse. My mother looked at her and tried to smile and then went over to the table and stood between my father and the red-faced man.

"These are terrible times," said the man. "But they are also glorious times. The signs are everywhere. You only have to read the papers. The world is consumed by war. The coming of the Lord is at hand!"

My father made a face, shook his head, and laughed, so that the little gray woman stepped back and knocked the washbowl from the table beside the door. The bowl clattered to the floor, clattered into our ears, and clattered into my father's head. My mother tensed. My father put his hand to his forehead and stood up as the women bent down to retrieve the bowl.

"Get out!" he said.

The red-faced man looked confused but immediately regained his ground. "We were hoping you might be generous," he said, and both he and his wife suddenly looked sunken and hungry.

"Out!" said my father. He took the man by the shoulder and pushed him to the door.

"You wouldn't put out a man preaching the message of the Lord. Can't you see the warnings? The end time is near!"

My mother said, "John," and put her hand on his arm, but he flung her hand away and marched the husband and wife out the door. The gray woman said, "Oh!" and trotted a little way. She was wearing town shoes with heels and she limped. My father watched the couple until they rounded the corner of the driveway out of sight. Then he went to the barn. I sat at the table watching as my mother stuffed a flour sack with jars of canned fruit, jam, and bread. She took me by the elbow so urgently that I stood.

"Go out our bedroom window and catch up to them," she said. "Explain your father's been ill this past year."

I pushed off my shyness and did as she asked, running the overgrown Indian trail that rounded the root cellar. I caught the strange couple as they were walking down Blood Road towards the reserve.

"Here," I called. "Wait."

The couple turned around and I handed the woman the bag of preserves and bread. "There isn't anything that way," I said.

"There's the reserve," the woman said. "We always do well on the reserve. The people are generous. They listen."

"I'm sorry," I said.

The couple exchanged a look, and I felt ashamed.

"God bless you, dear." The woman took my hand and gave it a squeeze.

When I walked back to the house, black lizards skittered away from my feet and ran for cover. I went after a couple of them, trying to step on their tails, but my mother clanked dishes around in the wash pan in front of the kitchen window, a hint that I'd better get busy. When I carried out my chamber pail to the manure pile to empty it of night soil, I saw my parents' pail was already there and opened the lid on it with the idea of emptying and cleaning the pail for them. It was full of water and at first I didn't comprehend why. Then I saw the dark bodies of the new litter of kittens I'd played with that morning. The stench of night soil on the manure pile became overpowering. I took a step back as my father passed by with a bucket of chop in each hand. He said, "Bury those cats, will you?" as if he didn't know what he'd done, as if it were just another chore for me to do.

5

I STOOD for a long time with my hand at my throat looking at the bucket of dead kittens. Then I removed myself and watched my hands take up a shovel, make a hole in the manure pile, and empty the foul water and the bodies of the dead kittens into it. Their bodies slid from the bucket like fish. I covered them over with manure, then followed myself to the other side of the barn, like a child following her mother. My father was there, throwing another bucket of chop to the pigs. He was wearing his town shirt, the white shirt my mother had mended for Sarah Kemp's funeral, and the black suit pants and suspenders he saved for funerals and weddings. I followed myself up to him and watched as my hand slid into a pile of warm manure and threw it at him, hitting him in the sleeve. In the moment he looked at me, I came back to myself and ran into the house. I stood in the kitchen washing my hands beside my mother, knowing he'd follow, knowing he'd lick me good. My mother didn't look up. She went on washing dishes even when my father stomped into the kitchen and grabbed me by the arm. She kept washing and clanking until my father let go of my arm and yelled at her.

"Stop that!" he said.

My mother stopped instantly.

"What the hell is the matter with you?" he said to me. "What did you do that for?"

I looked down at my dress because my father looked at it. I'd slopped manure down my front and it had dropped off as I'd run, leaving green stains over my breasts and on my skirt.

"Look at you!" he said. "You're filthy. Get that dress off. Wash it!"

I stepped back and my father rushed at me. "Now!" he said.

When I didn't move he swept me up. I screamed and that made him angrier. He carried me into my room, threw me on my blue quilt, and ripped the dress from me.

"That's enough," said my mother.

She stood against the doorframe to my room. Her hair was coming loose from the bun she'd wound it into. My father stopped, caught off guard. He stood up straight.

"Get out of the house," said my mother. "Now."

I held my breath and waited, but my father only lowered his eyes and like a kicked dog he slunk from the room. My mother turned sideways to let him pass, but she didn't let her shoulders fall, or let the air go from her chest until she heard my father's footsteps on the porch outside. She brushed her hair from her forehead.

"I hate him," I said.

"Get dressed," she said.

I put on a clean brown skirt and white blouse, combed out my curls, and padded out in my bare feet. My mother heated a little cream, poured it over a slice of bread, and sprinkled it with sugar. She set the bowl in front of me. The strangeness about her had dissolved into tiredness. She had rubbed rose petal into her cheeks and lips for a little color, but my father had either ignored or hadn't noticed this small vanity. She still had on the loose housedress that she wore to milk the cows and she smelled a little sour from the dairy. The bread and cream was child's food and I was no longer a child, but I was thankful for it. By the time I finished the bowl, I'd forgotten to hate my father.

6

MY FATHER wore his sheepishness like a sack over his back as he changed his shirt. He harnessed Cherry and Chief, our other horse, to the democrat himself instead of cowing my brother into it. He even helped my mother up into the buggy. But he wouldn't look at me; he ignored me as if I weren't there.

I sat in the back with my brother and the cream cans, watching the road unwind behind us. The road was a deep, rich brown-red, from iron deposits in the soil, I suppose, though I grew up believing the road was red from the blood of turtles. Blood Road was what the Indians called it, what everyone called it. The government maps, however, named it Caldwell Road after the first white landholder in the valley, a man who died alone in his cabin with no wife and no kids and no one to mourn him but his hungry pigs. The road had once been an Indian trail and had been expanded into a wagon road during the gold rush of 1867 that had founded the town of Promise. It had been a busy road until the new highway diverted traffic around Bald Mountain and through Promise. Now it was a quiet road through a quiet valley with only the rattle of ghost wagons and the crying songs of the berry pickers to tell us it had ever been anything different.

Towards the Turtle Creek Reserve, Blood Road wound through a valley so narrow that, even in summer, the sun didn't rise over the hills until nine A.M. and then set well before three o'clock. That end of the valley was damp and dreary without sunlight. The reserve stretched over part of Bald Mountain and down its slopes to the flat lands

beyond. Here a few Indians farmed and others made their living capturing and selling the wild horses that roamed across the flat lands. It
was a long walk to the reserve and going there was one of the many
things my father forbade. I was also frightened. You heard things then,
about the reserve; how white women were raped, how children were
beaten. Except for the times I walked up Bald Mountain to count the
wild horses, I stayed away from that end of the valley.

Towards the town of Promise, the valley opened up like a wound in
skin. The valley basin was rich and fertile because of the spring floods,
and the land along the road was cleared for pasture and crops, except
for trees that grew around the many sloughs. The road followed the
valley floor at the lowest point, and at spring runoff it became a muddy
mess. Three miles down the road from our farm was the Boulees' farm
and then the school, a small one-room building heated with a woodstove in the center that kept it too hot in the early summer and too cold
in the winter. I still went there, but Dan had quit school a couple of
years before. Beyond the school there were several smaller acreages
inhabited by families that I now had little to do with since the craziness
set in on my father.

The road followed the valley basin, along the creeks and swamps,
and now, in spring, the turtles crossed the road in thousands to lay
their eggs, so passing down it was a grizzly thing. Many of the people
who lived in the valley didn't stop but whipped their frightened horses
over the moving road of painted turtles. The shells were crushed under
the hooves of panicking horses and under the wheels of the wagons
and the few automobiles. Their smashed bodies were strewn all over
Blood Road, wherever the road met a swamp. But death didn't stop the
painted turtles. They came and came and came across the road, and by
their tenacity and numbers alone they succeeded in seeding the next
generation. The blood of the turtles seeped into the dirt of the road and
hardened, paving the road a brilliant red that turned to rust when the
season was done; this is what Bertha Moses told me, and the proof of
the story was there, on the road we followed.

In past years my father had held something like a worshipful respect
for that turtle pilgrimage. Only the spring before, perhaps a month
before the bear attacked our sheep camp, my father had pulled the
horses up short on the swamps just past our driveway, stepped down
from the buggy, and held his hand out to help my mother down. He

had gestured for Dan and me to get down, so we stood a little way behind my father and mother and leaned on the siding of the democrat. My father had put his arm around my mother's shoulders and together they watched the turtles climb from the swamp into the ditch, and then up onto the road. These were painted turtles, with yellow and olive-black shells that were edged with bright red crescents. They moved across the road in a slow, stubborn parade. Occasionally a little black lizard scuttled among them and hurried off into the cover of a ditch. That day Dan had picked up one of the turtles and turned her the other way. The turtle spun around slowly, using one front foot like an oar to push herself in the red dirt and paddled her way back in the direction she intended to lay her eggs. My brother turned around another turtle and another, and we watched them methodically right themselves. After a time my father told us all to pick the turtles from the road and put them to the side, and through the path we created he led the spooked horses down Blood Road until we were past the swamps.

But not this year, not on this trip to Sarah Kemp's funeral. The strange compassion my father once had for turtles and other things — the young robin that hit the window and lay dazed on the ground until he warmed it in his hands, the heifer born with a bum leg which he didn't kill but put a splint on, the newborn lamb he carried around all morning in his jacket to keep alive — had been broken up somehow, cracked into little pieces that made no sense to me. This year my father slapped the reins against the horses' haunches, forcing them, as they whinnied and shied sideways over the moving road. Rocking beside Dan, I held the side of the democrat against the swaying and jolts, clenched my fist, and closed my eyes against the sight of turtles cracked and bloodied in the ruts the wheels created. But I couldn't shut out the crunch and slide of them under the wheels and the hooves of the horses they crazed with their turtle selves. I opened my eyes long enough to see a turtle with her back legs crushed pull herself by the front legs over a last red rut and up onto the sandy banks where thousands had laid their eggs before her.

Promise was all the way down Blood Road, past the small acreages and fields, then down the new highway two miles. We made this journey every couple of days to take the cream to the train station, but we rarely went as a family. My mother and father went, or my brother went, or I went with my mother. But this day was different. This was the day of the funeral of Sarah Kemp, a girl I'd seen almost every day of my school days, and never talked to, not even once. She had sat in the corner of the one-room school, on the other side of the big wood heater, with her head down, her face towards the front of the room where Mrs. Boulee paced, but her eyes were always in the rapture of a daydream, and her arms were folded against her breasts, bracing whatever it was that would otherwise flow out and cause a thousand deaths of embarrassment. She was as unpopular at school as I and for that reason I thought of her as my secret sister, and I did not believe her dead. The story of her death was too fantastic; it was the sort of story told around the table on Halloween. She would be sitting there, I was sure, in the corner of the dark schoolroom opposite mine on Monday, and this day, this day, as I had promised myself every day this last year, I would conjure up the courage to go over to her where she sat alone, reading on the back steps during lunch, and touch the flowered material on the arm of her dress and tell her my name, as if she didn't know it, as if we were just now introducing ourselves.

We dropped the cream cans off at the train station and picked up the empty ones. Like the other dairymen in the area, we shipped our cream by train to Palm Dairies in Kamloops and received payment once a month, by check, in the mail. Once we had made our delivery, my father drove the buggy back up the street to the store and tied up the horses. His sheepishness had drained away. He said to my mother, "I want to see you at that church in fifteen minutes, not a minute longer," before he turned his back on her and strode over to Reinert's blacksmith shop. I followed my mother into the store. My father wouldn't enter the general store; he wasn't welcome there and he knew it. The last time he'd set foot in Bouchard and Belcham General Merchants was the day after the Dominion Day picnic, 1941, nearly a month after the bear attacked our camp. That day he walked into the store with my mother to buy the hard pink candy he loved so much, and when he stepped out of the store into sunlight again he had managed to start a fistfight with Morley Boulee, the teacher's husband, and to knock over a rack of ladies' silk stockings.

My mother and I, on the other hand, were welcome in the store, as long as we came without my father. My father had given in and let my mother go to the store alone over the necessity of having flour in the house. Bouchard and Belcham's was the only store in town. We either bought supplies there or made the daylong trek into Kamloops. The store was old, one of the first buildings in Promise. It smelled of sawdust and smoke from the big woodstove that the old men sat around. It had a very worn oiled wood floor and the walls were plastered with government posters. Some said DON'T BE A CUPBOARD QUISLING! and warned of fines up to five thousand dollars and imprisonment for hoarding food; others advertised Victory bonds or demanded that we all DIG FOR VICTORY and grow a garden plot, or KEEP IT DARK and cover our windows at night and close our mouths. Other posters explained the latest rationing regulations, which seemed to change monthly, on tea, coffee, and sugar. Sugar was limited to half a pound per person per week that month, down from three quarters of a pound.

Belcham sold everything in that store: coal oil, feed, dried fruit, split peas, beans, rice, barley, sugar and sago sold by the pound from hundred-pound gunnysacks, yard goods, galvanized tubs, milk pails, pitchforks, tools, binder twine, nails in bins, newspapers and magazines, tobacco, bluing, coffee, tea, canned vegetables that we never bought, and a few ready-made clothes. There was a cheese as big as a washing machine that we cut chunks from, wrapped in wax paper and then again in brown paper. In the back corner of the store was the post office wicket where everyone in the valley and in town went to pick up their mail. Belcham ran the wicket himself while his wife ran the till. Bouchard was long dead.

I waited on my mother, as she chatted with Mrs. Belcham, reading the covers of the magazines and newspapers that offered stories on how to grow a Victory garden and how to knit ten pairs of socks a day for the boys overseas, yet another way to eat rhubarb, and how to turn old pajamas into housedresses. I fingered the few pricey packages of nylons that Belcham kept in the store, until I noticed the old men around the stove staring at me. I stared back until they looked down at their feet and then went outside and sat on the steps. I pulled my skirt over my knees and hugged my bare legs. Dan had gone off someplace; he'd jumped off the democrat before my father had even pulled Cherry and Chief to a halt. But where he'd gone, I didn't know. There were few enough places for him to hide — the town was nothing but one long street of false-face businesses. It was framed by the United Church at one end, and the Anglican and Roman Catholic churches facing off at the residential end. Bouchard and Belcham's was just about in the center of town, across from the motel. The ancient little motel was then owned by the elderly Mr. and Mrs. Blundell and was fraught with stories of ghosts and the like. This one I know is true: the spring the grizzly attacked our camp and my father sold the sheep, Ginger Rogers and an unnamed male companion drove into town while on holiday and stayed the night at the Blundells' haunted motel because there was no place else to stay. Hanging on the wall of the room in which Ginger Rogers stayed was a photograph of Mr. and Mrs. Blundell standing on either side of the elegant and smiling movie star. The motel building was nothing but a frame of poles on which cedar shakes had been nailed. The floor and bunks were made of split cedar logs, the beds were straw mattresses. The only other furnishings were an airtight heater, a bucket of water, and an enamel washbasin that could be seen through the two little crossed windows in each unit. There were three units to the motel, all attached to one another and to the house in which the Blundells lived.

The doctor's house and office was on one side of the motel, and the blacksmith's shop was on the other. Beside the blacksmith's shop was the garage and gas station, the notary public, and the United Church. Opposite this, to the right of Bouchard and Belcham's, was G. Locke Drugs and the butcher shop. To the left was W. Clark Jewelers and a vacant lot. The little police office was down by the train station. Other than a few houses, that was all there was to the town of Promise.

The dirt road that was the main street was rutted and dusty, and when a horse and buggy went by the dust didn't dissipate but hovered, so the air was never free of it. Cars and trucks had seen their glory days briefly in the space where the Depression declined and the war and its gas rationing began. There were cars in Promise — the doctor had one, the one police constable had another — but many people went back to horse and buggy for the duration of the war.

As I was sitting on the steps in front of the store, a crow with odd coloring hopped across the street with a chunk of bread in its mouth. The crow was mostly white with black streaks running through its feathers. It stopped in the center of the street and busied itself prying the soft meat of the bread from the crust until a couple of black crows swooped down and went after the albino as if it weren't one of their own. The white crow fought them for a time and then gave up; it took off and landed on the church roof. I shooed off the black crows and picked up a feather the white crow had lost in the tussle; it was a beautiful thing, white with streaks and specks of blue-black.

Then Goat was there, right behind me. "Hello," he said.

Goat was the son of Dr. and Mrs. Poulin. His real name was Arthur. My brother said Arthur Poulin had the body of a man and the mind of a stupid dog. My father, surprisingly, was kinder. He said Arthur Poulin could play the piano and could be taught other things, if someone took the time with him. Half of Goat's face was that of a shy young man; the other was a cross-eyed child. His ears were small and square, his nose was flat and broad, his tongue hung out, his eyes were puffy-looking and slanted up. He was very short and his shoulders were hunched and he flopped around as if he had no muscle or joints. He had short stubby little hands that flew all over his body, all the time, scratching, pulling, picking. His constant nervous movements frightened me.

"Hello," he said again.

I looked at the faces of the town buildings and at the albino crow on the church roof and pretended Goat wasn't there. Goat stamped a circle in the dust. I flicked an ant off my skirt.

"I'm like everybody else," Goat said. "My dad said I'm like everybody else."

I looked up at him. Goat held one arm out and took a step towards me. I stood and ran, and after a moment Goat ran after me.

"I'm like everybody else!" he cried out.

Dan left the blacksmith's shop as I ran by. "Give her a kiss!" my brother yelled at Goat. "She loves you!"

"Kiss!" Goat yelled after me. "Kiss! Kiss!"

I left my brother's laughter behind and after a time I stopped running and watched as Goat caught up to me. He ran in an ungainly way, like a marionette. I bluffed. I put my hands on my hips like my father. Goat stopped running and walked towards me nervously.

"Hi!" he said.

I didn't answer. He stopped and started walking backwards. I stared at him. He turned and ran and disappeared among the buildings.

7

WHEN I WALKED back down the main street, Goat had already clambered onto the church roof. He sat with his back against the base of the steeple, his head down and lolling, playing with parts of himself that I knew should never be mentioned. Above him the anvil of a thunderhead grew in the sky. Morley Boulee, the man who shot the bear that killed Sarah Kemp, was standing by the newly dug grave near the church yelling at Goat to get down. Others were beginning to arrive at the church, on foot or by buggy. It was a funeral everyone would go to, whether they knew the family well or not. The school had closed for the day, and businesses would close down while their owners attended the funeral.

We hardly went to the church, but I knew it. I knew it from Christmas and Easter, from weddings and funerals and the fowl suppers. The church was a small wooden building painted white every spring so you never saw a crack in the walls. There was no fancy stained glass, only a row of small windows up and down each side. It had a rough steeple with a wooden cross attached at the apex, and it was against the steeple that Goat leaned to hide from the world and soothe himself as best he could. A new eight-foot-high fence made of chicken wire on wood posts went all the way around the church, all the way around the graveyard that sloped up the low hillside behind the church. The fence was not pretty and made the church grounds look like a farmyard — that and the Blundells' chickens, which pecked their way into the churchyard and then hid in the bushes surrounding the graveyard so no one could catch them.

I stumbled into the church behind my parents and my brother with the rest of the town, and stumbled out again propelled by the crowd when the casket was carried, by men I didn't recognize, to the grave. But I took nothing from the service. Through the hymns and the sermon and Mrs. Boulee's eulogy, I couldn't take my eyes off the casket. The church was filled with sweet peas, nasturtiums, marigolds, bachelor buttons, scarlet flax, and spiky delphiniums picked from the gardens of every woman in that church and arranged in what was handy: cups and coal-oil tins, glass canning jars and milk bottles. Garlands of deep purple lilacs were laid over the casket. Color all over, in the blue and pink dresses of the young girls, in the flower petals, and the blossoms of fruit trees outside the church windows. Yet there was the casket, under all those flowers, too large and black for that tiny church.

No one talked on the short walk from the church to the grave. No one even cried. My mother and I found ourselves behind the mourning family, but my father and Dan ended up standing at the back of the crowd. Sarah Kemp's mother held on tight to the arm of her own mother, Mrs. Anna Halley, and they both stood at the grave looking puzzled. Mrs. Halley was the only person I'd ever heard of who'd watched her stroke coming on. She'd been the church organist for years, and the day that eternity opened up and took her spirit was a Sunday. The story went that she was sitting at the organ at church, playing in front of everyone, looking at the music before her, when the black spot appeared on the page, just a little black spot at first, like a fly, but it grew, and grew, until it was a splash of ink across the page, obscuring the notes. She'd stopped playing then, just stopped and let her hands fall in her lap to stare in awe and confusion at the hole that had opened up in the universe, right there in the hymn "O Savior, May We Never Rest." She had talked in her marbled way about that hole for a time, but she'd lost her right side to the stroke, and so she lost her music, and after that the black hole slowly ate up everything that made her Mrs. Anna Halley and left behind a child in a crone's body.

Mrs. Halley moved away from Sarah Kemp's mother and touched my head, and said, "Sarah, your hair has gone so blond."

"I'm not Sarah," I said. I looked everywhere but at her face and finally settled my gaze on my feet, on the stitches in my shoes. The Swede spread his contempt over our family by not looking at us. Mrs. Bell watched me with a mask of patient charity, and Robert Parker, a boy my age from school, smiled his peculiar smile at me, half-hope, half-sneer. The whole crowd was still and staring expectantly, greedily, not shuffling self-consciously as they would if Mrs. Halley had mistaken one of the pretty Hambrook sisters for Sarah. They watched to see what would happen next. They watched to gossip later.

Mrs. Halley smiled and held her hands as if she expected me to embrace her. She had the stupid, pitiful look of one not living in her body, and that made me want to slap her. My mother mistook my anger for sorrow and held me closer. I struggled away. My mother gave me a pleading look, and I stood more defiantly than before and stared directly into the faces of the grieving family because I knew this would bother them. Mrs. Kemp took Mrs. Halley's arm and they stood nearer the grave. Mrs. Kemp caught my eye and looked away quickly; she began to cry. I felt remorse immediately and stopped staring. My mother whispered, "Stand straight!"

Mrs. Halley spoke very loudly, as if trying to get a message across a chasm. "Who are all these people?" she said.

"We're at a funeral," said Mrs. Kemp. "Sarah died. Your granddaughter. Sarah died."

"Who are all these people?"

In the time it took to lower Sarah Kemp's casket into the ground and fix the fact of death firmly in our minds, the ladies of the church had rearranged the pews along the walls of the church, put a long table in the middle aisle, and laid out a spread for those who'd worked up an appetite with their grieving. Everyone found a place in line for the food, and the line stretched out the door and into the graveyard. With their plates in their hands, my parents found a place to sit near the front of the church. I watched as several couples looked for seats, watched my mother smile hopefully at them, again and again, and watched her face fall when the couples turned and found spots at a crowded table rather than sit with my father. But my father seemed impervious to their rudeness. He kept his eyes on his plate and ate and ate. I don't think my mother ate a thing. When the line of people filling their plates finally came to an end, all the tables but my parents' were so full that people were mopping the sweat from their faces. The only one not afraid to talk to my mother when my father was around was Mrs. Bell. She ventured over to their table, and my mother's face lit up then, even for righteous, gloomy Mrs. Bell.

Well, I wouldn't make friends with any of them. Not with Mrs. Bell's silly daughter, Lily, not with that Parker boy, who tried, now and again, to catch my smile and got my hate stare instead. All of them, all the kids I knew from school, were sitting at one long table at the far end of the church wolfing down the lunch, laughing now and again even though one of their number had died, throwing the occasional snicker in my direction. My father's unpopularity had spread over me and my mother but left Dan alone. Because Dan had been out of school for two years by then, and had spent that time working on the farm, he didn't have to contend with the jeers of the kids at school. Even so, while I defended my father against the name-calling, Dan didn't do anything of the kind. He carried his plate around from conversation to conversation, adding to my father's misery by telling stories on him, about how my father brought porcupine home and tried to sell it as chicken; about how he forced Dennis to undo and rewind a haycock over and over, ten times, until Dennis had raised it to my father's sense of perfection and wasted half the morning; about how my father still hoarded flour and sugar, coffee and tea, in the hole behind my parents' marriage bed. That last one was a lie, and a dangerous story. It was my mother who stocked the hole behind the bed; that was her domain. And there were many who took those government posters in the store seriously.

Mrs. Bell sidled up closer to my mother, so close my mother moved away a little. Mrs. Bell was doing all the talking. My mother listened politely, nodding, smiling, glancing now and again at my father. My father ignored them both. When he got up to fill his plate for the second time, Mrs. Boulee went over to talk briefly to my mother. Mrs. Bell sat back in her chair and stared dimly at Mrs. Boulee as she approached, and when Mrs. Boulee and my mother spoke, Mrs. Bell looked away over the crowd. Mrs. Boulee kept an eye on my father and when he started back, she nodded at my mother and rejoined the women at her table. Mrs. Bell watched her leave and then sat forward again in her chair and took my mother's hand. My father sat without looking once at either of them and concentrated on eating.

I stood near the door, eating alone behind Morley Boulee, the hero of the day. He was a slim, tiny man who, though nearly fifty and creased around the eyes, looked no older from a distance and carried himself no differently than one of his wife's graduating students. I guessed that was part of the town's complaint against my father over the incident in the general store, that my father had picked on a man so much smaller than himself.

Mr. Boulee stood beside Robert Ferguson, the man with the property next to the schoolhouse, the dairyman who sold us the Jersey cows. Ferguson was a tall, knotty man with a thumb and index finger missing on his right hand who smelled of cigarettes. I began disliking him that afternoon. As my father got up to refill his plate for a third time, Ferguson nodded and glared at him.

"Look at that hoarder there, stuffing his face," he said. "Never seen a man eat so much. Can't believe I once liked the man."

Morley Boulee shook his head and nodded back over his shoulder in my direction. Ferguson glanced briefly at me, and, red-faced, turned his back further. I drilled hate holes into the both of them. Morley Boulee talked with a loud voice after that, so I couldn't mistake their talk for whispers about my father. He talked about the stormy summer headed for us, the Dominion Day picnic coming up, to be held, as always, at Boulee's Farm. He pointed out Mrs. Roddy, a tall, severe, elderly woman who still wore the long black dresses of her Victorian girlhood. Years of denying herself the love of a good friendship had left her without appetites of any kind; she was thin and righteous and mean and martyrly. She'd been widowed since the Great War and never took another husband.

"She got it in her head there was someone digging under her house," said Morley. "Told Constable Peterson there was a German hiding under her floorboards, coming to get her. Even got him to do a search. Can you imagine? Some German digging under her porch. Guess he dug himself a tunnel all the way from the war."

"Some dog likely, scratching under the porch," said Ferguson.

"Or a rat."

"Well, I can't blame her, living alone like that, and all the things you read in the paper. I heard the Germans are training dogs to rape women."

"I heard they nail women to barn doors, by their hands and feet, like they were crucified. Jimmy told me that. He knew someone who'd seen it with his own eyes."

The talk made my stomach turn and I moved off from the line and went to one of the windows. I had no appetite anyway for eating in the room where the coffin had been, and where my father flagrantly fed the gossip by filling his plate for a third time. I looked out over the grave-yard and thought of Sarah Kemp, and of the turtle that was crushed under our wheels and that nevertheless pulled itself, bleeding, across Blood Road. There was Sarah Kemp now in the ground; I could see her grave from the window, but I couldn't put it together with the image of that sullen girl hugging her breasts in the corner of the schoolroom, hugging whatever it was that she wished for. I couldn't believe her dead, because to believe that was to believe I was capable of dying.

Outside the sky had gone dark. The wind lifted up petals from the fruit trees on the church grounds and littered them over the graves. A thunderhead grew over Bald Mountain and had begun to rain over the summit; we'd have rain, then, in the valley, at home. If I pressed my face against the glass I could just see Cherry and Chief. They still carried the red of Blood Road on their legs and hooves and were pawing it into the ground, sending up little red dust clouds. The glass felt good and cool on my face and I lost myself to it, forgetting for a moment the room of judging whispers behind me. I placed my other cheek against the glass so I was staring at Sarah Kemp's grave. A figure turned up out of nowhere and slid up to the grave like a ghost. It was Coyote Jack, sure enough, here in town but looking every bit as bushed as he ever did, as ragged and nervous as a dog that's gotten kicked too many times. He placed a bundle of dying lilacs on the grave mound and stood looking at it for a moment. Then he was gone. He had on a red jack shirt and should have been easy to spot, but there was no flash of red in the bushes, no sight of him making his way past the church. I pushed through the crowd of people still lined up at the table of food and looked out the church window on the far side.

My brother came up behind me with his plate and looked out the window. "What you looking at?" he said.

"Nothing."

"I guess I wasn't being too smart," he said. "I mean, going on about Sarah Kemp's body. I didn't think she might be a friend of yours."

"She wasn't," I said.

Mr. Ferguson, the man who had just slandered my father, walked by and slapped Dan on the shoulder. "Why haven't you joined up yet, eh?" he said. "Got a wooden leg? Or has your old man got money?"

Dan laughed him off, but when Ferguson went to refill his plate at the food table, Dan leaned against the wall, blew the hair from his eyes, and looked like misery for a time. His suit was now too small for him. It showed too much wrist and too much sock, and his hands, as big as dinner plates, looked bigger still in that suit. He looked the clownish farmer and knew it; he played it up with mock clumsiness. The smell of his sweat drifted up, reminding me how unbearable the air in that building had become. The church was getting hot, and the mourners were generating a smell that the flowers couldn't cover. Mrs. Bell grabbed hold of my mother's shoulder, stood up, and then started coming our way with her dirty plate in her hand.

"Here comes doom and gloom."

"I'm getting out of here," I said.

I left my brother and pushed my way outside, through the crowd. The smell of rain and horses was infinitely more soothing than the smell of human grief. I stroked Cherry's nose and, having nothing better to do, looked down the main street for any sign of Coyote Jack. The whole town was shut down for the funeral. G. Locke Drugs, the butcher shop, the harness shop, the blacksmith's, Bouchard and Belcham's, and the Promise Cafe, the one lonely restaurant in town — everything was closed. No one was on the street; they were all inside the church eating, save a skinny wild dog at the end of the street that left his signature on the steps of the store, and slid, like a shadow, between the buildings. Horses tied to anything handy along the street shuffled and scratched themselves with their noses. Goat had left the church roof, scared off by all the people.

Coyote Jack was scared: of men, of town, of noisy cars, the occasional planes overhead, of small transactions with store clerks, the meaning of scratchy letters on paper, of church people and God, Indians and women, the sound of the human voice. He made his living trapping and never came to town, not even for provisions — he paid the Swede, his father, to box and ship his furs and to buy him coffee, sugar, flour, and rice and to leave them on the steps of his cabin. Most of the time he went around looking half-starved. He saw almost no one and washed his underwear by fixing them to the creek bed with a couple of rocks. I'd seen him just that week, through my bedroom window, drinking from our water pump outside. After he'd had his fill, he went skulking around the chicken coop, apparently looking for something, drumming up the will to come to our kitchen door.

I leaned up against the church and watched the petals from the apple tree flutter onto Sarah Kemp's grave until my mother, father, and brother left the church and got into the democrat.

"Can you believe that Swede coming up and giving me a lesson in table manners?" my father was saying. "He eats rotten fish and starves his chickens!"

"He said you eat like a pig," said my brother. "I'd say he was right there."

"You keep your mouth shut. He'll pay for that rudeness. He'll pay tonight."

My mother tensed and shut her eyes for a moment, then opened them with a forced smile.

"Mrs. Bell is coming to visit tomorrow," she said. "It's been such a long time since she's visited. Since anyone's visited."

"Beth got a kiss from Goat," said my brother.

"I did not!"

"Don't call him Goat," said my mother. "That's shameful."

"I'll tell you what's shameful," said my brother. "Them keeping that mongoloid idiot running around. They should lock him up. Send him to Essondale with the other crazies."

"Don't be stupid," said my father. "He can be trained. They can all be trained. You teach them something once and they'll remember it forever."

"They should at least have him castrated. He's disgusting."

"No more disgusting than you," I said to my brother.

My father grunted. My mother started up a sweet humming that could have been any song. Goat wasn't the only mongoloid in the valley. There were rumors about the Blundells, the owners of the motel where Ginger Rogers stayed. People said they kept a child in one of the motel units and never let her out. Or there was a ghost child there, in the room Ginger Rogers slept in, killed by her father, the senior Mr.

Blundell, a wispy gentleman with a cookie-duster mustache. Or the ghost of the very first owner of the hotel, a whore named Louise who kicked up her heels in the gold rush that founded the town, haunted the rooms.

"Stop that!" my father said to my mother, and she stopped humming.

I searched the windows of the Blundells' motel as we passed, but the face of the building was blank.

8

WHEN I BROUGHT home the cows down Blood Road that evening, the sky turned the odd green of a lightning storm, and then the lightning began. I counted the distance between lightning and thunderclaps with my footsteps. The cows, spooked by the turtles and the storm, kicked up their heels and ran off down the road. I let them run; they'd find their way home before me. Then I heard the slap of a man's footsteps behind me, following. I swung around, but there was no one there — only my own footprints followed, and even they were melting away in the rain. I stiffened in fear and listened. The wind whipped up the waves of alfalfa, corn, and flax in my father's fields and rain splattered around me, thrilling the back of my neck. My hair stuck miserably to my head. Trees along the road swayed, and the leaves of the plants turned the vibrant, glowing green that rain brings. The forest conjured up mists and little puffs of it spilled out onto the road and disappeared.

And there was Coyote Jack, standing near the forest edge. I gripped my gun tighter from surprise, but he only nodded. Then he wasn't there anymore, and I heard the mewing. I looked around and saw no cat, but as the thunder crashed the mewing grew louder. I called, "Puss, Puss?" and a little black cat jumped from the hollow of a log by the road. I looked to see if Coyote Jack was around, if this was his cat, but he'd long since blended into the forest.

The black kitten trotted over to me. I tucked it into my jacket and trembled all the way home, trying to think how I could avoid my father, where I could put the cat so he wouldn't find it, what story I would tell my mother about my wet and muddy blouse. When I reached the yard, I ran the cows awkwardly into the pasture behind the barn, still holding the cat in my jacket. My father was leaving the barn just as I reached it.

"What've you got there?" he said.

"Nothing," I said, and tried to walk around him, but my father would have his joke with me.

"Let's see," he said.

I opened my jacket a little, knowing he'd take the thing from me, this black heart, knowing he'd drown him like he drowned the others, to spite me, to get even for some outrage I couldn't have guessed at. The black cat stuck his wet head out and mewed.

"Look at him!" said my father.

"Don't kill him," I said. "Please."

"Why would I kill him?" said my father. "Black cat. Satan's cat. Call him Lucifer. Take him in and show your mother."

He was unnatural, turning like that, but I didn't question him. I took the little black gift to show my mother. She was stoking the kitchen fire, muttering to the ghost of my tiny grandmother. She quit mumbling when I came in and straightened her back.

"What do we have here?" she said.

"Father says I can keep him," I said. "He named him Lucifer."

"Well, there's no telling," she said. "Maybe he's coming back to his old self."

She took the kitten from my coat, checked his sex, put him in a box near the stove, and placed a saucer of cream before him. Then she insisted I take my blouse off immediately, to soak it in a washbasin, so I went to my room and changed into a clean blouse and one of my brother's sweaters. When I brought the dirty blouse back into the kitchen, my mother had the black kitten in her lap and was gently applying butter to each of its paws.

"This will keep him home," she said. "He won't wander."

I put the blouse into the soak in the washbasin and dried my hands. My mother put the cat on the floor and we both watched as he very deliberately licked his paws. Then my mother took my hand. Her fingers were warm and slippery with butter.

"I should have put butter on your paws," she said. "I worry, you know, when you're out in the bush. You never know what's out there."

"I take a gun," I said.

The kettle whistled and I made tea. My mother wiped her hands and brought out the tin of shortbread. We had an impromptu teatime alone, until my father and brother came in from the barn, yelling at each another.

"You aren't going anywhere," said my father.

"You can't tell me what to do," said my brother.

"Like hell I can't. You eat off my table. You do what I say."

"You've worked me like a slave. I don't owe you nothing."

"You leave and this farm falls apart. Think of your sister. Think of your mother."

"Don't give me that," said my brother.

My father scraped back his chair loudly. I threw on my coat and carried Lucifer outside, hugging him. The voices of my father and brother chased after me, chased me to the barn and the solace of the cows. The storm had carried the red dust of Blood Road to our farm and rained it down — on the windows of the truck and the poplar growing through it, the lumber and the pile of rocks — covering everything with the blood of turtles, the blood of our recklessness. The blood of a war a thousand miles away rained down on us.

9

THE MORNING of Mrs. Bell's visit, my mother baked as if her life depended on the fluffiness of her raspberry buns and the lightness of her daffodil cake. This was a woman's pride, to have a recipe worth stealing. To this end, my mother hid her scrapbook, slipped it away between bags of flour in the wall behind her marriage bed, before Mrs. Bell arrived. But while she baked, the scrapbook sat on the kitchen table in the light patchwork of sun that came through the kitchen window. She paged through it, anointing each page with the flour and butter that covered her fingertips. She'd changed into a clean dress after chores, a blue housedress with a lace collar. Her hair was wound up in a bun, and she'd rubbed a little petroleum jelly into her eyelashes to darken them, to make herself look as wide-eyed as a girl. She'd been up since before first light, stoking the kitchen stove, building the fire up until it was good and hot before we went out for chores. That's the secret to building a fire for baking: the trick is to build the fire up in the morning, get a good hot blaze burning, and then let it lick itself down and cool some. Once there's a bed of bright coals there, keep adding wood, one stick at a time, and don't add another until that stick is about burnt down; that way the heat stays constant, not too hot, not too cool, just right for baking. A moderate oven. Let the fire get too hot, and everything burns. Let the fire die down, and nothing bakes at all.

After chores that morning I got myself cleaned up in the washbowl on the bench by the door, then stole a look, over my mother's shoulder, at the scrapbook as I wiped off my hands. My mother had stopped on the page that contained the raspberry bun recipe. It was written on the back of a letter from her mother in thin black ink, and this page had a cartoon pasted onto it, of a man glaring at his watch as a woman hesitated by a shop window. The caption read "Time Is Money!" The page held many transparent spots where my mother had handled the paper with butter on her fingers; she added more spots this day.

"Think you can handle this one?" she said. "I thought I'd make a daffodil cake to use up some eggs. If you get started on this, I'll get the eggs."

She got up, and I sat in her place before the scrapbook. Raspberry buns weren't buns at all. They were more like cookies and something like dumplings. The recipe called for:

half a pound of flour
a teaspoon of baking powder
a quarter pound of lard or butter
a quarter pound of sugar
an egg
a teaspoon or two of milk
and jam to fill

Any jam would do, not just raspberry, though raspberry was the jam of choice. In our root cellar we had a few jars of huckleberry jam, strawberry jam from last year's garden, and a few tiny precious jars of wild strawberry jam from the berries my brother and I had searched out and picked the year before. That wasn't all we had stored in the root cellar, of course. There were rows and rows of bottled beef, canned in the cool of last fall; great haunches of beef that my mother and I cut into chunks, placed in sealed jars in pots of water, and boiled for four solid hours on a stove fueled by wood and our labor. On the floor close to the root cellar door, my mother and I placed gallon coal-oil cans, carefully washed and filled with a clear viscous liquid we called water glass, into which, each day, we placed the extra eggs brought on now by the increasing light and not used. The water glass would keep the surplus eggs fresh for use next winter when the pull of sunlight wasn't strong enough to convince the chickens to lay.

The raspberry buns were a standard treat for my mother's guests, and my mother knew the recipe so well she hardly needed reminding, so the instructions in the scrapbook were sketchy: *Roll out pastry into rounds. Put little jam in center. Roll little. Make cross on top.* This hardly described what I'd watched her doing. She'd roll out the raspberry bun dough and then cut the dough with a jar lid. Into each perfect circle of dough she'd place a dollop of jam and then roll the edges up, puckering them in the way you'd pucker up fabric to make a pouch, and pinch the dough together at the top. She'd cut a little cross on top, so the jam would ooze out as it cooked. When they were done, the raspberry buns looked like tiny precious pies and tasted of heaven. The smell of them coming out of the oven was more temptation than an appetite could bear. This is what I would do then, on the morning of Mrs. Bell's visit, fill the kitchen with the warm, happy seduction of my mother's little pies.

While my mother took the wire egg basket out to collect eggs for her daffodil sponge cake, I paged quickly, impatiently, through the stiff pages of the scrapbook, looking for anything new, or something I might have missed, but avoiding the page near the front containing Sarah Kemp's funeral notice and the warning of bear attacks. I flipped past the photographs of the king and queen and the various ghost stories my mother clipped from magazines, and went straight for my favorite page: the newspaper clipping of Ginger Rogers's visit of the previous year, next to my mother's recipe for quick Sally Lunn. There was plenty of room for additions on this page, but the only thing new was a sentence my mother had scrawled in sloppy blue ink that read, "Box of geraniums at open window keeps flies down." It was a hint she must have picked up from some magazine. I touched the fuzzy photograph of Ginger Rogers, but lightly, so I wouldn't smudge the newsprint. All that glamour so close to home. I hadn't seen Ginger Rogers, of course. We hadn't gone to town that day, but I wished with all my heart that we had. She was so beautiful, so foreign to anything I knew in the valley.

My mother's footfall approached the house, and I quickly laid the scrapbook as it had been, open to the raspberry bun recipe. Her wire basket was filled with eggs, and she put them carefully into the washbowl and scrubbed them clean with a fingernail brush, placing them one by one on the counter of the Hosier cupboard. Some cooks, to convince you of their miracle working, maintain that sponge cake is a difficult thing of chemistry, of eggs three days old and flour just so and the temperature and humidity just right, but making a sponge cake is the easiest thing in the world. A sponge cake is nothing but eggs, flour, sugar, and air; and if you're new to the sponge cake, a little baking powder too, to ease its way against gravity. The secret is eggs, lots of eggs, and eggs we had no shortage of now that summer was almost on us. My mother used an even dozen in each daffodil cake, then two cups flour, and two cups sugar. But here she did experiment; some days felt like a little more flour or sugar, some days a little less.

After separating the yolks and the whites into bowls, my mother added the ingredient of air, whipping the yolks until frothy, then adding half the sugar and flour and perhaps a little lemon juice or flavoring. In another bowl, she beat the egg whites until they stiffened, but not so much that the air bubbles began to break. She then added the remaining sugar and flour and a touch of real vanilla. There it was then: two frothy bowls of air and egg, one yellow and one white.

There are two more secrets to the sponge cake: a knowledge of folding and a clean pan. A sponge cake is nothing without a clean baking pan. A spot of grease on the pan from some other recipe, and your sponge cake will come out flat. So wash your baking pan ever so carefully, and never, ever grease it. The folding was so important that my mother spelled it out under her recipe for daffodil cake: *Take spoon under batter and gently fold over.* The spoon is important: it should be large and flat. The gentleness is important: you want to keep those bubbles of air intact. One fold is usually enough to mix the two colors. My mother poured a layer of the egg white mixture into the pan first, covering the bottom, then added spoonfuls of yellow here and there, folding them in as she went; then another layer of white, and so on. To bake she used a moderate oven. To cool the cake, she tipped it upside down over a bottle on the kitchen table, so the tube in the middle of the cake pan suspended the cake. After a couple of hours, gravity would pull the cooling cake down, so removing it from the pan would be nothing at all. My mother would then decorate the cake with an icing of butter, icing sugar, a little hot water, and vanilla, and top it with a few spicy yellow nasturtiums.

I laid out our best damask white linen tablecloth and four white napkins that matched, and the best dishes we had — a set of white teacups, saucers, and cake plates with tiny gold cloverleafs close to the rims. After arranging the plate of raspberry buns and the cake on the cloth, I put the sugar bowl with the bird on its lid at the center of the table, next to my mother's large brown teapot and milk jug and a glass pitcher I'd filled with lilacs and violets.

There was all our morning's work laid out on the table, all wealth and good eating and joy. But I couldn't enjoy any of it. During another visit, Mrs. Bell had shamed me, and my mother, by giving me a brisk lesson on sitting. She'd caught me on the bench near the kitchen door, sitting with my legs crossed, drinking a cup of tea. I thought I looked like the picture of Rita Hayworth in the magazine Mrs. Bell's daughter, Lily, had brought me once, in the days when she still visited us with her mother.

"Don't cross your legs like that," Mrs. Bell had said. "That's how the worldly women sit, the women who smoke. You sit like that and you're asking for something."

Mrs. Bell's wire-rimmed glasses and her hair, worn rolled back, made her face appear much rounder and larger than it needed to. Nevertheless, her resemblance to my mother's family was so uncanny that she could have been my grandmother come back from the dead. When she visited, she habitually sat with her back to the buffet, and I spent those visits looking from her to my grandmother's grim face in that photograph, trying to figure what it was that made them look so much alike. Maybe it wasn't her looks, exactly, maybe it was the way she held herself, or rather, the way her righteousness held her. The day she caught me posing like Rita Hayworth, she had taken me by the hand and had led me into one of the parlor chairs that pinched my thighs closed.

"Don't sit with your legs apart," she had told me. "Whores sit like that. Don't slouch. That's for the stupid and lazy. Don't hug your stomach like that."

I sat now at the parlor table as she had instructed, with my legs tucked together, feet firmly on the floor, arms on the arms of the chair. Of course there was no other way to sit on the parlor chairs. We all sat that way around the parlor table in those pinched chairs, my father at the head of the table with his back to the kitchen, my mother beside him and I beside her, and Mrs. Bell at the end of the table with her back to the buffet. Billy and Dennis were out seeding barley; hired hands never ate in the parlor when there were guests. My brother was out in the fields with them to keep him from spoiling my mother's time, to keep him from fighting with my father. Even so my mother and I waited for my father to come up with something, because he would come up with something, he always did when company came.

Mrs. Bell was complaining about headaches this morning. She was prone to small, undefined, and apparently untreatable illnesses: backaches and leg aches and stomach complaints that made her flatulent. My mother counseled her not to eat onions or fats, to get more rest, to put cold compresses on the back of her neck for headaches or bouts of panic, and to entertain a few lady friends.

"I wouldn't tell this to anyone but you," said Mrs. Bell to my mother, as if my father and I weren't sitting there listening. "Sometimes the pain is so great that I see lights, my eyes grow sensitive, and I must lay down because I fear I might fall."

My mother patted her hand, and Mrs. Bell grabbed on to my mother's wrist.

"You're such a comfort," she said. "Such a comfort. There's no one else I can turn to."

My mother smiled and pulled herself away under the pretense of pouring more tea.

Mrs. Bell helped herself to a heaping teaspoon of sugar from the little bowl with the bird on its lid and clanged the spoon against the teacup, knowing full well that it sent my father to hell and back again. My father rubbed his temple where the scar began but said nothing. He took another slice of cake.

"You have some appetite there, John," said Mrs. Bell. When he didn't answer, she said, "I see Johansson next door is taking down that old mess of a fence and putting up something practical, finally."

"No, that's me," said my father. "That Swede doesn't know where his property ends. I intend to let him know. Once and for all."

Mrs. Bell laughed a little, nervously. "What does Johansson think of all this?"

My father grunted. There was a long silence that my mother spent pouring tea, Mrs. Bell spent looking both horrified and pleased, and I spent staring into my plate. A shadow passed the window. It was Coyote Jack skulking towards the door in the hillside that was our root cellar. He looked up at the window and then he was gone. Just gone. For no reason at all, a panic came over me. The chair began to fold in on me, forcing down my arms, constricting my breathing. I couldn't catch my breath, my heart pounded. I stood up.

Mrs. Bell, my mother, and my father looked up at me.

"What's the matter, dear?" said my mother.

I leaned into the table, trying to catch my breath.

"Sit down, dear," she said. "More tea, anyone?"

I pushed the chair away from me. "I'll make tea."

"She's so helpful," murmured Mrs. Bell. She took my mother's hand again.

I opened the screen door to refill the kettle at the pump outside, and as I did, flocks of birds flew up and settled on the trees, on our house, and on the clothesline. Past the birds there was something else, the sound of women's voices singing, the sound of bells.

"Christ, that squaw again," my father said, but he stayed in his chair and helped himself to more of my mother's daffodil cake. Bertha Moses and her daughters and her daughters' daughters rounded the curve of our driveway and marched into the yard. Their jewelry shot sunlight in all directions, and the purple swallows zoomed around them. Bertha came to the kitchen door, but the daughters and granddaughters stood by the flower bed and didn't come any closer. The girl with the bell necklace stepped out from behind her sisters and aunts and looked at the house until she saw my face in the kitchen door. She smiled at me and touched the necklace.

"Bertha!" my mother said. "I wasn't expecting you today."

Bertha looked at my mother's tight smile. "Guests?"

"Yes," said my mother. "But maybe you could come by later? On your way back from town."

Bertha nodded, but she walked past my mother anyway and into the parlor. She walked right up to Mrs. Bell and shook her hand. My mother followed and stood at the parlor door with her hand at her throat.

"Good to see you, Mrs. Bell," said Bertha. She looked at my father and nodded. "John."

"Hello, Bertha. Where's the girls?"

"They're waiting outside."

"Well then, they should come in," said my father.

My mother's shoulders fell. She closed her eyes for a moment, then she regained herself and went to the kitchen door.

"Girls," she called. "Come in, come in."

I stood back under the coat hooks and watched them file in, a dozen or more of Bertha's daughters, granddaughters, nieces, and adopted daughters. The girl with the bell necklace saw me as she came in and stood in front of me. This close I could see that her eyes of two different colors, one green, one blue, were startling, the eyes of two women in one face. I looked from one side of her face to the other. She reached out her hand and was about to touch my hair when one of the women grabbed her by the arm.

"Come on," the woman said, with a voice so like a man's that it amazed me. "Out of the way."

The women streamed into the parlor. I pushed past them, picked up the teapot, and pressed my way back into the kitchen to refill the pot.

Mrs. Bell stared at Bertha's bright pink apron. Bertha smiled back at her. "You went to the Kemp girl's funeral?" she asked.

"Oh, yes," said Mrs. Bell. "A lovely service. All the girls were dressed so beautifully."

"Horrible death, eh?" said Bertha. "For one so young."

"Mauled to death by a bear," said Mrs. Bell. "Can you imagine?"

"It wasn't no bear," said the daughter with the webbed fingers. "A bear don't attack like that."

We all turned to look at her. She was dressed much like Bertha was, in a bright blue dress with the sleeves rolled back, but without the apron. I couldn't take my eyes off her. The skin between her fingers went right up to the first knuckle, and as she gestured light flickered through the webbing. She saw me staring and closed her hands into fists.

"He must have gone rabid," said Mrs. Bell.

"They killed that bear for nothing," said the pregnant daughter. "He didn't kill nobody."

Mrs. Bell looked down at the table, played with her fork, and stirred her tea. The pregnant daughter looked her over but went on anyway.

"That was a man that done the killing. Coyote's come and took him over."

My father laughed.

"You should be warned about talking like that," said Mrs. Bell. "You're saying it was murder."

"That was a man, sure enough," said the pregnant daughter. The dangling earrings she wore caught the light from the window and flashed around the room.

"No man's capable of that," said Mrs. Bell.

Bertha Moses gave a little wave. "She means to say the spirit took hold of him and made him do it. A man stays out in the bush alone long enough, and the bush changes his shape."

My father grinned and my mother looked horrified. The woman who had pulled the girl away from me, the one with the man voice said, "Mother. Don't."

"The thing is, Coyote keeps getting born, over and over," said Bertha Moses. "He rides on the spirit of a newborn into this world. It don't have to be a human newborn, it can be an animal, but once he's born into this world, he slips off and goes walking until he finds somebody to have some fun with, eh? He takes that somebody over, see? Possesses him, like them demons in the Bible. Coyote has an awful thirst. Can't satisfy him nohow, that's what makes him so bad. You got to stay away from Coyote." Bertha smiled, a little too sweetly. "Ain't that right, John?"

My father laughed, a long powerful laugh, and all of us watched him at it. My mother covered her face with her hands. Mrs. Bell stood up.

"Well, I have to be going," she said.

"Going?" said my mother. "So soon?"

"You have a houseful. There's no room for me."

"Oh, Flora, please stay."

Mrs. Bell pushed her way out of the parlor and found her coat on the hook in the kitchen. My mother followed her, pleading quietly. Bertha sat back in her chair, and called out, "Mrs. Bell."

Mrs. Bell looked back through the parlor doorway, tight-lipped, as she put on her coat.

"Your girl Lily called my granddaughter a squaw," said Bertha. "You make sure she don't do that again, eh?"

Mrs. Bell went red to her bones and pushed her way out of the house.

"Can't imagine where she'd pick that up from," Bertha said. "But I imagine she's got to learn those words from somewhere. Don't she, John?"

"Cookies?" said my father.

I looked over at the girl with the bell necklace and found her looking at me. She grinned and disappeared behind her aunts and reappeared just behind me in the crush of Bertha's progeny. Hidden within the crowd of women, she ran her fingers along the back of my hand, petting me. The thing was so unexpected, so thrilling, so soothing, I just stood there breathless, letting it happen. She stroked me like I stroked those kittens my father had hunted down and killed just because I loved them. I watched my father now, watched that he didn't see the girl standing behind me, petting my hand. After a time the girl took my hand, and I held on to hers like a secret.

"We better be going," said Bertha. "Maudie, can we buy a little cream from you?"

"You know I can't sell it off the farm. With the rationing."

"I thought maybe a bear could come raid your can, eh?" said Bertha. She clawed her hand in the air.

"Go ahead," said my father.

Every woman in the room looked at him. He shrugged and grinned.

The girl with the bell necklace squeezed my hand and disappeared into the crowd of women. Bertha's daughters and granddaughters filed out the kitchen door, and the flocks of birds lifted into the sky above their heads. My mother handed one of the daughters a syrup can, and the woman went to the well, brought up the shipping can, and ladled out some cream. Bertha, my mother, and my father stood on the steps admiring the day as it slipped into night. The sky had gone pink without any of us noticing or any of us getting to the chores.

"John," said Bertha. "You given my boys a raise yet?"

My father folded his arms. "You stay out of that, Bertha. It isn't your affair."

"Lots of my boys gone off and joined up. Soon there won't be nobody left to work on the farms, all the boys gone. How you going to manage then?"

"We'll manage."

"I think Dennis and Billy, they'll do well if they join up, they'll get money, and they'll see places they don't get to otherwise. I think I should say to them to join up. What do you think about that, John?"

"You don't want them enlisting. We both know that. You want to keep them here."

Bertha shrugged. "If they don't get paid like they should, I'll tell them to join up. They listen to their granny."

My father's face went red and he clenched and unclenched his fists. Bertha smiled.

"You get out!" my father yelled. "Just get out!"

"John," said my mother.

"Get off my property. Stay off it!"

Bertha Moses shrugged and smiled and signaled to her daughters and granddaughters to start down the road. She took my mother's hand and gave it a squeeze and then trotted over to the other women with her long braid and beads swinging. They marched down our roadway, a parade framed by the field of flax behind them. The girl with the bell necklace turned and walked backwards a little way behind the others. She smiled at me and gave the necklace a jingle and then turned back as they rounded the corner out of sight.

10

Sunday morning as I left the barn I heard a shuffling in the woodshed.

"Dan?" I said.

The shuffling stopped. I hesitated towards the woodshed.

"Dan, is that you?"

Dan poked his head around the corner and grinned. He was shirtless, a thing that wasn't done then, any more than a woman would go out without a blouse now. His nakedness embarrassed me but also fascinated me because he was so obviously no longer a boy. I felt awkward and fat in my heavy clothing. The day was unseasonably hot and muggy, but despite the heat, I wore a pair of my brother's old denim pants under my skirt.

"Everybody gone?" he said.

"Yeah."

"Dad not around?"

"He got mad and went off someplace."

"What say we go fishing?" he said.

He held open a duffel bag for me to see. I knew the type of fishing he was after. In the bag he carried several sticks of stumping powder, a roll of fuse, blasting caps, and a crimper — a tool that looked like a pair of pliers with a pointed end on one handle. The .22 leaned against one of the saddles on the dirt floor.

"Sure. Why not?" I said.

At the place where the hollow stump hid my treasures and blossomed yellow and purple violets, we dammed Turtle Creek with rotten fence posts and fallen trees until we'd flooded a deep pool. When we were done, Dan told me to go stand away from the creek, behind some trees. He slipped a blasting cap on the end of the roll of fuse, crimped the cap on tight, and used the sharpened handle of the crimper to poke a hole in the end of the stick of stumping powder. He slid the capped end of the fuse into the hole and cut the fuse from the roll with his jackknife. About sixteen inches of fuse stuck out from the stick of stumping powder; that gave him about two minutes to get away once he'd lit the fuse. He put fuses of longer lengths into the other two sticks of stumping powder. I'd watched this operation many times when my father blasted stumps from the fields we cleared. My brother lit all three fuses, starting with the longest fuse, and hurled the sticks into the creek, then ran like hell to my hiding place. The fuses fizzed a bit when they hit the water, then boomed, and a tremendous wave covered the sun. Out of the boom came a howl like a raging bull, or like a man in agony. When the splash and thunder of the blast left our ears, the howl went on; it came from up the path.

"We've woken a ghost," I said.

"Rubbish," said my brother. But he tossed me his jackknife, picked up the gun, and walked up the path. "Stay here and get the fish."

He was gone a long time. There were many brook trout, stunned or dead, floating belly-up in the water. To gather the fish, I cut several forked willow branches and sharpened the long end on each to a point so they looked like huge fishhooks. I took off the denims under my skirt, carried one of the forked sticks into the water and began swimming around in the creek, sliding the fish onto the willow by pushing the stick through their gills into their mouths. In this way I stacked the fish one on top of the other so they were easy to carry, and the forked branch at the bottom end of the stick kept them in place. After a while I got cold and swam back to the creek bank, leaned against the hollow stump, and warmed myself in the sun. There were sun dogs on either side of the sun, little red and yellow bits of rainbow that are a sure sign of an oncoming storm.

An ant crawled up my leg and I brushed it off. Another came. I pulled out my secret lipstick and drew a heart in the crook of my arm, and thought about holding hands with the girl with the bell neck-lace, about Bertha Moses, and my father's rudeness. I ran my hand down my bare leg and schemed on how I could come up with the money for a pair of nylons. I thought of what my father would do when he found out Dan and I had dammed the creek. I whistled. Eventually my brother marched down the path, weighing the .22 in his hand. I looked up at him, expectant.

"Must have been Sasquatch," he said, grinning. Then he said, "Look!" and pointed out a fool hen sitting on a fallen tree close by. A fool hen is a stupid bird that just sits there waiting to die. My brother took aim, squinting from one eye. Then he had a change of thought and handed me the gun.

"I saw Coyote Jack up the trail," he said.

"He's always around. He's been hanging around the house, looking like he wants to come in for a visit."

"Coyote Jack? A visit? Ha!"

I aimed at the fool hen. "Then I saw him in town, at the funeral. He put flowers on Sarah Kemp's grave. Can you believe it? Coyote Jack in town. Then he just kind of disappeared."

"Crazy," said Dan. "You know what the Indians say? They say Coyote Jack's a shape-shifter. He turns into a wild dog or something. That's why they call him Coyote."

I laughed and lowered the gun. "Who told you that?"

"I heard it all over. Jimmy George. Billy. Dennis."

"That's nuts."

Dan shrugged. "That's what they're saying. Jimmy George says some ghost took Coyote Jack over, like a demon possession, you know?"

Jimmy George was a farmer from the reserve and a friend of Dennis and Billy. He raised sheep and pastured them in the mountains over the summer, as my father once had.

"You really going to sign up?" I said.

"Better than staying here. Dennis is thinking about it too, you know, except Bertha won't let him."

"What does he care what Bertha says?"

Dan shrugged. "Why don't you go get yourself one of those factory jobs," he said. "Government's begging for girls."

I took aim again, fired, and missed. The fool hen only ducked her head, then sat up again.

"Can't even hit a fool hen," he said.

"Shut up." I tossed him the gun. He grinned at me, took aim, fired, and also missed. He swore and spit on the ground.

"Well," he said. "We don't need no fool hen. We got fish."

When we got back to the house it was early evening and my mother was out in the garden. "You went fishing!" she said.

I looked at my brother. "We went up to Mystic Lake," he said.

My mother touched my arm, pulling a spark that snapped us both. "Shock! Your arm feels like fire."

I laid my hand on my arm where she'd touched me, at the crook of my arm. I shrugged. She tentatively put her hand to me again, and when she felt no shock, she gave my arm a squeeze.

"Storm again tonight," she said. "You can feel the lightning in the air. Look!"

She ran her hand an inch above my brother's head. Fine strands of hair reached up to touch her hand. I put my hand above Dan's head and watched the hairs jump up to meet my hand. They crackled. I laughed.

"Time to get those cows down," said my mother. "Wear a coat. You're going to get rained on."

I went inside and threw on my brother's old tin coat — logger's gear that went so stiff when it was wet and cold that it stood up by itself — and took down my .22 from the gun rack. I cut through the fields of flax, corn, and alfalfa, which my father forbade me to do, and hiked up to the benchland. The sky above the bald spot had a greenish cast to it and thunderheads were growing. The air smelled of lightning, a smell that always got the cows dancing. I watched the storm as I followed the sound of the lead cow's bell. When I reached the cows, they spread off in all directions, kicking up their heels as if they were heifers, and attempting to mount the cows in heat as they ran. They were senseless, possessed. I started to turn back, to get help from Dan, and the storm seemed suddenly upon me. Lightning zigzagged across the sky and boomed immediately over my head. The hairs on my arms stood on end and my scalp tingled. The bell on the lead cow glowed blue. I looked to see that none of the cows had been struck, and lightning hit again, in the space of pasture between myself and the cows. In the fraction of a second that stretched on as if it were hours, the lightning rolled towards me in a series of loops, pinkish and sparked bluish white, like a snake all knotted up, evolving and transforming as I watched, straightening itself out and coming right for me, as if meant for me. Some of its power must have been discharged into the ground, because when it hit I didn't go black. I felt it, shooting through my right arm. Then it was gone. My arm was numb and tingling. I shook, my whole body shook.

I slapped my right arm as I ran home, trying to awaken it, comforting myself with the myth that lightning never hits twice. My whole body vibrated like a train. When I reached home, my brother was on the back steps cleaning fish. He sat on the dry steps, but the rain dribbled off the porch roof onto his boots.

"I can't get the cows home," I said. "They've gone stupid. The storm's making them crazy. I think I got hit by lightning. It came at me on the ground and hit me. My arm's gone numb."

"Yeah? You'd be dead if you got hit. I never heard anybody tell how they got hit by lightning."

"Cows get hit all the time."

"They're dead too."

"I got hit. Look, my arm's gone on me. Look!"

I held out my shaking arm. I had no feeling in it, and I couldn't make a fist.

"Yeah, yeah," said my brother, without looking.

I plunked myself down beside him on the steps and started crying. Until then he hadn't looked up from the fish; he hadn't even looked at my arm when I told him to. But he looked at me now and grinned, and I realized the mess I looked: hair flat to my head and misery all over me, holding that lightning arm like a martyr.

"I'll bring the cows home," he said, and pushed the wet hair out of my eyes.

I stayed out in the rain a few minutes longer, dragging my arm and pulling the small carrots with my left hand, digging new potatoes, washing them under the pump before taking them into the house in a sling I created with my coattails. If you don't grow your own, you don't know what a new potato is. The first potatoes of the year, the tiny white balls of perfection you can steal from the roots of a living plant with your fingers, no need for a shovel — now, that's spring. They take no time at all to cook and you need no butter to wake up their taste. They are like nothing you buy now in a grocery store, and when you put them whole in your mouth, you know they're something to celebrate.

I washed the new potatoes — there was no need to skin them — and snipped off the tops and scraped away the little whiskers on the tiny carrots. I coated the fish in flour and fried them in bacon fat and put the kettle on the fire for tea. My lightning arm came back to me slowly, tingling at first, then growing painful. But it stayed weak, making me clumsy. My grip gave out, and I slopped boiling water over my shoe, spread flour over my dress, dropped a cup on the floor.

My mother's scrapbook was there as always, on the rocking chair; its red cover was the only bit of real color in the kitchen. Once the fish was frying, I reached for the scrapbook with my good arm, but as I did I heard my father's heavy footsteps on the porch. I slipped back to the stove and kept my back to the kitchen door, turning the fish and feeling the hot tightness spreading up my neck and over my cheeks. My father sat on the bench, took off his boots, and dropped them on the floor with a bang that made me jump. He coughed.

"Where's your mother?"

"I don't know," I said. "The barn, likely."

He poured himself a cup of water, drank it, and poured another.

"Dan?" he said.

"Bringing in the cows."

He finished off the last of the water in the jug and poured himself a cup of lukewarm coffee from the pot and drank that too.

"Go to your room," he said.

"Dennis and Filthy Billy. They'll be in soon."

"They're still out in the alfalfa field," said my father. "They'll be late. Go to your room."

"I think I got hit by lightning," I said. "It rolled at me across the field. Got my arm. I can't hold anything. It hurts."

"Go to your room," he said.

"No," I said to the fish.

"Go to your room!" he yelled, and threw his empty cup across the kitchen.

I walked through the parlor and into my room with the blood thundering into my head. My father followed and closed my bedroom window.

"Lay on the bed," he said. "Pull up your dress."

I did as I was told and stared up at the forget-me-nots painted on the headboard, willing myself into them. My father started towards the bed, but the screen door slapped shut and my father flinched. I yanked my dress down. Dan looked at my father through the parlor, looked at me on the bed and looked away. I heard him flip the fish in the pan, turn them onto a plate, and put them on the table.

"Cows walked themselves home," said Dan. "Guess they got sick of the rain and followed you back."

"Clean your hands for supper," my father said to me. He sat in the parlor with his eyes closed until supper was ready.

Dan washed himself up and didn't try to talk or catch my eye, and I was thankful for that. I kept my mind on serving dinner and avoided looking at my father. My mother came in from milking, washed, and changed her clothes. A little while later, as I set plates on the table, Billy and Dennis shuffled in, slapping their wet hats on their coats. I filled my father's jug of water and served the men the bigger fish. My mother and I took the small ones. Dennis slid his hand along mine as I handed him his plate and he gave me a long look. When he saw me eating with my left hand, he asked, "You go hurt yourself?"

"Beth got hit by lightning," said Dan.

Billy looked up at me, and at my arm. I pulled it off the table and cradled it in my lap.

"Rubbish," said my father.

"She did!" He turned to me. "Tell them."

I didn't answer and, except for Billy's whispered swearing, the room went quiet for a while.

"Where did you catch this fish?" asked my father.

"Mystic Lake," said my brother.

My father pushed his plate away from him. "I won't eat fish from that lake," he said.

My brother immediately pushed his plate angrily across the table and stood up over my father. "My fish isn't good enough for you, eh?"

My mother and I stiffened for the confrontation, but it didn't come. My father took his pipe from his pocket and concentrated on lighting it; my brother stood frozen in his provocation, staring at my father, his big jaw moving back and forth. The fish was a ball in my throat. I saw that I held my fork in midair, and lowered it to my plate. My mother moved her fork from side to side on the oilcloth. When I thought the room might explode, my father said, "There's bodies in that lake."

His voice punctured my brother's anger, and my brother sank back into his chair.

"There was a ferry lost in 'twenty-one," he said. "Twenty bodies went to the bottom of Mystic Lake. Storm came up out of nowhere, drowned them all. We went out with poles and nets, tried to drag the lake, but of course we found nothing. A week or so later a lightning storm brought up a corpse, that's all. Found it floating in the middle of the lake the next day. For a long time after, the fish caught in that lake had rings and jewelry in their guts. Other things too, coins, buckles, buttons, anything shiny. Made me sick. I won't eat fish out of that lake."

Though I knew where the fish had really come from, I didn't want it now either. It smelled of death and discord.

"I got a story," said Dennis. "Jimmy George was down in Horse Meadows last week with my uncle, working on the fence near Jimmy's place, when they come across this bear eating on one of Jimmy's sheep. Neither of them got guns on them. The bear doesn't take off. Just goes on eating the sheep. So Jimmy picks up a fence post and hits him over the head with it. The bear goes on eating and both Jimmy and my uncle hit him with fence posts. That bear didn't stop eating on that sheep until they conked him out."

"That's the biggest load of rubbish I ever heard come out of your mouth," said Dan. "And I heard lots."

"It's in the paper this week and everything."

"Still rubbish."

"We're going to operate on that brindle tonight," my father said.

My stomach knotted up to nothing. I'd named that brindled cow Gertrude. Gertrude hadn't caught, that is, she hadn't become pregnant, so she was no good as a milk cow. She'd be sold as beef. My father's notion was to remove her ovaries so she'd gain weight, in the way a steer puts on fat much faster than an uncastrated bull. It was a foolish idea, and my father should have known it.

Filthy Billy and Dennis looked at each other.

"I pay you to work and you'll work," said my father.

"Not tonight," said Dennis. "I put in a full day already. You got to pay me better if you want me to work nights."

"Fine then, Billy will."

Dennis looked over at Filthy Billy and Filthy Billy looked at his plate. "Nope," said Dennis. "Granny's right. You got to pay us better."

My father stood up and flung his arms up. "Then get out. You won't eat at my table."

Dennis shrugged and stood up. He picked up his plate to take with him and tried to pass me a look, but I kept my head down. Filthy Billy played with his food for a moment, then grabbed a bread bun and ran out of the house so quick he upset his chair and it fell crashing to the floor. My father kicked the chair and sat heavily on his own. He rubbed his face, and looked over at my brother.

"Oh, no," said Dan. "I told you I'm having no part of it. It's a dumb idea."

My father slammed his fist on the table. My mother and I both jumped. "You'll do as I say!"

"Forget it," said Dan.

My father stood up. "I'll whip you good."

"You don't scare me," said my brother. "You're nothing."

Dan grabbed the .22 from the wall rack and marched out the door. My mother and I sat frozen, our forks in the air. Finally my father sat again.

"Then you and the girl will help me tonight."

"Oh, I don't think so," said my mother. "I have some things to catch up on. Beth has school in the morning."

"You'll do it! Christ, why doesn't anybody listen to me around here?"

My mother poured my father coffee and set it down in front of him.

"We'll do it now!" my father said.

He stood quickly, grabbed his jacket from the hook by the door, and went outside. My mother hurriedly put on her coat and she gathered up a bowl of water, some towels, the curved needles, and linen thread. I put a pair of my brother's pants on under my skirt, lit the kerosene lantern, and followed my mother outside. My father had brought the cow in from the pasture. Her head was held in a stanchion, and her legs were roped together and tied to posts, so if she struggled she would only bind herself tighter. My father pulled up the empty stumping powder box my mother sat on when she milked the cows, and my mother placed the bowl of water, the towels, needles, and thread on the box. My father took a whetstone and his jackknife from his pocket, and sharpened the knife. He told me to hold Gertrude's head by her halter, and to hold the light up higher. My mother pushed her weight against the shoulder of the cow, and my father cut into the cow's hide just before the hipbone; he made sawing motions, as if he were carving the Sunday roast, and the cow struggled violently against her ties and the weight of my mother. A jet of blood spurted up from the muscle at the incision. The cow bawled and kicked out but only managed to tie her legs tighter. My father rocked with the struggles of the cow and kept cutting into her until he'd made an incision about six inches long in the dip before the hipbone.

"There!" he said.

His face shone and he sweated in excitement. The cow bawled and bawled. I wanted to stroke her, to offer her some comfort, but I had to keep her head straight, as my father had instructed, and keep the lantern up.

My mother removed her apron, which had become filthy in the struggle, and threw it to the floor of the barn. "I'm going inside," she said.

I watched her walk down the alleyway of the barn and disappear into darkness. A little while later, a light flared up in the yard as my mother broke the blackout and lit a lamp in front of the kitchen window. The hazy light of the lamp moved through the parlor and went dead as my mother closed her bedroom door. Over the dark house, the Milky Way stretched out forever.

"She can't take it." My father grinned at me. "We can do it by ourselves, then."

He whistled and worked with agonizing slowness. His hand, his wrist, his elbow, disappeared into the cavity of the cow. She moaned and struggled now and again, then the bawling became less frequent. I looked for Lucifer in the rafters. My father began swearing. The ovaries were not where he had imagined, and he searched inside her body until his arm was bloody to the shoulder. He rinsed his hands off in the bowl of water again and again. The cow's head rested heavily on the stanchion and her eyes rolled in her head; she'd bit her tongue and the blood congealed on her nostril. I held the lantern up until my arm grew numb and tingling, then switched hands. A cat, one of the unnamed, slunk up to the bloody dish, sniffed it, and slunk off into the shadows. Lucifer appeared and wrapped himself around my leg and that was a comfort, but when I gave him no attention, he trotted over to a pile of loose hay and curled himself up there. As the night stretched on, the nausea of sleeplessness came over me in waves. I dreamed on my feet and when I jerked awake the barn seemed filled with the tinkling of bells. My father rinsed his knife in the bowl of water and its blade clanked against the side of the dish.

"Higher!" my father said. I switched hands and held up the lantern. I was cold, but the sweat dripped from my father's face. "Damn it!" he said. The old white tom, ears bitten down to nothing, crept up to Lucifer asleep in the hay and tried to do his dirty humping business on the black cat, but Lucifer squirmed away and hissed at the old tom, and the tom danced off. My sense of time dissolved. My arms grew numb, and I switched hands again and again. I dreamed.

"There!" my father said. "There!"

He pulled something from the body of the cow and dropped it in the bloody dish. "Now," he said.

He went to the other side of the cow and made a second incision just in front of the hipbone. The cow struggled for a moment, but she gave up quickly. She didn't bawl this time. My father's search here went more smoothly. He found the second ovary and slopped it into the dish. He stretched his back and wiped the sweat from his forehead with his shirtsleeve. Then he took the two ovaries from the bowl and held them out for me to look at. The ovaries were oblong and purplish red, like the egg plums that grew in my mother's orchard.

"You have these," he said. "This is what makes you female."

I looked at the bloody things, not comprehending what he was trying to tell me. He laughed and threaded the curved needle with linen thread and sewed the hide of the cow together. The sound and texture of the needle going in made my teeth ache. He worked, now, without swearing. His face grew red from the strength of his concentration. But the cow was sinking. She didn't have the strength to stand on her own, and it was the support of the stanchion and post she was tied to that kept her up. What sky I could see out the barn door was growing pink. The rooster crowed and was answered by a rooster far up the valley. Cats fighting, or mating, screeched someplace behind the barn. The homesteader's children clanked rocks in their graves. A black lizard slid across the floor.

My father untied the binds that held Gertrude as I released her head from the stanchion. The cow slumped to the ground. As he bent down to arrange her legs to relieve the pressure of her guts on the incisions, and to pour disinfectant on the wounds, I slipped from the barn and ran to the house. My mother was sitting at the kitchen table, writing on one of the pages of her scrapbook, mumbling to my dead grandmother. Her eyes were puffy, her face was creased where she'd lain on her pillow. She closed the scrapbook as I closed the kitchen door.

"Go catch a little sleep," she said. "I'll wake you for school."

She pushed stray hairs away from my eyes and tucked my hair behind my ears. I pulled my head away.

11

MY MOTHER woke me with a butterfly kiss. She grazed her eyelashes across my cheek, fluttering them, and entered my dream as a moth. I shook my head awake, and my mother stood straight and produced a butterfly from behind her back. It was made from petals of scarlet flax and my mother's fingers breathed life into it. This was a child's game; it made me angry. I threw back the covers and turned my back on her as I dressed for school in a blue pinafore over a white blouse. I ate breakfast in silence and walked out of that kitchen and down Blood Road without saying so long to anyone, triumphant in my crankiness, knowing full well that my mother's sorry eyes were following me.

Lucifer tried to follow me too, mewing, onto Blood Road. A black cat on a red road, he was a sight. But I had no time for him that morning. I threw rocks, harder than I needed to, and he trotted back to the farm.

Halfway to school the anger lessened, and in an act of appeasement for hurting my mother I picked up a turtle straining her way back across the road and set her at the edge of one of the many sloughs. As I did, several turtles splashed from logs into the swamp. The red and yellow of their painted shells reflected like cats' eyes. I watched the turtle I had helped ease into the water become a graceful and swift-moving thing.

The sky was stormy and threatening to rain again. The low clouds and the effects of the sleepless night made me feel heavy, made the day seem out of my control. Just before Boulee's Farm I heard footsteps behind me — I know I heard them — but when I turned no one was there. I ran the rest of the way to school, hugging my lightning arm.

The small one-room school building, with its wood heater in the middle, had cloak hooks at the back. The walls were bare wood except for the blackboard, a framed photograph of the king, and a map of the world. All the grades were jumbled together. I had sat in this same classroom with my brother until he left school to work full-time on the farm. I knew the names of all my classmates then, and I can still remember some of their names now, but I'd never been popular like Dan. I'd been heavy and shy as a younger child and was still dogged by the stigma of that early awkwardness. The only friendship I'd had my father had undone with his strange rages in this last year since the bear attacked our camp. Lily Bell, Mrs. Bell's white-haired, white-faced daughter, had come several times with Mrs. Bell on her visits and we'd become something like friends. Lily Bell had brought me old magazines full of movie stars and beauty secrets, and we had lain on my bed, giggling at the pictures and gossiping about other kids at school. During one visit just the summer before, the summer I was fourteen, Lily Bell brought eyeliner, and we sat at my orange-crate vanity and tried to apply it as the magazines described. My father heard us giggling, came into my room, and slapped the eyeliner from Lily's hand, then slapped her face. Lily Bell burst into tears and ran to Mrs. Bell, who sat with my mother in the parlor. My father stomped after Lily and yelled at Mrs. Bell.

"Your sluttish daughter brought make-up into my house!"

Mrs. Bell sputtered, shamefaced, and said, "I don't know what to say."

But of course she had plenty to say. She said it all around town, to anyone foolish enough to listen to her. And although even my father couldn't scare Mrs. Bell away, Lily Bell had never come to visit again.

Now, at school, when she wasn't ignoring me, Lily Bell joined the other kids in taunting me over my father's craziness. I sat at my desk in the far corner and ignored them all. Opposite me, at the back of the room, the desk where Sarah Kemp had sat was left empty.

During hygiene inspection, Mrs. Boulee found a yellow streak of manure on my forearm, from helping my father in the night, and my nails were dirty. She wasn't all that unkind, saying only I should be more careful about washing up after chores, but that singled me out for Robert Parker and his thugs. I'd been their victim before; years before I'd been forced to steal rhubarb from the abandoned Fraser property next to the school. The house was haunted and I was terrified. One of the boys jumped at me from a derelict window and I ran home, screaming, sure that Old Man Fraser had risen from the dead.

At noon Robert Parker and Lily Bell led a group of kids that surrounded me as I read on the back steps of the school. Robert Parker was a short boy who wore nothing but baggy work denims to school. He'd been trying to catch my eye all that school year, but he had a funny way of going about it. He'd smile at me one minute. Then, when the other boys were around, he'd call my father down. He tried giving me his half smile, half sneer even there, with all those kids around, but when I ignored him and went on staring at my book, he said, "Dirty Beth, never takes a bath!"

I ignored him. I ignored them all.

"Your mother's a witch," said Parker. "She talks to the Devil."

"She does not," I told the book. "That's stupid."

"She talks to herself anyhow," said Parker. "I seen her."

"She's an Indian lover," said Lily Bell. "Lives with Indians. Lets Indians into her house."

Lily Bell was ridiculous in a frilly pretty-girl dress much too young for her. Nevertheless, I felt poor and clumsy in my plain white blouse and pinafore. I looked down at my rough red hands, and the book that trembled in them.

"Squaw," Parker said. "Beth's a squaw."

"I am not," I said.

"No, she's not a squaw," said Parker. "She's a sheep tick."

"Her dad's a hoarder," said one of the other kids. "They get fat while the rest of us starve."

Parker shoved his hands in the pockets of his denims and rocked back on his heels. "Your father's gone crazy," said Parker. "Turned into a wild man. Too long in the hills, eh?"

I looked up into the faces of every one of those kids, Lily Bell and Robert Parker too. "None of you is starving," I said. "You're a bunch of fatheads, the lot of you."

My lightning arm went dead on me suddenly, and the book leapt out of my hands onto the step. I bent to pick it up and, as I did, Parker jumped on the steps behind me, clapped his hand over my mouth, and, together with a couple of other boys, picked me up and carried me, as I squirmed and kicked and tried to scream, over to the abandoned Fraser property. When I bit Parker's hand, he took up a stick and forced it sideways into my mouth. I screamed, but the scream came out only as an indignant grunt. Once in the old house several boys held me down to the floor.

"Let's see how dirty Beth is!" said Parker.

They stripped me of my underwear and pulled my pinafore over my head and ripped my blouse off me. They pulled off my brassiere and laughed at my nakedness. I looked off into the corner of the creaky old building. Decades' worth of dusted cobwebs draped the ceiling like a canopy on a bed. Floorboards were missing in places, and the windows had long ago been knocked out. Parker and the other kids knelt around me, not letting me get up, pushing me. I gathered my knees up and hugged myself. Somebody started up a chant: "Slut, slut, slut!"

Lily Bell stood a little away from the group, watching without an emotion on her face, with her hands on her frilly hips. After a time she picked up my clothes, pushed the other kids out of the way, and threw my clothes at me.

"Let her up," she said.

"She's nothing but a slut," said Parker.

"Leave her!" Lily said again.

I dressed quickly, sobbing, still sitting on the floor, fighting the clumsiness in my lightning arm. When they finally let me go, I ran from the old house and went on running, home.

Parker and the chorus of kids chased after me a little way down Blood Road, yelling, "Slut!" until one by one they stopped chasing me. I ran anyway, crying, following Blood Road through an ocean of alfalfa and young corn, flax and wheat, barley and oats. The clouds finally broke and the downpour began. The thing that had followed me that morning hopped up onto the road. I heard it first, scuffing behind me, and when I turned I saw its footprints, a man's footprints, picking up the wet dirt on Blood Road and leaving dry red tracks that quickly disappeared in the rain. I ran harder until I saw Filthy Billy sitting against a pile of hay in the alfalfa field, with his collar up against the rain. He smiled and waved, swore at me and apologized.

I shouted at him. "Billy," I cried, "something's following me."

"There always is," he yelled back.

I ran up to him, but the thing still followed, and Filthy Billy began swearing and apologizing profusely, and there was no comfort there with him. I left Billy to it and stumbled into the house. I turned to see that the footsteps ended outside, on the front steps. I ran to my room and threw myself on the bed, sat with my back against the wall, and clutched my pillow. The voices of Parker and the other kids who had stripped me filled my head, pounded on the walls. Their hands tore at my clothes. Their laughter beat down on me. Then it seemed if I were to stay very still everything would stop. I lay down and held myself rigid on the bed and closed my eyes. After some time like that, the hand on my lightning arm began to expand, spread out like a balloon, take on proportions much too big for my arm, big enough to hit back. I opened my eyes and looked down my arm and was surprised to see just an ordinary hand. I stared up at the blue forget-me-nots on the headboard of my bed and put myself there, in a stream full of them. The voices faded away and became the rain beating on the roof, the wind howling around the house.

I heard my mother's footsteps and then her face was over me. She called my name and shook me, but I stared through her at the headboard. She called my name louder and slapped my face. She said, "Oh God," and left my room. A little while later she came back with my father. His footsteps shook the bed, so I knew he was angry. He looked distorted and huge.

"She saw me, she's awake," he said.

"Whatever could have happened?" said my mother.

"She should be at school."

"She wouldn't have come home unless something happened," said my mother. She looked into my face. "Beth, dear, what happened?" she said.

Her voice was so tender, so forgiving, I almost answered. But there was a new peace here, in not reacting. Everything seemed in my control. As long as I didn't move, no one could hurt me, nothing could penetrate. She tried for a long time, talking sweetly to me. My father stomped from the house, and my mother cried. Then she left my room and fussed in the kitchen, and I must have slept. When I woke, there was no one in the house, and Lucifer was mewing on my windowsill. He was wet through and looking scrawny, comical. I opened the window, picked him up, and carried him into the kitchen, where I poured him a bit of cream. I drank a cup of milk myself and ate a piece of unbuttered bread as I listened to the rain beating down on the roof and watched it slide past the window sideways. My mother's scrapbook was there on the table in front of me. A pair of scissors sat on top of the red cover, so I knew my mother had added to it, but I felt no desire to find out what was new. I felt no desire to do anything at all but sit there. Even eating the bread was a labor I put myself through to quiet my stomach. My father opened the kitchen door and caught me like that, staring at the scrapbook, petting the black kitten, stuffing bread in my mouth.

"What the hell's the matter with you?" he said.

He stepped towards me, and Lucifer jumped from my arms. I ran around the table and fled from the house across the yard and into the field of violet flax. My father didn't bother to follow me out into the rain. I was soaked through in seconds; my hair was pulled by the wind from its barrettes and pushed around my face. A little while later I saw Lucifer streak from the house, through the rain, into the barn. The storm had taken on a new fury. Wind blistered the rain, and it boiled in all directions. Birds struggled for cover and were carried in the wind like sheets of newspaper. A whirlwind zipped by the hung laundry, flinging my father's underwear and socks up to heaven. The fields were a tumult of motion, pushed, lifted, and cracked by the wind.

I ran back into the house as my father stumbled to the pasture with his coat over his head. From my bedroom window I watched as he struggled to get the animals into the barn. The cows were excited by the storm and his attempts at chasing them looked clumsy and foolish. Seeing him pitted against the storm in this way, I wondered how I could be frightened of him.

As I watched my father bring in the last of the heifers, the anger of the storm ended abruptly and an awful calmness smothered the house. I pressed my face against the window and saw a rain begin to fall, so gently the raindrops seemed to float. Then I saw they weren't rain-drops, they were flowers, violet flax, fluttering to the ground. In no time at all the rain covered the earth in flowers. I opened my window and crawled out onto the purple carpet, took my shoes off and paddled around in pools of flax. The fragrance was intoxicating. The clouds moved on, and still the violet flax drifted down from a blue sky.

12

WITH BLUE FLAX in my cupped hands, blue flax on my hair, my face, my dress, I looked over a world that was blue and as strange as a dream. The shame of nakedness in front of the kids at school seemed so far from this blue world. The wet petals of blue flax plastered the barn roof and the skin of the poplar growing through my father's old Ford truck. Petals littered the window of the truck, covered over the rust, and gave the Ford a moment of new life. Blue flax covered the pile of rocks that marked the graves of the homesteader's children. Chickens pecked and scratched blue petals in their yard. The roof of the house was blue in petals, and on the roadway, the blue looked deeper, vibrating against the red of the dirt.

Out in the pasture, my father's struggle with the calves and heifers had ended. The cows were in the barn calling to one another, springing in the excitement of the storm. My father now stumbled down the length of the wheat field where the young wheat was lodged, fallen over but not flattened completely; each stalk leaned on its neighbor. The flax field was nothing now; its fragile flowers had been whipped by the wind into the air and had showered down on us, a harvest ruined. Even so, the blue. Blue around my toes, blue in the trees. I threw up my handful of wet blue petals and let them rain down on me.

My mother stood at the barn door, hugging herself, looking around in amazement and horror at all that blue. Out in the field, my father turned and started kicking his way back to the house.

"Are you all right?" said my mother. I nodded. "Then go find Dan," she said. "See if he's okay. And Dennis and Billy."

I followed the Swede's fence to the creek, instead of cutting through the field to the benchland where Dan had been working earlier in the day, to avoid my father. The petals of blue flax speckled the morning glory growing up the Swede's fence. I picked some of the blossoms and put them in my pockets. The Swede had been at work again on the disputed fence line, moving it a greater distance yet into my father's field. He had placed deer antlers along the top of this section of his uprooted and dying fence line, making the fence look fierce and ragged and foolish, a portrait of the old Swede himself. My father's bit of fence lay, once again, on the ground: a tangled roll of wire and fence post. Nothing of it reminded me of my father. I touched the antlers of the Swede's fence and tugged at the vines that held them. Honeysuckle vines came off in my hands. An unnatural fear that I would be punished for this act came over me, and I looked around quickly to see if the old Swede was watching. Then I bolted. I followed the creek up to the benchland overlooking my father's property, running until the fear exhausted itself. Dan and Dennis were nowhere I could see, but Filthy Billy was walking around in the field below, looking over the damage. It occurred to me that if I ran down that hill, I could fly. I spread my arms and it felt like that: the air carried me.

Filthy Billy was wet through; his hair was flat to his head from the rain and he was sprinkled all over with blue petals. "Hello (fuck)," he said. "Excuse me, hello (fuck)."

"Hello," I said.

"(Shit) Excuse me. Sorry (fuck). Some storm, eh? (Shit)."

"You seen Dan and Dennis?" I said. "Mum's worried."

"(Fuck) Sorry. They snuck off (shit). Excuse me. Into town before (fuck) the storm. They'll be okay. (Fuck) Excuse me."

I looked off down the fields to the tiny black figure of my father kicking and tramping the wheat field by the barn. Clouds of birds circled over him and the piles of wet and steaming alfalfa hay. Where the blue lake of flax had been, there was now a green patch of flattened plants. Filthy Billy swore under his breath, apologized, and scratched the skin on his forearm.

"Why do you scratch so much?" I said.

"Sorry. I can't (fuck) help it. Excuse me."

"What does *fuck* mean?" I said, to taunt him.

"(Shit) You should go," he said. "(Fuck) Your dad's (shit) going to be mad. (Fuck, shit) Excuse me. After this storm. (Shit) If he sees you and me (shit). Sorry. (Fuck) You should go. (Shit) Excuse me. Please. Go."

I walked through the grass that hemmed my father's fence along Blood Road, watching the grass part for my feet and watching, also, for the tiny black lizards that would climb inside you and eat your heart.

Then I heard it, as if my fears had conjured it, the swooshing behind me, the sound of grass opening a path to the wind. But it wasn't the wind. Something followed me in the grass. There was a second path through the long grass behind mine, coming at me. I walked faster and then ran. The path through the grass chased me. I jumped over the fence behind the pile of rocks, the homesteader's graves, and leaned against the back of the barn out of breath, my heart pumping fear into me. A pair of hands clutched the boards of the fence, as if someone were leaning on it, but nobody was there. I kept my eyes on the hands on the fence, backed around the corner, and ran smack into someone. I jumped and squeaked. The girl with the bell necklace was standing right there.

"Hi!" she said. She bent forward and looked at the fence line. "What you running from?"

"Nothing."

"You home early from school?"

I looked for the hands on the fence which were no longer there, and nodded.

"Hey, you okay?"

I became aware of the noisy chattering of birds. "Where is everyone?" I said.

"In the house."

I sighed and braced myself against the wall of the barn, catching my breath. Despite the storm, the wood in the wall of the barn was warm. I pressed the palms of my hands against it.

"Some storm, eh?" I said. "Look at all those blue flowers! Ever seen anything so pretty?"

"Yeah." She grinned at me. Her two-woman face lit me up inside. I looked from the blue eye to the green and back again, in love with the wonder of them. The blue eye had specks of yellow radiating out into the blue; the green eye held enough brown to be almost hazel. There was little of the white man who had fathered her in the rest of her face, though. She was Indian enough to be an outcast in town and white enough to be an outcast on the reserve. But she looked at me like I looked at the barn kittens, and that was enough for me.

Lucifer wrapped himself around my legs and then lay on my feet. The girl took my hand, and we stared up at the petals dripping from the edge of the red barn roof against the blue sky. Her hand in mine made Parker and Lily Bell and the other kids look foolish in my mind, criminal.

I tried to think of something smart to say, to conjure something smooth and shiny to show her. I wanted to give her something, but I couldn't think what. My stomach bundled up into a new ache, a delightful need to please. The children in the homesteader's graves knocked rocks together briefly. A crow flew off the barn roof over our heads; its wings were transparent.

"There's children buried there," I said. "Under those rocks."

"I know it."

"How do you know that?"

"Everybody knows it," she said. "And how they died."

"How'd they die?"

"You don't know that?"

"Dennis says some bear got them, like what got Sarah Kemp."

"It was Coyote," she said.

"A coyote? A coyote got them? That's crazy. A coyote wouldn't kill those kids."

The girl with the bell necklace spread a know-it-all smile on her face but didn't answer me.

"I think I hear them sometimes," I said. "Knocking around."

"Coyote killed them, so they know when he's around," she said. "They get all excited. Try to warn you."

"That's silly."

She turned my way, leaning her shoulder against the warm barn wall, and looked at my face up close, so I could feel her breath on my cheek. She studied my hair and petted my hand. After a time I heard my father yell, from some distance away, at the end of the wheat field near the creek. I couldn't hear what he said, but I could see he was angry. Lucifer ran off. We let our hands fall. Finally my father came close enough that we could hear him.

"You!" he said. "You deaf? Get off my property. Get away from here. Lousy Indian! Get off my property."

He marched at us. I looked at the girl with the bell necklace and saw that her face had gone stony. She turned and fled, jingling, into the house, followed by my father. The birds on the petal-blue roof of the house lifted. Presently the women of Bertha Moses's family filed out the door. They jingled, sang, and fluttered, and the birds accompanied them. The girl with the bell necklace looked back at me several times, but neither of us waved.

13

I HESITATED back to the house. The door to the kitchen was open, but the screen door was closed. Through it I saw my father kneeling before my mother as she sat in her rocker. My mother held my father, like she used to hold him in the days before the bear attack, and he cried. She was dressed in her sour milking dress, and he leaned into her breast, heaving with the sorrow of that lost harvest. It wasn't until then that the tragedy of the storm hit me. I'd been flirting with a girl who petted me like a kitten while my father was out there taking stock of the damage. I was wondering, tickled, at the blue that was our ruined flax crop spread all over the yard. We made our living out there in the field. Those crops fed the cows, fed ourselves, and brought in the money to buy the flour my mother hoarded behind her marriage bed. There was still time to replant, and my father would do that. But if the weather didn't help us along, if that crop failed too, then how would we live? I backed away from the kitchen door and stood for a while looking over the yard feeling sick with worry. The homesteader's children clanked the rocks in their graves, as they almost always did this time of day. Over them, on the edge of the barn roof, a crow paced back and forth, back and forth. The voices of Parker and Lily Bell and the other kids slipped in under the worry and pounded louder and louder at my head until they took over. My lightning arm went numb, and I nestled it against my chest as if it were a frightened child.

Lucifer trotted up to me, mewing, and wrapped himself around my leg, then flopped himself over on the red dirt, offering his belly to me. I rubbed him with the toe of my boot, and then wandered over, through the orchard, to the Swede's fence. The Swede's billy goat was ramming his head into one of the trees that made up the fence, but our sheep ignored him and went on grazing between the fruit trees. The bell on the lead sheep rang out as she ran up to me and nosed my fingers for feed. They were a strange sight, sheep out of dreams. The blue flax had clung to their coats along with everything else. I sunk my hands into their blue wool and rubbed next to their skin, where the lanolin lay, to smooth away the dryness on my hands. When Dan and Dennis sheared the sheep for my father, as they would sometime this month before the real heat of summer began, their callused hands went as soft as any city man's. The smell of wool on a live sheep is the same as the smell of lamb meat you eat at a restaurant or buy in a supermarket. This was the smell my hands carried, as I plucked blossoms off the Swede's dying fence and threw them in the air so they would rain down on me.

I went back to the barn and checked the cow my father had operated on. She was still lying as she had that morning. I nudged her bony back and slapped her, to try to get her up, but she wouldn't move. There wasn't much hope for her now; a cow that can't get up is a dead cow. I filled a bucket with water and put it in front of her and smoothed the hair between her horns. Because she lay, the skin across her belly stretched the wounds open. Flies landed on the wound, darted away, and landed again.

When I finally went back to the house my father was no longer there. My mother was feeding the fire and whispering, explaining something to my dead grandmother. She looked sideways at me as I came in, and said, "Hello, dear."

She'd taken a bag of flour from the hole in the wall behind her bed and leaned it against the kitchen cupboards. Flour was on the floor and on the kitchen table where she'd been mixing a batch of bread in a large ceramic bowl. Flour was in her hair, on her nose, and down the front of her dress. Though there were bread recipes within the pages of her scrapbook, the scrapbook remained on the rocking chair while she made bread; my mother never needed the recipes to guide her. She made bread so frequently that it became one of those mindless habits that made hours disappear into daydream.

"Are we going to be all right?" I said.

"I don't know. I don't know anything anymore."

I sat on the kitchen chair beside her.

"Are you ready to tell me what happened today, at school?" She didn't look up and talked through pursed lips.

My stomach tightened up. I searched my hands and picked dirt from under my nails. "Nothing happened," I said.

"Why were you home early?"

"Mrs. Boulee let us out early."

"You were so strange on the bed. Like some kind of fit."

"I felt sick. I fell asleep, then I couldn't come out of it."

My mother stopped working the dough and looked me up and down for a moment. "You made your father very angry. He doesn't like it when you don't answer him."

"I was asleep," I said.

"With your eyes open?"

"I don't know. I don't know what happened."

"Is it the boys at school?" said my mother. "Are they teasing you?"

"No!" I said. "Nothing happened. I just wasn't feeling well. I'm all right now."

My mother added more flour to the dough and set the bowl in front of me. "Well then," she said, "you can knead that for me."

"What's going to happen with the crops?" I said.

"I don't know. We'll plant again, I guess. It's a lot of money lost on wages."

I washed my hands and went to work. My mother insisted that I knead the dough in the way she did, bringing the dough forward with my right hand, and pushing it down back into itself with the heel of my left palm. Pull forward and push down. My whole body rocked with the effort of it. I was tired and cranky from lack of sleep and shamed by the day. Though I was used to physical work, kneading dough always left an ache in my upper arms, and tensed the back of my neck. But at the same time the rocking motion was hypnotic, calming. I pushed the day's events into that dough, brought them up, and beat them back down again. Parker's laughing face, then the girl's hand in mine. My father's anger, then blue petals drifting. Pull forward, push down.

14

MY MOTHER woke me very early, as the sky was growing light, before my father and brother were up. Her face was still puffy and creased from sleep and she wore her milking dress and kerchief. She stood over me patting my shoulder.

"I need help," she said, and when I sat up to clear the dreams from my head, she left my room. I threw my brother's jeans on under my nightgown, put on a sweater and some socks, and went into the kitchen. My mother had lit the lamp on the kitchen table and now sat in her rocking chair, holding one elbow and covering her mouth as she did when she cried. But she wasn't crying. She was laughing, or rather, trying to hold in a laugh. My mother had thrown my father's jack shirt over her big bowl of bread dough, to keep the dough warm overnight, but she must have miscalculated the amount of yeast, or else the fire in the stove was too hot for the warm night. Whatever the case, her bread dough had risen out of the bowl and oozed into the arms of my father's jacket and over the edge of the bowl into a heap. In the uncertain light, the bread-filled jacket looked like a drunk taking a nap face-first on our kitchen table. I laughed too, but silently. My mother and I held in the noise of our laughter until our eyes stung.

"Well," she said quietly. "We better clean this up before your father wakes, or he'll be livid."

She scraped the bread dough away from the jacket with a wooden spoon, then gave the jacket to me. While she cleaned up the mess on the kitchen table, I took the jacket outside and washed it down under the pump water in the early morning light. I scraped the bits of dough off with my fingernails and took the coat back inside to hand wash it in the washbasin. I hung the coat on a hanger behind the stove.

"If he asks, we're just getting a start on cleaning winter linens," said my mother.

My father didn't ask. He didn't even notice the coat hanging there, in the shadows behind the stove. He sat at the kitchen table with his back to the coat, hunkered over his coffee. My brother came out, yawning, and after a time Billy and Dennis scraped their boots off on the porch steps and came inside. They all sat around staring into their coffee mugs, too sleepy to talk at first, as my mother and I served up a breakfast of porridge, toast, and marmalade.

"That cow's dying," said Dan. My father looked up at him. "You don't shoot her today, I will."

"Give her time," said my father.

"Christ, she's suffering. Have you looked at her? There's maggots in that wound you made."

"She'll heal up."

Dan stood up. "If you're not going to, I'll kill her myself."

My father stood up and leaned over the table at Dan. Dennis went on eating. Filthy Billy went on staring at the table and cussing under his breath.

"Leave her," said my father.

"She's dying," said Dan. "She's in pain. Can't you hear her moaning?"

"You eat here, you do as I say. Leave her."

"Cutting that cow open was just stupid."

My father hit his fist against the table, sloshing the coffee in his cup. Filthy Billy stood up beside Dan. We all looked at him, surprised.

"(Shit) She's dying," said Billy. Then he was overcome by a wave of cussing so violent it took the breath from him and made him sit down again. We watched him at it, amazed.

My father, still standing, bowed his head for a moment. "I'll do it," he said.

"What?" said my brother.

"I said I'll do it, goddamn it."

"Then I'll give you a hand."

"I don't want your help. The girl."

"She'll be late for school," said my mother.

"Let her."

"Let Dan help," said my mother. "For heaven's sake!"

"(Fuck) I'll do it," said Billy.

"No!" said my father. "The girl."

My mother quickly packed a sandwich of new bread, butter, and last year's strawberry jam into the syrup can that was my lunch pail, muttering all the while to the ghost of my grandmother, and handed it to me as I followed my father out the door. "Try not to be late," she said.

My father strode off to the barn so quickly I couldn't keep up to him. The petals of flax were turning brown on the barn roof and over the old Ford. When I got to the barn door, my father was already at the other end with the cow he'd operated on. The old white tomcat was walking circles in front of the barn door, and the morning sun scattered his shadow around the barn. I all but tripped over him as I came in. His eyes were glazed and paralysis had mounted one side of him, just as the stroke had mounted one side of Mrs. Halley and pushed her world into a black hole. It looked like the old tom intended to cross to the other side of the barn, but sickness reined him in like a rider turning a horse. I lifted the cat by his belly and carried him halfway across the barn. He hung limp in my hands and when I put him down again, he created a new orbit in the middle of the barn, round and round. I put my hand up to test his sight, but he had become blinded by his intent. He could see nothing but the other side of the barn.

At the far end of the barn, with the sledgehammer in his hand, my father motioned me to come and hold the rope halter on the cow. I held her so her head and neck were pulled flat out on the floor. My father knocked the sick cow squarely on the forehead, then took out his jackknife and cut her throat. The cow jerked from the impact of my father's blow, but that was all.

"Why do you have to go around hurting things," I said.

My father turned and looked at me.

"Operating on that cow was just stupid," I said.

My father got up so quickly that he stumbled over the empty stumping powder box I sat on when I milked. When he steadied himself, he took me by the shoulders and slapped my face. It stung, hot, and I was frightened, but I said, "You don't scare me," and surprised myself with the saying of it.

That creepy darkness spread under my father's eyes, and I felt sick. He walked at me slowly, undoing his belt, and then Filthy Billy was there, at the doorway of the barn. As he came in he nearly tripped over the old tom. Nevertheless he walked up the aisle of the barn slowly, too casually, muttering obscenities. He picked up the stumping box that my father had tripped over, looked inside, and put it down again.

"Went and forgot (shit) my canteen someplace," he said. "Don't know (fuck) where I (shit) put it."

My father watched Billy stumble around the barn for a few moments and then walked around me, without looking at me. He said, "Crazy man," as he left the barn.

Filthy Billy bent down to pick up one of the grain pails and watched my father leave. Then he came over to me.

"You (shit) okay?" he said.

I shrugged.

Billy pointed out the tomcat turning circles in the alleyway. "(Shit) He's got a (fuck) demon riding him (shit)," he said.

"Nah, he's had a stroke," I said.

As we watched, the old tom carved out the same circle over and over again, never varying. His white coat was stained in patches. His eyes weren't registering what was before him.

"I should do him in," said Billy, and for once his speech was clear of obscenities.

I said, "Yes," and we looked at each other, both of us surprised that he wasn't swearing for that moment. But as soon as we did, he was back at it, cussing under his breath. Lucifer bounded into the barn, stopped short at the tom, hissed, and arched. When he got no response, Lucifer walked carefully around the tom and wound himself around my feet and then around Billy's, round and round in a figure eight.

"Maybe leave him," I said. "Maybe he'll get better."

"(Shit) Maybe," said Billy.

We watched the old tom for a little longer and then Billy tipped his hat to me and left the barn.

I didn't go to school that morning, or any morning after. By running around the back of the root cellar and following the old Indian trail, I could reach Blood Road without anyone seeing me. My mother would take the democrat into town later in the day, to take the cream to the train station, so I turned left and followed Blood Road towards the reserve. There were only one or two turtles still making the trek across the road. Lucifer followed me a little way, mewing several yards behind me. But he got nothing in the way of loving from me that day and disappeared into the woods, just as I turned off Blood Road to follow another of the old Indian trails. The bush this low on the mountain was dense, and I was glad for the trail. I swung my syrup-tin lunch bucket and looked up into the roof of trees. Branches were broken at eye level along the trail, breaks fresh and deliberate: a birch branch was stuck in the crotch of a fir, a willow sapling drooped in the arms of a spruce, bits of trees that didn't belong together, that didn't grow anywhere near one another, trees with different needs. The branches were pointers, like those Dennis or Filthy Billy used when hunting with my brother. If the hunting went on for more than a few days and the party split up, sometimes Dennis or Billy grabbed a handful of grass and left it near the dead fire. Whoever followed could tell how long ago the rest of the party had been there by the state of the grass. Then they'd put branches in the trees like those on the trail, pointing the direction they'd gone. People hunted here or on our land, but they didn't need markers. My brother and I shot deer eating off the wheat stacked in stooks in the fields, and the occasional cougar, and many coyotes skulking behind the sheep in the pastures.

I took the birch branch from the spruce and walked with it, driving myself that fingernails-on-blackboard crazy with the feel of birch bark under my callused fingers. I followed the pointers out of listlessness and boredom more than curiosity. At first, the forest was quiet. Then I began hearing the noises that made up the quiet: trees aching, birds whistling, someone chopping wood way off. There was something else, too. A metal sound, a tinkling or clanking, like the sound of a horse harness, but it was too far off and receding to hear clearly. I branched off the many trails, following the sound, and when I was about ready to give up and turn back I came on the girl with the bell necklace, Bertha Moses's granddaughter, walking some distance ahead of me in the bush. She was dressed as she always was when she came to the house, in boy's jeans, a western shirt that was too small for her, and of course she wore the bell necklace; that was the sound I'd heard. The sight of her slim back in that clearing lit me up inside. She was bending over, working with something very tiny in her hands. She turned and I ducked down behind a wild rose bush.

"Beth Weeks, I see you," she called out.

I stood up from behind the bush and grinned, all shyness and delight.

"You were sneaking up on me," she said.

I took a few steps forward, holding my syrup tin with both hands.

"Scared me too!" she said.

She looked sideways at my wool skirt and shook her head. My eyes were drawn to the necklace. It was made from bells of many sizes, all cheap and a little tarnished, and strung on one thread of red yarn. I was tempted to pull the necklace because one good yank would send the bells tinkling into the air. She jingled the necklace.

"Like it?" she said. "I made it."

I nodded, then noticed the bloody cuts on her arm.

"What happened to your arm?" I said.

She pulled her sleeve down. "Nothing."

"Let's see." I reached to take her wrist but she pulled her arm away. "You did that, didn't you?" I said.

"So what if I did?"

"Doesn't it hurt?"

"Mind your own business." She buttoned her shirtsleeves. "What're you doing out here anyway?"

"Walking. What're you doing?"

"Nothing."

"No, really. What's that you've got in your hand?"

The girl tried to hide what she had in her hand, but I pried her fingers open. She had two live crickets, tied together with a blond hair. She let them go and they struggled on the ground for a time, to free themselves.

"What're you doing?" I said again.

"Nothing."

"You killing them?"

"No!"

"What then?"

She nudged the struggling crickets with her toe. "It's a love charm," she said finally. "You tie two crickets together with the hair of whoever you love."

"Who are you in love with?" I said.

The girl shrugged and went shy. She looked up and around at the sky through the trees. I flicked a ladybug off my skirt.

"I never seen you in pants," she said. "You don't ever wear pants?"

"When I do chores. Under a skirt!" I giggled.

"Your dad say so?" she said.

"My mum doesn't let me wear pants."

"Granny says your father's gone stupid."

I was immediately angry and felt my face flush, but I said nothing.

"I'm sorry," she said. "Granny says that about a lot of people."

I shrugged.

"Is it true he's got metal in his head?"

"A bomb blew up right next to him. In the war. Covered him right up. Left bits of stuff in him. Mum says they couldn't get it all out. She nursed him for a while, after. That's how they met."

"Is that what makes him like that?" she said.

The anger lit up like a match. "Like what?"

"I don't know. Yelling all the time. Or not even that. Like when he's all nice one minute and then he's crazy. Like how he gets so jealous if a man even touches his cap at your mother."

The fire licked around inside me and sputtered out. I kicked the ground in silence for a while. "He wasn't always like that. You seen him. Even last spring he wasn't like that. After that bear attacked our camp, after we sold the sheep, he wasn't right after that."

"Bet it was Coyote. Granny says that. She's scared Coyote's back, sneaking around. Granny says if a man's got something wrong with him, if he's a drunk or got hit on the head or bushed or something, then Coyote can get inside him and make him crazy, make him do stuff. Bad stuff."

I laughed. "Like Coyote Jack. I heard that. Dan told me you guys think he's a shape-shifter."

"Yeah, like him."

"You really believe that?"

The girl shrugged. "Granny's stories. Sometimes she swears it's the truth. Sometimes she says it's just stories."

I kicked the ground. The girl looked down at the crickets and then back up at me.

"I like your hair," she said. She reached out and ran her fingers through my hair for some time without speaking. It felt good and calming, like my mother brushing my hair before bed. After a minute I closed my eyes and enjoyed it.

"You're beautiful, like an angel," she said, and just then, I felt that way. She stopped stroking my hair and sunk both hands into her jean pockets. I tried to think if there was something in my lunch can fit to give her; I tried to think of something to say. I felt silly asking her name because I already sort of knew her. She'd been at the house with the rest of Bertha's family so many times, drinking coffee, looking at the walls.

"Want to come to my place?" she said.

I nodded and began walking with her before I thought about where it was she lived. She lived in Bertha's house on the reserve road with all the other women in Bertha's clan. At that realization, all the name-calling Parker and Lily Bell and the other kids from school did rose up in a hot wave that burned my cheeks and made me sulky. *Indian lover. Squaw.* I walked on with her anyway with my fear of the reserve making me silent. The girl with the bell necklace walked ahead of me, breaking off branches now and again and sticking them in the crotches of trees. Her walk wasn't a walk at all; it was a skip, a dance. I found myself copying her. She put another branch in the crotch of a tree.

"What are you doing?" I asked.

She shrugged and kept walking.

"I saw Filthy Billy the other night tying his pants legs together before he went to sleep," I said. "And he jumped over the fire because a lizard chased him."

"So the lizard don't come eat his heart."

"Yeah."

"My great-uncle did that too before he died. Some of the old people are still scared of those lizards. Filthy Billy's just plain crazy. Granny says she's seen a man die from his heart getting eaten that way, by one of them lizards. Can't believe half what Granny says."

"I like her," I said. "I still have that velvet she gave me."

We walked on a little longer in silence. The girl put branches in the crotches of trees now and again, and I found myself doing the same.

"I'll show you something," said the girl.

"What?"

"You'll see."

15

THE GIRL with the bell necklace left the trail and pushed her way into the bush. I followed with my hand up to protect my face and my skirt from catching on every branch. "Dennis is scared of those lizards too," I said.

The girl grinned at me. "So am I."

"They're not even lizards, you know," I said. "They're salamanders. My dad says they'll live through fire. You can throw them in the fire and they'll live. They live forever."

"Don't tell Billy that, eh?"

We came on a clearing and what looked like a mound of dirt overgrown with moss and weeds. Bush was all around us, and someplace close Turtle Creek burbled away. "This is Granny's old house," said the girl. "A winter house."

"Where?" I said.

She took me by the hand and led me forward slowly, testing the ground with her feet, as if we might fall through to China. "Careful," she said. Then there it was, a hole to China in the ground, an opening into darkness at the center of that mound of dirt and weeds. I could clearly see the old posts and sticks that served as supports.

"There'd be a ladder there," said the girl. "Right down the center where the smoke came up. You'd climb down into the smoke to get into the house. Sometimes there was a door on the side for women and old people, so it was easier, and so the women were never higher up than the men. It was bad luck to have a woman over you if you were a man."

"People lived there?" I said.

"Granny lived there, when she was small. That was my great-granny's house. Then it was Granny's house. My mum wants nothing to do with it, so I guess it's mine now, eh?"

"My dad wouldn't give nothing to me," I said. "The farm goes to Dan when he's done with it, even though Dan wants nothing to do with it."

The girl led me back down the bush trail, and before I knew it we broke out onto the road that led right through the reserve village. Women watched us from inside their houses; I saw them from the corner of my eye and when I turned to look at them, they disappeared. Two old men sat on the steps of one of the houses, laughing and playing ball with several small children. When they saw me they stopped laughing and watched as we passed.

The reserve was overwhelmed by the church. It sat up on the hill at the far end of the reserve road, painted white with new shingles on the bellcast roof of the belfry. Children played all over the churchyard. Two little girls ran, laughing. The older of the two grabbed the other and made her stand still. The older girl put her hands on her hips as her mother might, wagged her finger, and said, "Shut up, you just shut up," and then they ran off, giggling. A small boy with a dirty face held a dog at the hips and made humping motions against its backside. I looked away.

The church was ringed by an unkept graveyard dotted with simple white crosses, no big headstones or stoic angels, no fence to keep the chickens out. Children played there now, in the graveyard, pitching a baseball, batting, catching, and running from cross to cross as if they were bases. As we got closer, I saw objects on the graves. In one case it was a frypan; in another, a teacup without the saucer; in another, the head of an ax; in another, the black lid off a woodstove. Whether children's playthings or tokens to take to the next life, I never asked. Before I had the chance, two boys were on us, following our footsteps, capturing our shadows in their arms. They were dressed up like cowboys, and one wore chaps. He said, "Hey, half-breed, you gonna come to my house tonight, drink some booze, eh?"

"Go shut up," said the girl.

"What, you too good for us now, running with a white girl?"

The other one called, "Hey, white girl, what time is it? Got to hurry, eh? Got to be on time, eh?"

"Wouldn't touch no half-breed anyhow," said Chaps. "She's got fleas."

"No, she got ticks from that Weeks girl. Sheep ticks. That's what them Weekses are, a bunch of sheep ticks. Whole town knows they're sheep ticks."

"She's a Cockney. Go back where you belong, Cockney."

Without a twitch to betray her, the girl swung around and pushed the boy without chaps down. Her necklace swung around too and tinkling accompanied her attack. The other boy moved at her.

"You gonna hit a girl?" she said. "You're a big man, Jason, hitting girls. Real big man. Bet you learned that from your dad. Bet you watched him beat your mother. You learn good, eh?"

The boy took a step back. "You're no girl," he said. "You're a sheep tick. Stupid, dumb half-breed, got no father."

"You got no mother. You got a woman beater for a father."

"Least my mum and dad was married when they had me."

"That don't stop you from being a bastard."

The other boy rose up through this and pulled on Jason's sleeve. "Come on," he said. "That's the white in her talking. She ain't worth nothing."

The unnamed boy spit in the red dirt at our feet and backed off down the road. When they were far enough for me to be brave, I said, "I think he likes you."

"Sure he does."

I ribbed her, and she jostled me back and then raced me up to the porch of the log house that could belong only to Bertha Moses. A patchwork quilt with big red scraps of that velvet she had given me hung over the porch railing along with women's bloomers, stockings, brightly colored blouses, and skirts. The house was an unpainted, weathered gray. It wasn't a government house like the others. It looked as if it had been built someplace else and then reassembled in this spot because old chinking was blended with new in the gaps between the logs and in some places the wood wasn't weathered as much, as if it had been snug against another log for a time and then exposed in the rebuilding. The house was on the reserve road but wasn't on reserve land. There was a huge, neatly kept vegetable and flower garden in front which we had to walk through to get to the porch; the garden was fenced off from the chickens that pecked and scratched the yard. Bertha had made patchwork curtains, the same as the quilt that hung over the railing. I stopped at that quilt and pinched the softness in the velvet squares.

"I helped make that," said the girl.

"My mum used to quilt," I told her. "Used to get the neighbor ladies over and set up the quilting frame in the parlor. I used to play under the quilt like it was a tent and pick up all the scraps and pretend to make quilts for my dolls. She hasn't made a quilt for years."

"No use quilting by yourself," she said. "Come on."

We entered the house smells of strong coffee, bacon, and women's sweat and talc. More clothes were strung from wall to wall across the stove. The cabin was divided into several small rooms with partitions that didn't quite reach the ceiling; clothes were draped over the spaces between the walls and the roof. A ladder by the stove led up to a square hole in the roof; each rung of the ladder held some garment drying. There were objects everywhere, hanging from nails or dangling from the ceiling or over chairs: half-finished baskets, bundles of grass, skeins of wool, bundles of fabric, a flour sack full of socks. There were several braided rag rugs on the floor. The door to the room behind the stove was open; the room contained a bed that filled almost the whole room and was covered in piles of fabric and clothing, books, magazines, boxes, brown bags, and sugar and flour sacks trailing fabric and bits of yarn. Bertha Moses slid past the bed and came out of the room, concentrating on threading a needle. She looked up and smiled at me.

"Beth!" she said. "Come sit down, sit down."

She offered me one of the many chairs crowded around a table no bigger than the one we ate at in our kitchen. Several of Bertha's daughters and granddaughters appeared from the rooms; the granddaughter with webbed fingers climbed down the decorated ladder in her stocking feet. They all took a chair and sat without saying anything, watching their hands and snatching looks at me. Bertha picked a piece of fabric from the table, the beginning of a red dress, and threw it on the mattress under the window beside the door. The mattress was covered in a blanket made from strips of rabbit fur and on top of that were several worn copies of movie tabloids with the faces of movie stars on their covers. A few coyote pelts were nailed to one wall. Like many of the women on the reserve, Bertha and her daughters ran traplines over Bald Mountain and parts of the benchland. On the reserve the women trapped and the men hunted, although in Bertha's house, as in our house, the women hunted too. The house had to be fed. One of the daughters opened the window, looked around outside, smiled, and sat down again.

"You watch that window," said the girl with the necklace.

"How come?" I asked.

"Just watch."

"Why aren't you in school today?" said Bertha. I shrugged. "Well, you tell your mother and I won't have to, eh? Nora, get me the coffee going, and there's those cookies in the tin."

The girl with the bell necklace jumped up and busied herself around the kitchen. Her name was Nora, then. I tried it out. "Nora showed me the old house in the ground," I said. "She said you lived in it."

"Sometimes," said Bertha. "We moved around a lot more back then. Before, in my mother's time, there were winter houses like that all over, and every year we rebuilt them. Now it's all caving in. I think sometimes I should rebuild it, but what good is that? No one wants to live in the ground."

"I'd live in the ground," I said. "Sometimes I go into the root cellar. It feels safe."

"My mother used to say the winter houses were safe like a mother's hug," said Bertha.

"I'd die from the smoke," said Nora.

"There's that too, isn't there?" said Bertha. She took her tobacco and papers from her apron pocket and winked at me.

"Granny, ladies don't smoke," said Nora.

Bertha Moses pointed over at the pile of magazines on the bed. "Them movie stars smoke," said Bertha.

"They aren't ladies," said Nora.

"You getting to sound more like your mother all the time," said Bertha. She looked over at the woman who had pulled Nora away from me when they last visited, the woman with a man's voice. The woman looked away and unfolded her hands. For the first time I saw she had an extra little finger on her right hand. Behind her a window looked out over a ragged pasture with a few fat cows and skinny horses grazing on it. Over her head there were two clocks with two different times, neither of them anywhere near right. One clock was more than an hour ahead, the other more than an hour behind. A plaster of paris Christ on a crucifix hung between them.

"Your clocks don't keep time," I said.

"Hmm?" said Bertha Moses. I pointed at the clocks. Bertha and several of the daughters laughed. "Whites and your clocks," said Bertha. "You've got a love affair going. Got to go. Got to be on time. Rush, rush."

Nora came close to refill my cup with coffee and for the first time I smelled the talc on her, violets, cheap violets like my secret bottle of perfume. Under that the smell of liver, the smell of coming-on-sick time, warm though, not unpleasant.

Bertha reached across the table and patted my hand. "I think it's just time runs different for you people."

You people. I looked around at the women, and they stole quick shy looks at me that made me sit up straighter and start judging the room as if I were a stranger. I didn't know what to say so I took sips from Bertha's coffee. The coffee ran through me and got my hands shaking and my skin prickling. Nora brought out bread and cheese and bully beef and we ate. The women began talking quietly among themselves. Then there was a flap and hullabaloo and a chicken flew in the window. The women all laughed. I started to get up, to help catch the chicken, but Nora held my arm. We all watched the chicken nestle a place for herself among the magazines and rabbit fur on the mattress, cluck and croon and lay an egg. The women all laughed again and watched me watching the chicken. When the hen had done her business, she hopped back up onto the windowsill and flew off. Nora picked up the egg and gave it to me. It was warm and still a little wet.

"How's that for service?" she said.

"Your daddy sent us some missionaries the other day, eh?" said Bertha. "They come to my door and want to make me listen and then they want handouts. Crazy people. I told them to go away, and then they tell me I got to get born again. I tell them I had enough trouble getting born the first time."

"You sent them away, all right," said Nora's mother. "With jam and bread and eggs."

"No one leaves my house empty-handed," said Bertha. "Speaking of which, you take that back with you."

Bertha reached over to the crowded little table behind her and slid a jar of huckleberry jam across the table to me. Nora watched my cup and filled it with coffee as soon as it was half empty. She filled the cookie plate and placed more bread and cheese in front of me. She smiled at me under those strange two-woman eyes and watched for my every need, in the way my mother now served my father.

"I heard you go walking lots in the bush," said Bertha.

"Sometimes," I said. "Sometimes I go up to watch the wild horses."

"You be careful running around in the bush." said Bertha. "You'll end up like that Kemp girl. She's not the first to go like that. You got some kids buried on your place that went the same way."

"What do you mean?" I said.

"Just be careful," said Bertha. "And don't go out after dark. You neither, Nora."

"There's nothing else to do," I said. "There's no place to go."

"Listen to me, Beth," said Bertha. "Those Christ people rule this village here, but Coyote owns the bush. He always has."

"Coyote Jack, you mean?" I said, but she didn't answer. She took up the red dress from the mattress and went back to her sewing. Nora patted my arm.

"Is the smoke getting too much?" Nora said. "Granny's always got to have a cigarette in her mouth."

She got up to open the window by the stove, and I put my hand up to stop her. "No, I'm fine," I said.

"Cookies?" she said.

"I'm full," I said. "They're good. I'm just full."

"I see John's been at that Swede's fence again," said Bertha. I drank my coffee and didn't look at her. "No good can come from that," she said.

Nora and I sat in silence for a long time listening to the other women chat quietly about their neighbors, chores to be done, the sickness that was coming over several of the children, the young child who had gone missing the day before, and their fears for their own children, how they weren't letting them out past dark. I watched Bertha sew.

"I'd like a red dress like that," I said. "I'd make it from velvet — like that piece you gave me — and I'd buy a pair of nylons and red shoes and I'd go dancing."

"You want to be a stepper, eh?" said Bertha.

"No, not that," I said. "Just to dress up, you know? Be someplace with people. We never go out anywhere, except church sometimes. Dad won't let me wear anything red. Like it's some kind of sin. He made Mum send back a coat she ordered for me once, just because it had red pockets. It was supposed to be my school coat."

Bertha nodded. "When I was a girl I wasn't allowed to wear red either," she said. "You never knew who had a wild animal for his spirit. If somebody had a predator for a spirit, a bear or a coyote or a cougar, and he saw red, he might think it was blood and go crazy, eat you up. So no girl wore red. Now I wear red any chance I get."

"Don't talk about that," said Nora's mother.

"Why not?" said Bertha. "That was the way. I tell you something else. We had parties in those underground houses. Sometimes forty people in there, dancing and eating and having a good time. But it was sacred too, like going to church. When I was little, I saw a man dancing with a rope tied around his waist and four men pulling on each end of the rope. Those men pulled that man's waist in two so his legs were dancing at one end of the winter house and his chest and head were dancing at the other. When the dance was over he was back in one piece again."

"Nonsense," said Nora's mother.

"You talk worse nonsense than that," said Bertha. "Baby born with no man fathering him. Man comes back to life after three days dead. Man walking on water. *That's* nonsense. I was there. I saw that man dancing in two pieces."

"There's nothing here to go to," said Nora. "No dances, nothing. You got to leave the valley to see anything at all. I'm going to leave, get out of here. I'm going to get a factory job. Live in Vancouver."

Nora's mother didn't say anything to that, but she set her coffee cup down a little too hard and stared at Nora.

I became drowsy from lack of sleep, too much food, and the warmth of Bertha Moses's house. My eyelids began to fall, and I jerked awake when Nora lightly touched my shoulder.

"I'll walk you back," she said.

We walked the way we came, back through the trees behind the church, and down the trail to Blood Road. I followed behind as the girl broke branches off the trees and placed them in the crooks of others. "What're you doing?" I said. "With the branches."

She shrugged. "It's something my mother did, and my grandmother. Only they did it at night. My uncles won't let me out at night. They watch so I don't go. They're afraid of Coyote Jack."

"He's just scared," I said. "He's a silly old man."

"Not so old," she said.

"Anyway, the sticks?"

"It's a thing you do when you become a woman. It's a kind of marking. You go out at night and you leave a trail."

"For who?"

"Nobody, I guess. I don't really know." After a while she said, "I just like the walking. To get away, you know?"

"I know," I said.

"I'm kind of old, I guess. I already had regular periods for a long time. But I didn't hear about it 'til now. My grandmother never told me. She thought my mother told me, but my mother thought it was stupid. She said going out at night into the woods would only get a girl pregnant or eaten by a bear. She says almost everything my grandmother says is stupid. They fight a lot. My grandmother says the worst thing she ever done was let my mother go to that residential school. She said it poisoned everything for my mother. They told my mother everything was stupid. I'm never going to that school."

I heard all this, but I was still vibrating from the word *period*. In my house no one talked about that. Sometimes Mrs. Bell complained about "coming on sick," and my mother blushed at that and said nothing.

"Your mum's got an extra finger," I said.

"What about it?"

"Nothing, I guess."

"You ever see things?"

"Like what?"

"I don't know. Things in the bush."

"Sometimes I think I'm being followed," I said. "I never see it, exactly. But it leaves footprints. It's got hands."

"You got the invisible man following you?"

I didn't answer.

After a while, Nora said, "You think you got that following you, you should talk to Granny. That's Coyote."

"Coyote Jack?"

"Kind of. Just talk to her, eh? She's got stories. Spook you silly."

After a time, she said, "I just seen a ghost."

"Really?" I said.

"I got out past my uncles and went out walking and there was this sound and then a thing, like a light, like a blue light or white went up this tree, zoom, and went up into the sky and was gone, and I knew it was a ghost. That was the night Sarah Kemp got killed."

"No," I said.

"Really."

"You know her?" I asked.

"Nope. Just to see her."

"How did you know it was her ghost?"

"'Cause it was right near where they found her dead."

"You were out there? You could've come across her dead there at night. You could've got killed."

"Yep." She smiled. "I still go out, you know, at night, when I get a chance."

"You're crazy," I said, but I thought she was brave and she knew it.

"Sometime maybe I'll come to your place at night," she said.

"You be careful of my father," I said.

"Always," she said.

"I got hit by lightning."

"No," she said.

"Yes! Came at me on the ground. Got me in the arm, so I can't hold nothing. Now I can't milk very well. My arm goes numb. It takes off by itself."

"You just want to get out of chores," she said.

"You don't go to school?" I said.

"No," she said. "Don't tell nobody. My mum's scared somebody's going to find out, but she's scared of Granny too and Granny won't let me go. I don't want to go. I'm not real Indian anyhow. Now I'm too old and she can't tell me to do nothing anyway."

"I hate school," I said.

"Yeah, well, I wouldn't mind going, but not to the residential school. They made my mother crazy. They beat my uncle. They wouldn't call him by his real name. They called him Samuel. What kind of place takes away your name?"

16

MY FATHER was standing on the porch when I reached home. "Where in God's name have you been?" he said. "You've been keeping your mother waiting. She goes and makes you dinner and you don't have the decency to be here to eat it? Where the hell have you been?"

Something got a hold of me and I just walked right by my father without saying a word, just like Dan. I walked right by him and into the house. He watched me go inside and didn't immediately follow. My mother was just putting dinner on the table. Everything was steaming hot. She smiled at me.

"Hello, dear," she said. "How was school?"

My father stomped into the house and grabbed me by the shoulders and spun me around. He slapped my face. "You answer me when I talk to you. Understand? Where the hell were you?"

I looked right at him and didn't answer. He went to slap me again, but my mother said, "John!" He lowered his hand and sat at the table. Then my mother lied for me. "After school, Beth took some bread to Mrs. Slokum," she said. "How was Mrs. Slokum?"

The Slokums were farmers with property next to the Boulees. We never went to visit them anymore.

"Fine," I said and held up the jam Bertha had given me. "She gave me this jam."

"Go wash up," she said.

Filthy Billy was calm that night, too tired for nerves, likely. He sat through almost the whole meal without scratching and he ate with a delicacy that didn't fit with his whispered profanity. His face was sun-dark and unlike Dennis he'd taken the time to wash up and shave. He caught me looking at him and smiled shyly. Dan gave him a little nudge in the ribs and they exchanged a grin.

My father finished off the last of the water in his jug and reached for the teapot.

"I'm going to get that Swede," said my father. "He went and dammed the creek off the north field. Dead fish floating everywhere, stinking up the water. It's a good thing we got the well. He knows what he's doing, and he's going to pay for it, I can tell you that much."

I looked sideways at Dan. He had a grin on his face that I wanted to slap off.

"You see what he's done to the fence now?" he said. "Planted bramble all over. That'll be a mess coming into my field."

"You don't know it was him that dammed the creek," said my mother.

"I know."

"What do you plan to do?"

"I'll get him all right. Don't you worry."

"Please don't do anything stupid," she said.

My father slammed down the cup he'd been drinking from, and that set Filthy Billy to scratching his face, his arm, his legs. "I don't do anything stupid," said my father.

"What did the homesteader children die of?" I asked.

The question was so out of place and so unexpected in the silence surrounding my father's anger that everyone looked at me. My mother stopped clanking dishes and wiped her hands on her apron.

"What do you want to know that for?" she said.

I shrugged.

"I guess they died of the usual things. Whooping cough, measles, scurvy, fevers."

Dennis shook his head.

"What does it matter what they died of?" said my father.

"Just wondering," I said. "Bertha says they died like Sarah Kemp."

"They did," said Dennis. "Like I told you. They were picked off one by one by some crazy bear or cougar or something and found half eaten."

"That's nonsense," said my father.

"No," said Billy.

We all turned to him and watched him scratch. He looked at each of us and at the table and scratched harder. He stood up, scraped his chair loudly on the floor, and ran outside crying out a string of curses loud enough to wake the dead. Somewhere back of the sheep pasture, a coyote yipped.

17

AFTER SUPPER, as she washed and I dried the dishes in the kitchen, my mother said, "Where were you off to today after school, making me lie like that?"

"I went walking. Met up with Bertha's granddaughter. The one with the bells. Her name is Nora. She took me to her place, Bertha's place. They don't have much. They live poor. A lot of the little kids are sick."

"Well, that's the way it is. They live their way. We live ours."

"We don't live so different," I said. "Bertha's house is nicer than ours. She's got colors up all over. It's so dark in here, I feel like I'm suffocating."

"Do something with your room, then. Put up curtains."

"I don't have any material."

"Use scraps. You got that blue dress to cut up."

"Bertha thinks Dad is possessed, doesn't she?"

"Bertha says a lot of things she doesn't mean."

"There's a child missing," I said. "On the reserve."

"Whose child?" asked my mother.

"I don't know. I don't know anything more than that. Bertha's daughters were talking about it."

"Well, there's always something going on there," she said. "We don't hear the half of it."

I didn't say anything to that. On impulse I flipped open the scrapbook lying on the kitchen table.

"Leave it!" said my mother.

"Okay, okay." I slammed the scrapbook shut.

My mother took down the jar of marbles she kept in the cupboard and gently poured them into the big pot she used for canning. As the water got low, the marbles would begin to rattle and bang against the bottom of the pot, letting my mother know the pot would run dry and burn if she didn't add more water. After a time, she said, "I didn't mean to snap."

"It's okay," I said.

"I'm canning peas tonight. You want to help?"

"Dan and me are shooting some targets."

"Is that really necessary?"

I wiped my hands, took down my coat and gun, and left the kitchen without saying any more to my mother. Dan was standing by the implement shed, cleaning his gun. He was letting his beard grow a little, against my mother's wishes. In his ragged field clothes, he looked like the hobo characters we used to dress up as at Halloween.

"Ready?" he said.

Together we walked through the orchard grass, following the Swede's fence to Turtle Creek. The Swede's goat stared at us from the other side of the fence, curling his lip and sniffing the air as he did when checking a nanny for heat. He stank.

"You really have to do that?" I asked, pointing at the damage Dan and my father had done to the Swede's fence.

"Sometimes it's just easier to give in, you know?" said Dan.

"I know," I said.

"Anyway, it doesn't hurt me none."

We reached the creek, and I followed my brother across it, hopping from stone to stone.

"Where you been going in the evenings? You got some girl?"

"No girls," he said. "Nothing's going to tie me down here."

"Where then?"

"Just walking. I shoot coyotes if I see them. Sometimes I spend some time with Dennis and Billy. I got to get away from here, you know?"

"I know," I said.

He looked back at me and slowed his pace so I could catch up and walk beside him.

"You ever see anything weird?" I said. "Something following you?"

"No. Well, a cougar once. And every once in a while I see Coyote Jack out there. He's pretty weird. Why, what'd you see?"

"I don't know. Something. Most of the time I think I'm imagining it."

We reached the clearing where we had set up tin cans as targets, and loaded our guns. Dan took a couple of shots at the cans, hitting both times. I fired once and missed, shot again and hit a can. We went together to set them upright again.

"You take that gun with you when you go out?" he asked.

"Sometimes. Most times."

"Take it all the time," he said. "Dennis and Billy have been telling me stories like maybe that bear Morley Boulee shot wasn't what got Sarah Kemp. They say there's this animal out there, like what I was telling you. A ghost that takes men over, a shape-shifter."

"Yeah? You believe that?"

"No! I don't know. Just take the gun, okay?"

I shrugged. "Okay."

"Dennis is sweet on you," said Dan. "He took the job this summer because of you." When I didn't say anything to that, he said, "Billy likes you too, I think."

"Billy!" I said and slapped him on the shoulder.

"What? You don't want to go out with Billy? You'd make a sweet couple. Made for each other."

He took a step back when I slapped him again and he pushed me to the ground. We horsed around for a while, then he sat on me and held down both my shoulders. I struggled to get up and then I panicked. He didn't see my panic and went on holding me, giggling. I struggled to get my breath and my face went red.

"Stop!" I said. "Stop!"

"Say 'uncle,'" he said. "Say it."

"Uncle!" I said.

He rolled off me, still laughing. I was suddenly angry. I slapped him hard on the side of the head and picked up my gun and popped off the tin can targets one after the other, not missing even one.

"What was that all about?" he said, holding his head. But by then the anger had already faded, and I couldn't remember what had caused it. I put my gun down and held my face and started to cry, hard.

"Hey," said Dan. "Hey, there. What's up?"

He took me by the shoulders and tried to get me to look at him. When I wouldn't, he put his arm around me and held me until I stopped crying.

"You're getting to be a good shot," he said. "Eh? You'd outgun Filthy Billy, even. You two would make a good match."

I hit him in the chest. He laughed, and got me laughing and crying at the same time. "I don't want you to go," I said.

"Why you think I'm still here? Can't leave you with him. He's crazy. You've got to think about leaving yourself. Find someplace to go. There's lots of jobs now, in Vancouver, Calgary. They say all a girl's got to do is walk up to the factory door and she's got a job."

I shrugged.

"I can't stay here forever," he said.

Dan set up the cans and shot them down. A coyote howled someplace off towards the reserve and that started all the dogs up and down the valley barking.

"You know what Billy says?" said Dan. "He says a coyote howling sounds like a whole bunch of them howling because a coyote howls from both ends."

He passed wind and I laughed at that. Dan set the tin cans up once again and together we shot every single one of them down.

In the morning, instead of going to school, I slipped across the orchard, heading for the bush. Something dead was stinking up the orchard. I followed the smell and wasn't surprised to come upon the body of the old white tom. There wasn't much left to identify him except the white fur in the tail. Maggots were squirming all over him, so many moving so fast that they made a rustling sound. The maggots had taken over the head of the old tom and eaten it down to nothing. One tooth stuck out of the squirming mass.

I put my hand over my mouth and left following the orchard fence line bordering the Swede's property, heading towards Turtle Creek. After the storm that took out all the flax crop and much of the corn, you'd have thought my father wouldn't have had the time for replanting and messing around with the Swede's fence too. But he had found time for both, and more, because he stepped up the pace of dismantling the Swede's lovely living fence. I hardly ever saw him at it, but the evidence was there. The Swede's fence along that property line was either lying on the ground as next winter's firewood or was new growth wilting to nothing in the summer heat. There was only one precious chunk of that Swede's fence left alive, down near where our cherry trees now held out hard green marbles of promise, and it was thriving. Wild rose crawled up and blossomed pink and fragrant all over the crooked and reaching trees that made up the fence. Honeysuckle and morning glory wound around everything, and the low morning sun shining through it cast a shadow of lace all over the pasture grass. Along one section of fence that my father had dismantled, the Swede had planted several thorny blackberry bushes. The bushes were drooping and would soon die, but they were still a huge tangled mess covered in delicate pink and white blossoms. I foolishly moved in to smell them. The prickly tendrils grabbed my socks and bound my skirt and when I pulled my skirt away, the bramble caught my blouse and tugged at my hair. I struggled, trying not to snag my clothing and only getting more entangled, and in the midst of it my lightning arm went dead again. I turned to stretch it and work out the tingling, and I saw a motion in the grass coming towards me, a splitting of the grass as if an animal or a man were running through it, but there was nothing there. Terrified, I pulled harder from the bramble, tearing my skirt. The swishing of grass filled up my ears and came at me faster than anything possible. Then a hand was on my shoulder.

I swung around and Nora was there, her hand on my shoulder, grinning, her necklace tinkling. She said, "What's up?"

I looked back at the pasture grass and the trail that ran through it and ended at my feet. My lightning arm tugged from the brambles like an alien thing and moved through the air in front of me as if searching for something in the dark. Then all at once the lightning arm was mine again, the tingling and feeling returned. Nevertheless, I felt through the air a moment longer and ran my hand through the grass trail at my feet.

"Lose something?" said Nora.

"No. I don't know."

"You got yourself stuck there." She made me stand still and, vine by vine, she untangled me. I stood like a child or an old woman getting serviced, thankful for her company, more for her soothing touch. A wind stirred up the ghost scent of the violet flax and messed the trail in the grass so it was hardly visible. A whirlwind will play tricks like that, run itself out in a straight line and create a trail in its wake, spawning stories of ghosts and making you see things, hands on fences. So I told myself, as Nora untangled me.

"You okay?" she said.

"Yeah, fine."

"You got some scrapes there."

"They're okay."

"You're not going to school anymore?"

"I don't know," I said.

"Your mum doesn't know, does she?"

"No."

Nora looked down the line of blossoms on the Swede's fence, and around at the sheep grazing in bunches under the fruit trees. She took the hand on my lightning arm.

"You got scrapes here too," she said. I shrugged. "You should come home with me. Granny will clean them up."

"I don't know."

"She won't tell."

"Sure she will."

"You should do something. Granny told me about a white woman who died when she pricked herself on a rosebush."

"Yeah, I heard that too," I said.

"See. Come on."

We walked a little ways up the Swede's fence towards Blood Road.

"Mum will make me go back to school," I said.

"Okay, we won't go to Granny's. But I'll go get something to fix them scratches. You could die."

We walked along for a while longer, listening to the sound of Nora's bells and the birds in the trees.

"I wanted to go to that school," said Nora. "I don't no more."

"Me neither."

"We could have our own school," said Nora. "We could sit someplace and teach each other things. Today, we could do that."

I shrugged.

"What do you want to do, then?"

"I don't know," I said. "Where's that hole in the ground? The winter house."

Nora sprang ahead of me and walked backwards, facing me, skipping like the Swede's yellow-eyed dog, grinning and needy.

"That's something," she said. "We could rebuild the winter house."

"Rebuild it?"

"Sure. It'll be our house. No one can find us. We'll bring stuff there. Food and blankets and things, and make a house. It'll be hidden."

That lit me up inside. A place to go to that my father wouldn't know about. A place no one would know about. I'd take my little treasures there, my violet perfume, my nail polish, the scrap of red velvet, and other things too, that I'd planned on getting, a pair of nylons, a tube of lipstick, a dress with a bit of red on it, maybe at the collar, a racy girl's dress, something to dance in.

"We could decorate it," I said. "Hang some things up on the walls."

"They're dirt walls. But yeah, we could hang things. Granny's got a bolt of red material. She'd give me some."

Nora took my hand again and we walked like that, my hand getting sweaty in hers from the plans we were making. Shared secrets, a new thing for me. Most secrets I kept to myself and squirreled away in the holes of trees.

"The Georges' little girl's gone missing now too," she said. "She didn't come home last night. My mum says I got to stay around the village, don't go in the bush."

"You're still out."

"I'm not scared. I was out walking the night Sarah Kemp got killed. Saw her ghost."

"Yeah, you told me."

We came onto Turtle Creek on the place where it switched back on itself. Nora pulled me by the hand to the creek bank and washed the scrapes on my shins and arms in the cold creek water. I flinched at her nursing.

"Lots of blood from nothing scratches," she said. "You won't die."

"What do you think happened to those kids?" I asked her. "On the reserve."

"Who knows," said Nora. "Granny says an animal spirit's gone crazy, out for blood. Coyote, she says, like I told you. He gets inside a man or a bear or a coyote — any living thing walking around — and makes that man or bear do crazy things. Everybody's talking like it's Coyote Jack gone crazy. My mum says stay away from him."

"You really think he'd go around eating people?"

"Granny says that sometimes. Other times she says they're just stories people tell when they get scared and don't know what's out there."

"He left his cat," I said. "I found his cat."

"His cat?"

"Beside the road. He left his cat for me. My dad called him Lucifer because he's black."

"How did you know it was him?"

"I saw him. He was watching me."

Nora shuddered dramatically.

"He's not so bad." I said. "He's just shy."

"Coyote Jack's not shy, he's bushed. He really is a coyote. He fades into the trees like magic. I've seen him. Granny says he's lived too long in the bush. The bush makes you change shape, takes away your man-body, makes you into an animal."

I picked up a stick, dipped it into the water, and watched it slide into two pieces where it met the surface. Nora washed my blood from her hands and then lazily let water drip from her fingers onto my lightning arm. She caught a drop sliding down my arm and smeared it in slow circles around the blue veins in my wrists.

"Your skin's so see-through," she said. "Like I could look inside and see your bones."

She looked up at me and made me look a long time at her two-woman eyes. Looking at her confused me. I went back and forth between each differently colored eye held in a different face. She was two women — or girls. We were both just girls. Nora leaned her two-woman face into me and kissed me like a lover, there, at Turtle Creek, with my feet in the creek water to cool me, my lightning arm tingling as if it might die.

18

DURING THE WEEK or so that followed, Nora and I never met at the winter house, never planned for its construction. I'd just go walking, down the Swede's living fence, or along Turtle Creek to the place it bent in on itself, or maybe up over Bald Mountain to count the wild horses grazing miles away, it seemed, on the plains below. Somewhere on those old trails she'd find me, or I'd find her first, in the way I'd find the sheep, or the cows to bring them down from the benchland for milking, by the bells around her neck, by the steps that jingled them. Then we'd go walking together and sooner or later we ended up at the hole in the ground that led to China, the winter house.

"We've got to take it apart first," she said. "Fix it right."

So we took apart and rebuilt our winter house, over the course of a week or so. We constructed a frame of old lumber and logs over the hole, and laid sticks and brush over the frame. We covered this with mud and dirt, so our hut looked like nothing but a mound of earth, and then covered that with more brush. The winter house already had a worn ladder, a pole with chunks taken out. We went down the hole through the center. We didn't build a side opening.

I wanted to give Nora something so badly that I stole my own treasures from the hollow stump and brought them to the winter house and shared my secrets with her. I pulled the top from my violet perfume and handed her the bottle.

"That perfume stinks," she said.

I smelled the violet perfume again, and all the richness I'd felt when I put it on my feet was gone. Its sweetness in the confined space of the winter house made my head hurt.

"How long you had that stuff?"

I shrugged. I stoppered up the perfume bottle, lifted my skirt, and tucked the bottle into the pocket of my brother's jeans, next to the scrap of velvet and the bottle of nail polish. Later I would sneak it back into my hollow stump by Turtle Creek.

"What you got there?" said Nora.

I rubbed the sticky perfume off my hand onto my skirt and pulled the bottle of nail polish from my pocket. She took it.

"Now that's something. My mother won't let me wear nail polish."

"My father neither. He threw it into the manure pile," I said, and immediately regretted it. Nora held it up between her fingers. "I washed it," I said. "It's all cleaned." She sniffed it and handed it back to me. "What've you got?" I asked.

Nora dragged her red carpetbag over to the circle of light around the post ladder. She pulled out a ragged gray camp blanket and a box of wood matches.

"All we need now is food and we got a house," said Nora.

"Wait here," I said. "I'll go back home and get some jars from the cellar."

"What if your mum sees?" said Nora.

"She won't. She'll be out serving lunch in the fields now."

"You're taking a chance," she said.

"I'll be careful," I said. "Can I use this?" I held up the red carpetbag.

Our root cellar was cut into the bank of the low hill behind the house. Its roof was held up with heavy timbers and covered over in dirt and grass and weeds so it looked like nothing but a door in a hillside. It smelled of darkness and damp, the haunt of last year's apples and sprouting potatoes laid out in bins on the floor along the dirt walls. Before the snow fell, the apple bins would be full of fruit from the trees that bordered the sheep pasture: Russets, Grimes Golden, rich red Jonathans. The smell of apples still ripening would be everything in that dirt house, but now that sweetness was subtle. On the cellar shelves were jar after jar of sweet promise: raspberry jam, strawberry jam, cherry jam, sweet whole cherries pitted and sugared and cooked in their own juices, huckleberries that Bertha Moses and her daughters had brought round in big stained baskets the fall before and traded for cream and butter; plums boiled and sugared into jam, or left whole in syrup to cleanse away the sins of beef from the body in midwinter. There were jars and jars of chutneys made from apples, raisins, sugar, vinegar and spices, and squash jams — marrow and citron jams that tasted of candied ginger — but no canned tomato relishes or pickles, save the beets, as ripe and rich as bottled blood: my mother regarded tomatoes with suspicion and considered pickles foreign and largely indigestible.

I looked up at the blank windows of the house for any sign of her. Seeing none, I opened the door in the hillside slowly, watching for the place where it squeaked. When the squeak began, I set the carpetbag down to hold the door open. I'd never stolen from my mother; there'd been no need. I never went hungry and the things I really wanted never found their way to this farm, so theft was never on my mind. Still, here I was thieving.

I backed out the hillside doorway with my hands full of jars, and Dan was standing there, wearing his ragged field denims, a short reddish beard over his heavy jaw, smelling of soap, hanging on to the door. He scared me half to death. "What you got there?" he said.

"Nothing."

"Looks like a lot of nothing. You wouldn't be taking that over to the reserve, would you?"

"No."

"Don't worry, I won't tell anybody. I sometimes snitch a jar of strawberry for Dennis and Billy."

I gave him a thankful look and put the jars into Nora's carpetbag. "Dad isn't around, is he?" I said.

"He's still out in the wheat field. He's eating lunch out there with Mum."

I picked up the bag and carefully slung it over my shoulder.

"You're not going to school?" said Dan.

"Who says?"

"You're here now, aren't you?"

"Don't tell Dad. Please don't tell."

"They're going to find out sooner or later."

"I know," I said.

"If those kids give you any more trouble, you come to me, okay?"

"What kids?"

"Robert Parker and the others."

"How'd you hear about that?"

"People still talk to me, you know," he said.

I looked over at the house and didn't say anything. The blood pounded into my head so I couldn't think.

"Why don't you give Dennis a chance, eh?" said Dan. "He's a good guy. The girls like him. Even Lily Bell likes him."

I kicked dirt.

"Is it 'cause he's Indian?"

I shook my head. "Dad would kill me," I said.

"There's that, isn't there," said Dan. "Jesus, he's so loony these days. I wonder if things will ever get back the way they were."

I looked out past the house at the tiny figures in the field.

"What do you do all day?" he said. "You go wandering around in the bush?"

"Sometimes," I said.

"There's kids, young kids, gone missing on the reserve. Dennis is right. Killing that bear didn't fix anything. There's some animal out there gone crazy and it's attacking people."

"I heard," I said.

"I don't want you running around in the bush alone. Go visit Bertha."

"She'll tell Mum."

"Then hide out in the cellar, or the barn loft. Just don't go in the bush."

"I've got a place."

"I'm not kidding about this," said Dan. "There's something crazy out there."

I stumbled back a couple of steps and swung around to the trail behind the cellar. "Be careful," my brother called out.

19

I CLIMBED DOWN the makeshift ladder to our winter house and sat on the blanket that Nora had spread on the cool ground.

"Your mother home?" she asked.

"Dan knows. About me not being in school. He was there."

"Your mum's bound to find out sooner or later. She talks to Mrs. Boulee."

"She hardly ever sees her. She takes the cream into town in the daytime, when Mrs. Boulee is teaching. When Dad's with Mum, Mrs. Boulee won't talk to her, not after Dad punched out Mr. Boulee."

"She'll hear about it," said Nora. "Somebody will tell her. Or she'll see you."

"What if she does? I'll leave. She can't tell me what to do. I'll find a job."

"We'll find a job together. We'll go to Vancouver."

Nora took off the bell necklace and held it out for me. I took it and jingled the bells.

"Roll on your stomach," she said. I rolled over and lay full length, resting my chin on my hands. The bells smelled tinny. She arranged my hair to one side and smoothed the material of my blouse as if cleaning a blackboard. She began to draw on my back. It felt smooth and ticklish and I relaxed under her hands. After a while, I said, "What are you drawing?"

"I'm writing," she said.

"What are you writing?"

"You have to guess," she said.

I followed the circles of her hands on my back. "I don't know," I said.

"Guess!"

Slowly she formed the big looped letters of three words, and repeated them over and over. I understood quickly, but didn't know what to do. I turned over and she continued to write, spelling the words over the sides of my breasts. "You," she said, mouthing the last word, and forming a *u* that cupped my breast.

20

MY MOTHER SANG, my brother whistled, the birds fluttered around us following the ribbons my mother had tied to the horses' reins, and even my father smiled as he whipped those ribbons into confusion. All of us, Billy and Dennis too, rode the democrat down Blood Road, thumping and jostling over the red ruts, to the Dominion Day picnic at the Boulee's Farm. I was squashed between my brother and Filthy Billy in the back of the buggy, thrown into Billy at every rut we thundered over, sick with the motion and dreading the picnic because of course Mrs. Boulee would be there and of course she'd tell my mother I hadn't been in school and of course there'd be hell to pay. My mind was full of confrontations. Would Parker be bold enough to taunt me in front of all those people? If he did I would push him down. Would Lily Bell swing by in her too pretty dress and call me "Indian lover"? If she did I would slap her rouged cheek. Would my father's face turn beet red over the sound of a spoon clanking against a coffee cup or some neighbor tipping his hat to my mother? If so I would make myself as small as those black lizards and slink away.

Mrs. Boulee had made some attempt at gaiety by tying ribbons in the fruit trees under which everyone sat. But the feel of celebration wasn't there. A few very young children tried jumping around in potato sacks and fell. The Swede's three-legged dog ran around begging for food, sniffing crotches and getting slapped away. In other years, the Boulees' Dominion Day picnic had danced. Children had hopped down the length of the orchard, their arms around each other, their ankles tied together, sweat holding their hair to their necks. They'd raced each other in potato sacks from the apple trees to the pear trees for the glory of a pretty red ribbon. Mr. Aitken's son Henry played a fiddle and Arnold Stowards or Mike Heatley pulled out a mouth organ, and the women and their husbands danced in the long orchard grass in broad daylight.

But now the war was on, and Henry Aitken, Arnold Stowards, Mike Heatley, and almost all the young men of age were gone, and that was at the front of everyone's mind. The women were hungry for them. You could see it in them, in the way they leaned towards my brother, Dan, in the way they fawned over Dennis and even Billy, bringing them sweating glasses of lemonade or slices of cherry pie, and in the way they lingered, as the boys accepted these gifts, smiling grins as big and foolish as that of the Swede's begging dog.

You could see it, too, in the way the women both ignored and snatched glances at my mother. My mother had her son still at home, and a handsome buck named Dennis working for her. Though they pitied my mother because they now feared my father, she had the power these women lacked: she had men to care for.

The food, though — you couldn't help but get distracted by the food. Cherry pie, strawberry pie, store-bought ice cream stored away from the heat in a little steel bathtub filled with ice, rhubarb-strawberry pie, raspberry pie, and cookies, cookies, cookies. And every perfect pie was laid out on the prettiest plate in the household of whomever had brought the pie. This was a time to show off, and every woman there chose the best recipe in her scrapbook and picked the freshest, most perfect ingredients from her garden. A few of the women, including my mother, had early cucumbers grown against the sunny side of the house where the heat was trapped, and, like my mother, they sliced the cucumbers so thin they were transparent, and placed them between thinly sliced buttered bread. That was the thing, at the time, to make the thinnest sandwiches.

I stacked my plate with the too thin sandwiches to feed the butterflies gnawing at my stomach: sardine, ham and onion, egg, my mother's cucumber, and Mrs. Bell's ribbon sandwiches that were nothing but white and brown bread sliced paper-thin and rolled together with butter. Mrs. Bell was there, of course, filling her plate behind me, wearing a new tweed swagger coat with pleats in the back in the style of the day. She was simply showing off because the day was much too hot for any coat, much less tweed.

"Stuff's going on at the reserve all the time," Mrs. Bell was saying. "We don't hear the half of it."

She was talking to Mr. and Mrs. Ferguson, who'd sold us the Jerseys. I watched Mrs. Ferguson's ugly mouth, looking for that crooked, tea-stained tooth.

"You hear about those Indian kids gone missing?" asked Mrs. Ferguson.

"Can't get a word out of them dumb Indians," said Mr. Ferguson. "I asked Jimmy George about them missing kids and he just looked at me and didn't say a word. Not one word. He was sober too."

"Bertha Moses told me some crazy story about a coyote that eats people," said Mrs. Bell. "Then she accused Coyote Jack of Sarah Kemp's murder! Coyote Jack! Sarah would have scared *him* half to death, poor little thing."

"I'm starting to think maybe Morley shot the wrong animal," said Mrs. Ferguson.

"He's saying that himself," said Mr. Ferguson.

Mr. Ferguson drank from his cup. Because the thumb and index finger on his right hand were missing, he held his cup in an odd way, hooked over the three remaining fingers.

"Could have been a cougar," said Mrs. Bell. "Remember years ago that boy got scratched up pretty bad. It was a cougar then."

"A cougar will go after a little one, maybe," said Mr. Ferguson. "Sarah Kemp was almost grown. Never heard of a cougar going after an adult."

"If it's hungry enough it'll go after anything, don't you think?" said Mrs. Bell. "Or if it's frightened?"

"Got to wonder how any wild creature could be hungry enough to go after a child, let alone an adult, with all the livestock around," said Mr. Ferguson. "Never seen a thing like it. Most times coyotes go after livestock in the winter, when game's low. But not this year. There's no shortage of deer and rabbit. Louise can't keep them out of her garden. I don't know. Maybe them Indians are right. Maybe there is something crazy out there."

"I don't think we should let the little kids go out hunting for strawberries alone like we did last year," said Mrs. Bell. "Send the bigger kids out with them. Keep an eye on them."

"No argument from me," said Mrs. Ferguson.

I picked out cutlery and sat on the grass beside my mother, opposite my brother and Dennis, careful not to look at Dennis, lest my father see. Billy wasn't swearing much. He pushed food into his mouth so fast the words didn't have a chance to come out. My mother touched a napkin to the side of my father's mouth and wiped off a bit of mayonnaise.

"Morley says Goat's got a new perch," said Dan. "The old men put rolls of barbed wire along the top of the fence around the church, so now Goat climbs up on top of Blundell's Motel and plays with himself up there. Morley said he saw the idiot slide down the side of the roof and nearly fall right off! Sooner or later he's going to kill himself. That would be the best for everybody."

"Don't talk like that," said my father.

"I'll talk like I want," said Dan. "He should be locked away in Essondale. They should castrate him."

"Enough!" said my mother.

"You don't know what you're talking about," said my father.

"Yeah?" said Dan.

We watched for a moment as my father closed his eyes and breathed out long and slow, pushing the anger down to his boots. "Goat and Billy here and those like them, they know things we can't possibly know," he said. "They have talents that come from God alone. Goat can play piano like he was made for music. I've heard him myself in the doctor's parlor. Hum him a tune, and he'll play it, though he's never heard it before."

"Yeah, yeah, I heard that," said Dan.

"You heard it, but you've never seen it, and that's the thing. If you'd seen it, you wouldn't be talking like that now. And Billy here, he can find water anywhere if you give him a stick to find it with. It's like their minds aren't all cluttered up with useless things, so God can work straight through them."

Dennis and Billy looked at each other. I'd never heard my father talk about God in this way before. Mrs. Bell had called my father a faithless man, to my mother's face. Bertha Moses had said my father's spirit was an empty jug just waiting for Coyote to pour himself into. My father bent his head into his plate and played with his food, and in the silence that followed his little speech my mother reached over and put her hand on his. He took her hand and for a time they sat there looking at each other lovingly, as if all the events of this past year had never happened.

Filthy Billy didn't look up. He stirred his food around in a circle on his plate. Then he talked at it. "(Shit) My mind (fuck) ain't empty. My mind's so full it's going to (shit) split open one of these days."

All of us looked down into our plates and snuck looks at Billy and at one another. Billy had shaved, combed his hair back with bear grease so it shone, and put on a clean white shirt and wool trousers. He looked kindly, not crazy. He went back to filling up his mouth so it wouldn't spill out filth and further embarrass my mother. None of us said any more until Mrs. Bell waved at my mother from the food table and made her way over.

"Here comes doom and gloom," said Dan. "She got herself a new coat, I see."

"Enough of that," said my mother.

"Well, I'm not going to sit here listening to her." Dan stood up and Dennis and Billy stood with him. They carried their plates to a plum tree nearby and sat under it, laughing at something Dennis had said. Mrs. Bell ran over and sat right next to my mother so their knees were touching and grinned so foolishly I wanted to slap her.

"Well! I've got you to myself!" she said, as if my father and I weren't there.

My father shook his head and stared at nothing, chewing his food.

"How are you today?" said my mother.

"I have an ache in my back," said Mrs. Bell. "The weather's about to turn, I can feel it. We'll have rain this weekend. It'll be a rainy summer, a bad year for crops, and coyotes all over the place. There'll be plenty of farmers ruined, I'm afraid."

"Well, it's a beautiful day today," said my mother, and she nodded at the girls skipping near the Boulees' house. "The children are certainly enjoying it."

"They should enjoy themselves while they can," said Mrs. Bell. "I'm afraid we'll have another dead child before the year is out. Morley Boulee says he shot the wrong bear."

"He talked to you?" said my father.

Mrs. Bell glanced at my father but answered looking at my mother. "Well, no. But Mr. Ferguson says he said that."

My father smirked and went back to eating. Mrs. Bell stared at him for a moment and then took my mother's arm.

"Well, here we are," she said, again dismissing my father and me both. "Alone! Every time I see you, you're talking with someone else."

"I wish that were so," said my mother.

I put my plate down and Mrs. Bell looked over at me as if she had just noticed me. "Tuck your skirt over your legs, dear. You are showing too much leg."

I ignored her and looked over at Dennis, Dan, and Filthy Billy. Mrs. Ferguson, who had bawled me out for my father's misdeeds, was serving sandwiches to my brother and my father's hired hands. Dennis laughed at something she said and then saw me looking at him. He winked and went on looking at me so long that both Billy and Mrs. Ferguson glanced my way. I grew shy and pulled my skirt down over my knees. When I looked up again to see if Dennis was still watching me, I saw Mrs. Boulee, my schoolteacher, leave the house and head our way. I picked up my plate and started walking off.

"Where are you going?" said my mother.

"For something to drink," I called back.

I went over to the food table and poured myself lemonade from the glass jug my mother had brought and watched, with my knees going weak on me, as Mrs. Boulee sat beside my mother, even though my father was there, and began talking. They both gestured in my direction. It had finally happened, then. Mrs. Bell moved away from my mother, adjusted her skirt, and turned her back on Mrs. Boulee.

Suddenly Lily Bell was there, standing beside me. "How come you're not going to school?" she said.

I didn't answer. I didn't look at her. I drank my lemonade as if she weren't there.

After a time she said, "I'm sorry, about what happened at the old Fraser place. It was a game. I didn't think it would be like that."

When I still didn't respond, she said, "You didn't tell no one."

I gave her a mean-mouthed look and turned my back on her. She left me and I watched as she swayed over to Dan, Dennis, and Billy and offered them yet another plate of cookies. She had on another dress too frilly for the war rations or her age but again I felt clumsy and out of place in my pinafore made from two old dresses, bare legs and gillies, though many of the women there wore dirndl skirts sewn from old curtains. Lily wore lipstick and a little eye shadow and, compared to her, I felt as plain as paper wrapping. Dennis and Dan laughed at something she said, and she sat down in front of them, with her back to me.

The Swede came by, followed by the three-legged Lab, and offered my father a swig from a brown paper bag, and I watched, amazed, as he and my father went around to the back of the Boulees' barn. My father and the Swede had been something like friends before the bear attacked our sheep camp, but ever since my father had started up the dairy there'd been nothing but grief between them over that fence. My mother watched him go as Mrs. Boulee talked to her. Then Mr. Boulee shouted out that all the little kids should go hunt for strawberries now, and could they please be accompanied by an older sibling?

I had no younger brother or sister to accompany on the hunt for wild strawberries, but I went anyway, to get away from Lily Bell and her pretty dress, Mrs. Boulee's concerned looks, and my mother's tight-lipped stare.

Wild strawberries like meadowlands, clearings, and the edges of forests and roadways. The sides of Blood Road were thick with them, and the young kids and their older brothers and sisters scrambled along the ditches to find them. It was a contest, of sorts, to see who could bring the most back. As tradition had it, the children weren't looking for strawberries for themselves, though their tongues became bright with the red of them, nor for their parents, but for the old women and old men, to decorate the old-timers' ice cream.

I crossed Blood Road, pressed the wild strawberries into the mossy ground with my feet, and entered the bush. There were no paths here that I knew of, so I made my own, cracking twigs and swishing through undergrowth until I came across a deer path that opened a way into the bush. I reached a place where sunlight slanted through the trees and into a clearing. Then I was far enough away that I couldn't hear the laughter from the Dominion Day picnic. There was a bath of other noises here, birdsong and trees shushing, and I closed my eyes and let these wash over me.

Then there was that other noise, the dull roaring and crackling I knew but didn't want to believe. It filled me up and took away my breath. My stomach gripped it.

"Nora, is that you?" I called. "Come out, Nora. I hear you."

The roaring went on, came at me.

"Who's there?" I said.

The birds went quiet, and the roaring grew. I walked slowly at first, back towards the farm, with my whole body listening. The roaring seemed to come from all directions and grew louder and louder and then suddenly the sound was on me and Parker was there, pushing me down and holding my squirming body with his own. He put his hand up my skirt and pulled down my panties. He undid his pants and pushed himself between my legs, hurting me, unable to find an opening. The roaring enclosed me, deafened me, held my screams and curses to the ground.

As suddenly as it started, the roaring stopped. Filthy Billy was there, over Parker, poking the gun into Parker's rear end. "Get off!" he said.

Parker went still, looked over his shoulder at Billy and the gun, and slowly moved off me. Billy kept the gun pressed into Parker's buttocks until Parker had crawled away from me on all fours, clownishly, with his pants around his knees. Billy pushed the gun inward once, just for the justice and meanness of it. It was so unlike him that in my fear and nervousness I laughed a little. Billy tipped the gun up and watched as Parker quickly pulled his pants on and stumbled down the path. After a time I heard him crash through the bush as he headed towards Blood Road. Filthy Billy turned his back to me so I could arrange my clothing.

"He doesn't know what he's doing," he said.

"He knew."

"He won't remember. Or if he does, he won't know why he did it. You'll see."

"I don't want to see him ever again." I leaned against a tree and hugged myself. Billy squatted near me.

"You okay?" he asked. And as soon as he said it, I started crying. Billy brushed the hair from my eyes and cupped his hand around my cheek.

"Don't tell anybody," I said. "Don't tell my father."

"No. That wouldn't do no good."

"How did you know to come?"

He shrugged.

"You following me?" I said.

"You got to be careful," said Billy. "You hear? Real careful."

"You're not swearing," I said.

"Swearing?" he said. "Oh!"

Then the roaring sound was on us again. Billy looked suddenly confused, moved back from me, and began swatting some invisible thing away, as if he were being attacked by a swarm of wasps. Then he was at it again, swearing under his breath and scratching. The muscles under his eyes twitched.

"Billy?" I said. But he didn't seem to hear me. He ran off down the path towards the farm, batting away whatever it was that chased him.

21

I RAN AFTER BILLY, but when he reached Blood Road and turned again into the bush, throwing up his arms like a crazy man, I didn't follow him. I crossed Blood Road in time to see an even crazier sight than Filthy Billy: my father and the Swede walked arm in arm towards me through the Boulees' orchard. The Swede still carried the bottle in a bag. They both stumbled and swayed and talked so loud that people at the picnic watched them. Parker was nowhere in sight. Lily Bell was still with Dan and Dennis, though all three of them stood near the food table now with cups in their hands, watching my father and the Swede make fools of themselves. Dennis looked over at me and I looked away. I turned through the orchard to avoid my father and the Swede but couldn't help but hear them. The sentimental cloud that comes over some drinking men had descended on Johansson.

"We were best friends," said the Swede.

"Best friends?" said my father.

"We hunted together," said the Swede.

My father took the bag from the Swede and drank and drank, and the Swede watched him, looking dismayed.

"We never hunted," said my father, still holding the bag. "You shot deer on my land and left gates open so my sheep got out."

"I gave you meat, didn't I?"

"You gave me nothing."

"Well, I meant to."

"You stole game off my land."

"You seem to be a bit confused about who owns what land," said the Swede. "Anyhow, nobody owns the game."

"What?"

"I saw you took a bit of liberty with the fence line."

"What do you mean?"

"You came over onto my property."

"You saying I stole land?"

"Not saying that at all. I'm just saying maybe you made a mistake."

"I made no mistake. I fenced on my property line."

The Swede and my father were no longer arm in arm. They stood a little apart, facing each other. My father clenched and unclenched his free hand. The Swede tried to take the bottle from him, but my father wouldn't let him have it. "What exactly are you saying?" my father demanded.

"I'm saying if you didn't make no mistake, then you're a damned thief."

My father threw down the bottle and punched Johansson. The Swede was on the ground, feeling the side of his mouth, as Mr. Ferguson and Morley Boulee ran up behind my father and held his arms back. He shook them off and kicked the Swede as he was getting up. The Swede feigned agony in his leg until my father was close enough, then butted my father in the stomach with his head. My father picked the Swede up by the belt loops, threw him on the ground again, and kicked him several times in the side as the Swede writhed this way and that, trying to avoid my father's boots. Another two men pulled my father off and held him as Ferguson punched him in the stomach and as Morley Boulee tried and failed to stop Ferguson. My father buckled in, twisting to avoid the blows. Some other men who'd been drinking started pushing my father and then each other around, and women ran up, yelling for them all to stop, but they wouldn't. My father was drunk. All the men in that fight were drunk. The Swede's three-legged dog ran circles around them, jumping and barking.

My mother abandoned my father, left him to his foolishness. She pulled me away from watching the fight and told me to drive her home and, as she did, she held my arm so hard I feared she might hit me, or worse yet have one of her spells and go cloudy-eyed and start talking to her dead mother there, in the middle of Dominion Day picnic.

"What about Dad? What about Dan and Dennis and Billy?"

"They'll find their own way," she said.

I helped my mother into the democrat and slapped Cherry and Chief with the reins to get them going. Mrs. Boulee and several other women watched us drive off. My mother sat upright in her seat until we were well out of sight and then all the air seemed to go out of her. She sank into the seat and cried for a time. I put my hand on her arm, but she pulled away.

"Mrs. Boulee says you haven't been going to school over the last month," she said. "I had to lie. I told her we needed your help on the farm after that big storm flattened the flax field. How many times do I have to lie for you?"

"You didn't have to lie," I said.

We swayed down Blood Road for a long time in silence, listening to the wheels creek and jump. A coyote yipped. A pheasant leapt out of the bush and flew up at us, startling us both.

"Tell me where you've been," said Mum. "Have you been with some boy? That Parker boy? Mrs. Bell says she saw that boy coming out of the bush from the direction you'd gone."

"I haven't been with anybody," I said.

"You're lying to me. Tell me the truth."

"I am telling the truth. Sometimes I was with Nora. Only Nora."

My mother stared at me. I kept my eyes on the horses and the road. "Your father's right. She's a bad influence."

"No she's not."

"Does she put you up to it? Does she make you miss school? What happened that day, when you came home early, when I thought you were sick?"

I didn't answer until my mother raised her voice to a shout. "Answer me!"

"They were picking on me," I said. "Lily Bell and Robert Parker, all the kids, but them especially. They call me sheep tick and Indian lover and hoarder. They carried me into the old Fraser house and took off my clothes."

My mother slapped me, setting my cheek on fire, and the horses, made nervous by the shouting, worked themselves into a run, so we had to hang on to our seats to keep from falling. I held the reins with one hand and clung to the seat with the other.

"Enough lies!" she said. "You tell me the truth!"

"They came and pushed me down. Parker and Lily Bell and those kids. They took my clothes. Parker, again today, he pushed me down."

"That's nonsense. Lily wouldn't do a thing like that. She's a nice girl."

"They did!" I cried. "It happened."

"Nothing happened! Nothing happened at all. You just don't want to go to school. Don't lie to me. Tell me where you've been all day. Where you go."

"Out walking."

"You go to the reserve?"

"Sometimes. Sometimes I just walk."

"Where do you walk to? You don't see some boy?"

"No!" I said. "I just walk. Sometimes I see Nora and we do things."

"Things? What things?"

"She shows me things. Indian things. We built a house."

"A house?"

"A place underground. Like a root cellar. A winter house. Like they used to live in, underground."

"You're talking nonsense. No one lives underground."

"What good is it telling the truth if you're not going to believe me?"

My mother didn't say another thing as I drove the rest of the way home. When I pulled Cherry and Chief to a halt in the yard, my mother leapt from the democrat and marched to the house, leaving me to deal with the horses. I took my time taking off their harnesses, and when I finished I fed the pigs, brought in the cows, and milked alone. My mother never once came out to offer help. She wrapped the house up in her anger, made it a fortress I couldn't enter. Sometime during the milking I heard a buggy pull in the yard and out again, and heard the voices of Dan, Dennis, and Billy heading towards the hired hands' cabin. A little while later my father stumbled across the yard, carrying a bottle and heading for the Swede's fence.

When I finally went into the house, my mother was already in bed and her bedroom door was closed. My father was still out. Dan was still over at the cabin with Dennis and Billy. I went to my room and took off my clothes in the dusk. As I undressed, I became aware that I was being watched and turned to the window. The hands, from the thing that followed, were on the outside window ledge. I jumped onto my bed, threw a blanket over myself, and looked again. The hands were gone, but a darkness moved in front of the window. The window slid open, and Nora climbed in, with her necklace jingling.

"You were asleep," she whispered.

"No."

"What's wrong?"

"Nothing."

"Your dad isn't here?"

"No. Just Mum. He's taking down Mr. Johansson's fence. Dan's out someplace."

"I saw the fight," said Nora.

"You were there? Where were you?"

"Looking for you."

"I didn't see you."

"Your mother was dragging you off."

I opened my blankets to her, and she lay in bed beside me, fully clothed, and eventually we fell asleep like that, holding each other. My father came home swaying in the night, drunk and hurting. When he came into the house we jolted awake. Nora leapt out of bed and, as my father marched into my room, Nora climbed out the window.

"Get out of my house," my father yelled, but of course she was already gone. "I'll skin you! Stupid little squaw."

Then he flipped me over onto my stomach, turned up my nightgown, and slapped my bare bottom with his bare hand. Dan ran into my bedroom.

"Get your hands off her!" He took my father's arm and pulled him off.

"You will not have that girl here," my father said. "Do you understand? She's a breed. They're filth. They carry lice. Do you understand? It's for your own good. I'm only trying to protect you. Do you understand?"

His breath and clothes stank of booze. Blood was smeared on his face, his cracked lips were bleeding, and a splotch of red was growing where his cheek had met with a blow. He scared me so that I could barely breathe or answer him. I crouched against the headboard decorated with forget-me-nots, held my ears, and sobbed. My father stamped a circle in front of the black window screaming words I only half heard.

"Did that breed make you miss school? Here I am working. Sluttish girl! Were you with some boy? Who is he? Answer me!"

But I couldn't answer. I couldn't say anything at all. My mother stood at the doorway to my bedroom in her nightgown with her arms crossed, not intervening this time. Dan slapped the wall and pushed past my mother. I heard his bedroom door slam shut.

My father shook me by the shoulders and my head hit the headboard so hard I cried out. My mother came around then. She stepped forward and put her hand on my father's arm. "John!" she said. "That's enough."

My father shook her off, but he stepped back too, letting me go. On the back of my head a pain swelled. The room sparked with little bits of light for a moment or two, then the dizziness passed. I slumped forward on the bed just the same.

Mum said something quietly to my father, and he started out the door, then yelled at me. "You'll stay in the house. Understand? You won't leave this house!"

He stomped from the house himself, and spent the whole night cutting down and tearing up what remained of the Swede's living fence. My mother sat on the edge of the bed beside me, feeling for the growing bump at the back of my head. Dan shuffled through the parlor and stood at my bedroom door.

"She all right?"

"I don't know," said my mother.

"She tell you about the kids?" said Dan.

"What?"

"Robert Parker, Lily Bell, and some others. And Billy said Parker went after Beth today in the bush."

"Nothing of the sort happened," said my mother. "She's just been lazy and lying to cover it up."

"It did happen. Billy was there."

"No!"

Dan crossed his arms and looked back into the parlor. My mother sat on the bed and held my shoulders and made me look at her.

"Did a boy get inside you?" she said.

"No!" I cried.

She shook me as my father had done. "Did a boy get inside you? Answer me!"

"No!" I said. She slapped me hard.

Dan said, "Mum!"

"Did a boy get inside you? Did he? Did he?"

She went crazy, shaking and slapping me and pulling my hair. I cried out, but she kept at me. Dan pulled her off and held her arms until she sank to the floor crying. We melted there together in my room for a long time, my mother crying and me sobbing and Dan rubbing his embarrassment into the floor with his foot. He tried once to pick my mother up and carry her out, but she was a limp sack of potatoes and he ended up only dragging her to the door. He gave up, said "Jesus!" and stomped the same steps as my father had out the door. I didn't see him again that night.

As soon as Dan shut the door my mother started talking to her dead mother, just mouthing the words at first, and staring at something just in front of the window as if listening to a reply.

"We've got to clean you up," she said so quietly that I thought she was still talking to my dead grandmother. But she said it again, louder, as she turned to look at me. Then she slid up the doorframe, magically, her skirts hiding the effort.

"Put yourself together," she said, and went into the kitchen. I heard her rattling around in there, stoking up the fire, filling the kettle with water from the bucket, pulling the little tin washtub from the pantry.

I put on my nightgown, sweater, and slippers and shuffled into the kitchen. My mother had lit a lamp and placed it on the table. She stood at her prized cupboard with her back to me, mixing something in the half dark. She poured the mixture into a wine bottle and handed it over to me. I took the bottle and sniffed it. It was a vinegar solution of some kind, likely just vinegar and water. I smelled nothing else in it.

"You know what it is to douche?" she said.

I nodded.

"Go to the outhouse and douche with that."

"Why?"

"Just do it. It will help stop anything that might have started."

"What do you mean?"

"Just go do it. Take a towel."

I did as I was told, sitting awkwardly in the outhouse with one knee up, then dropped the wine bottle down the outhouse hole. When I went back into the house, my mother had a bath ready for me. She made me take off my clothes, there, in the kitchen by the fire, and step into the little bathing tub in front of her, and, while I cried at the injustice, she scrubbed my skin until it bled.

"If a boy got inside of you, or ever gets inside of you, you take care of it. Understand? You're too young for mothering. Too young for any of it."

I felt dirtied by my mother's talk, confused by what she was telling me. The sting of embarrassment reddened my face and churned in my stomach.

"I didn't do anything," I said. "I won't do anything. Parker pushed me down, that's all. Pushed me down."

"I don't want to hear about it," said my mother. "I don't ever want to hear about it."

22

I SPENT the next day in bed, staring out my naked window at the barn wavering in the heat, replaying the events of the day before over in my mind, sometimes as they happened, sometimes as I would have liked them to. I grabbed the gun from Filthy Billy and shot Parker in the butt as he retreated. I gripped my father by his collar as he opened his mouth to yell at me, and pushed him through the window. I replayed that scene in my mind until I had it perfectly: my father lifting from the floor, coasting towards the window, smashing into it and through it, the glass floating off in all directions and tinkling to the floor, the look of fear, surprise, and shock on his face.

My mother made no demands on me that day, but my father came into my room to interrogate me after he woke late in the morning. He stomped the same circle as he had the night before, in front of the window, round and round, shouting and not waiting for an answer. I flinched and shook through it all, hugging my knees.

"You tell me where you were! Why didn't you go back to school? What happened that day you looked so strange? Were you with some boy? Who was it? Who was it?"

Exhausted and frightened by my father, my nerves shot by the events of the day before, I giggled. My father roared — *roared* — and took me up by the arm and slammed my whole body against the wall. I didn't cry that time. I stared at him, running that perfect scene of him breaking through the window over and over in my mind. My lightning arm reached out and tried to grab him, though the rest of my body was numb and useless with fear. My father took a step back; he was stunned a little, I think, at the thought that I might try to protect myself or hurt him. I took the arm by the wrist and pulled it down to the blankets and held it there. But he grunted and left my room. He was gone for the day. My arm came back to me slowly, but anger took me over, leaving me breathless, shaking, sick to my stomach. I sweated and my heart raced, although I did little that day but lie in bed staring at that window.

My mother came into my room silently once with a jug of water, an empty glass, and a ham sandwich, and left them for me on my vanity, but I didn't eat them. Sometime in the afternoon, Dennis came up to the window. He looked over his shoulder, then cupped his hand against the glare of the glass, tapped once, smiled when he saw me, and left a bowl of cherries on the windowsill. Then he was gone again. I got out of bed and opened the window and realized just how hot I'd been, cooped up in there. Sweet air flowed through in waves, fluttering my nightgown, refreshing me. Lucifer jumped onto the windowsill and rubbed himself against me. No one was around in the yard. The outhouse door was ajar. I caught a glimpse of Dennis running across the fields to where my father, brother, and Filthy Billy worked to cut the alfalfa hay. I ate the cherries that Dennis had left and spit the pits out the open window, petting Lucifer and conjuring, once again, the vision of my father cutting through glass.

23

RASPBERRIES HANG like nipples on tall, thorny stalks. If a raspberry is ripe, caressing it with your fingertips will bring the berry rolling into your hand. But wait for that ripeness. A berry plucked too early has no sweetness, only a coarse flavor that will pucker your lips up tight. When a berry is ready you'll know by its softness, the deep purple-red color, and the ease with which it gives itself to you.

But that's just raspberry. You approach each fruit, like each lover, differently. For cherries, you roll your sleeves up. Otherwise you'll stain them purple. And look into the sun when picking cherries, so you can see their dark silhouettes hanging there. And of course you must reach up, so find yourself a sturdy ladder. When you eat a ripe cherry straight from the tree on a sunny day, its juice is so hot, thick, and red that it has the feel of blood running down your chin, staining your lips, and filling your mouth. Once you've sucked all you can from it, you spit out the pit and go for another warm cherry off the tree, and another and another, because the cherry will seduce you every time. The cherry becomes a compulsion, a thing you must have, a passion. You don't see that ripeness, that hot blood juice, in a store-bought cherry. But a cherry sun-hot off the tree, well, that's where it came from, the insinuation of lust in the cherry, the smut-name put to the ripe button-love of a woman. Cherry. It's all juice and warmth, an O in your mouth, a soft marble for your tongue to play with, a sweet soft thing with a core cloaked in flesh.

A few days after the Dominion Day picnic, I was picking cherries, stuffing my mouth with those sweet cherries, when Nora appeared under the tree as if she'd always been there. She touched my knee, scared me half to death.

"What're you doing here?" I said.

"Come to see you."

"You know Dad says no."

"Hasn't blown over yet?"

"No."

I dropped cherries into her waiting hands, and she hung them over her ears, colored her lips with their juice, spit their pits at the sheep grazing around us. When we were both sick-full of them, Nora took out her knife and carved the bark of the tree below me.

"You'll kill it," I said.

"I won't kill nothing." She went on carving and I went on picking cherries.

"Why don't you come with me now? Your mum's gone. I seen her driving into town."

"She was just taking the cream in," I said. "I don't know when she'll be back. If she catches me gone, I'm in for it."

"You're in for it anyway."

I shrugged and went on picking. Nora pulled a little bark from the tree with her fingers.

"Chicken," she said. "Your mum don't even hit you or nothing. She's not half crazy like my mum."

"Crazy enough. She talks to my grandmother's ghost. I see her listening, like she hears somebody."

"Lots of people haunted by ghosts," said Nora. "Come down. See what I did."

I climbed down and sat my basket of cherries on the ground. Nora had carved our names, hers and mine, in the trunk of the tree, and surrounded them with a heart.

"Somebody could see that," I said.

"Let them."

She pushed me against the tree and kissed me. I pushed her off.

"Somebody could see," I said.

Nora stepped away and kicked the ground.

"I'm sorry," I said.

Nora cleaned the dirt from under her nails with the blade while I tried to think of what to say.

"I'll come tomorrow," I said finally. "I'll tell Mum that I'm going and I'll go. There's nothing she can do to stop me."

"Come now," said Nora.

"Tomorrow," I said. "I've got chores. I'll come tomorrow. I'll meet you at the winter house."

She didn't say anything to that. She turned her back on me and walked back to Blood Road through the orchard. Lucifer tripped along behind her, parting a second path through the grass. I watched her for a time, then — cherry juice coloring my lips tart red, cherry juice leaving stains like blood down the front of my blouse — headed back to the house with one of Bertha Moses's red cedar baskets filled with sun-hot cherries.

That afternoon my mother came back from town loaded down with several elegant wine bottles. Mrs. Boulee, the schoolteacher, had asked her to fill them with beet wine for her as a favor, and my mother had felt obliged, after all that had happened, to comply. She got to work on the beet wine that very afternoon. There was sediment in the bottom of almost every bottle, so she filled them half full of warm water and added a drop of ammonia and a bit of crushed eggshell to each one. We shook each bottle so the eggshell stayed in the bottom to scratch away the sediment. It didn't take long to clean those bottles.

Beet wine was a common wine in the valley, as beets grew well there, and a wine of an uncommonly lovely rich red color. My mother's recipe called for:

> *six or seven pounds of beets*
> *a gallon of water*
> *four pounds of sugar*
> *a pound and a half of seeded raisins*
> *the peel of one lemon and one orange*
> *a slice of toast*
> *one ounce of yeast*

My mother put the water on to boil first, of course, because that could take forever on a woodstove. Then we went outside together to pick the beets. Even before you pull the beet from the ground you can clearly see the beet draws its blood from the earth: red runs through the veins of the green leaves, making it the prettiest plant in the vegetable garden. When you pull the root up, you'll see the long whipping tail of the beet that reaches far down into the soil. Slice the beat crosswise and you'll see deep red growth rings, just like what you'll find in a tree. Run your thumb across the cut root and your thumb will turn the color of a tatty girl's lipstick. A cut beet will bleed into your soup pot and color everything in it. That's why, if you want to keep the color of a boiled beet for your table, you trim off the tail and snap off the greens but don't cut into the root itself.

Color is what my mother wanted in her wine, so she and I spent the better part of the afternoon cutting the beets into little cubes and boiling them slowly for two hours until the pot appeared to be a kettle of boiling blood. Later I would hold cheesecloth across the mouth of a crock as my mother ladled the beet blood into the cloth to strain it. She would then add the sugar and raisins, orange and lemon peels, and float the slice of toast covered in yeast, yeast-side down, on the mixture. We would let this stand in the root cellar for a fortnight, stirring several times each day. Then my mother and I would very carefully strain the beet wine and bottle it for Mrs. Boulee.

I stood next to my mother at the kitchen table on the afternoon that Nora and I had picked cherries, dicing a pile of cleaned beets. On the table before us, the scrapbook was open to the recipe for beet wine. My mother's beet-bloody fingerprints covered the page. As I was cutting, I sprayed a bit of beet juice on this page, so I grabbed a dry dishrag and dabbed it up.

"Leave it!" said my mother.

"I was just wiping it off."

"I said leave it!"

I threw the cloth on the kitchen cupboard. "How long do I have to stay around here?"

"I don't know," said my mother. "The way your father's talking, he may never let you out of the house."

"But I'm going out of the house. When he's not around."

My mother looked at me sideways, and I grinned at her.

When she smiled back, I said, "I'm going to go see Nora tomorrow."

"You know your father doesn't want you seeing that girl."

"He doesn't want me seeing anybody. He'll keep me locked in here forever."

"Maybe it's best for now. It's not safe walking in the bush. Anything could happen."

"Billy scared that Parker kid off," I said. "Scared him good. With a gun. Wish I'd done it."

"I don't mean Robert Parker. He wouldn't hurt anyone. I mean a bear or cougar. There's those children missing on the reserve. It could be Mr. Boulee didn't shoot the right animal. I couldn't bear it if you were out there and some animal. . . . No, Robert's a good boy. You must have misunderstood. He was having a game with you, I'm sure of it. He helped me carry my flour out to the democrat just today."

I watched my mother for a long time. She wouldn't look at me. She went on dicing beets. Her fingers were bloody with their juices.

"I'm going to see Nora tomorrow," I said. "While Dad's out in the field. He doesn't have to know."

"You'll stay here," she said. "I need your help."

"I'll do the work and then I'll go. You can tell him or not. I'll leave after he's gone out for lunch and come back before supper."

"You will not leave this house."

"What are you going to do to stop me?"

My mother looked away. She went on chopping beets. After a time I went back to cutting them as well.

"I have some preserves for Bertha," she said. "Remember to ask me for them before you go."

My father ran into the kitchen then, holding a hand that was bloody, howling like a child, crying real tears, so panicked he walked right into the table that was filled with beets before falling onto the seat of a chair. My mother pulled off her apron to use as a tourniquet and my father sank into her, hid his head between her breasts as she tied her apron around his wrist to stop the bleeding. When she washed the blood away, it turned out to be nothing but a nasty cut to the meaty patch at the base of his thumb, but she held him anyway, rocking him as if he were a child, and I watched him hold on to her as if he were hanging on for dear life.

24

THE THING that followed hopped onto Blood Road and followed me, I heard it, but I held my breath and told myself it was my own imagination at work, nothing more, and that time I came to believe it because the sound stopped. I turned then, more from curiosity than fear, to see if there were footprints following mine in the red dirt. There were none. Instead, a little way in the bush, I caught sight of a coyote nervously watching me. Since I had no gun I left him to his curiosity and went on walking. He followed me; I caught glimpses of him trotting parallel to me in the bush.

My mother had given me two tiny jars of wild strawberry jam for Bertha and I carried them in my skirt pockets. I had walked past the root cellar into the bush, so my father wouldn't catch a glimpse of me leaving from the field, and then followed Blood Road towards the reserve.

Nora was standing, waiting, at the last corner before the reserve. She was dressed as she always was, like a cowboy, with her bells around her neck. She waited in the middle of Blood Road with her hands in her jeans pockets, and when she saw me coming she grinned a little shyly and scuffed her feet in the red dirt.

"What're you doing out here?" I said, as I came up to her.
She shrugged.
"I was coming to the winter house to see you," I said.
"I know."

She didn't reach out to pet me or say anything to settle my nerves, so I put my hands in my skirt pockets and looked around behind me for signs of the coyote. Nora stared off down Blood Road.

"You know what we could do?" said Nora. "We could walk right down that road, and keep on walking and catch the train this afternoon for Vancouver."

"We don't have money."

"Don't need money. We could jump a train. Get a job in Vancouver soon as we get there. They're begging for girls to work the factories. We could go right now."

"Nah." I looked down at my shoes, then caught sight of the fresh cuts on Nora's arms. She saw me looking and pulled her sleeves down to her wrists.

"I got a coyote following me," I said.

She squinted past my shoulder into the bush. "Where's the coyote?"

"He's there, sure enough."

"Come on." She took my hand and we pushed into the bush, heading towards the winter house. "There's coyotes everywhere. Coyote got our cat. Too many of them living off farmers' garbage and chickens, then they breed. Soon enough you got too many and they starve and go after the sheep."

"We lost a ewe and a calf to coyotes already this year," I said.

"Everybody's losing sheep. My uncle Louie lost a sick cow to them coyotes. She was too sick to get up and the coyotes ate her cunt."

"No!"

"I saw it!"

I took Nora's arm and we shivered through the bush.

"Maybe Coyote Jack's following you," said Nora.

"He's around. He comes to the house sometimes. I see him through the window, hanging around. Sometimes he gives me the creeps."

"You ever been to Coyote Jack's cabin?" said Nora.

"Don't even know where it is. Dan said it's someplace on the mountain."

"I been there," said Nora.

"You're crazy."

"Maybe. It's just a little house. Smaller than Dennis and Billy's cabin. I looked in the window. Everything's really tidy. You wouldn't think he'd be neat, but he is. He keeps a garden behind the cabin. I took a carrot and ate it."

"No!"

"Let's go there now," she said.

"I don't think so."

"Come on. What else you got to do?"

"I've got to take this jam to Bertha."

"It can wait. Come on!"

We followed one of the many Indian trails up the mountain. The path was winding, steep, and overgrown, as if it had not been used for some time. We climbed it with our breath short and our hearts clanging with the outrageousness of what we were doing. After all the terrible stories of Coyote Jack, we were seeking him out, we were following his trails, we were tracking him down.

"What if he's home?" I called up to Nora's back.

She looked over her shoulder once and kept on climbing up the slope. "What if he is?" she said.

"Bertha thinks he's dangerous."

"Granny thinks every man's dangerous. She had some things done to her when she was young."

"You said yourself he's crazy, that he scared you."

"Yeah, well, you scared now?"

"I'm not scared," I said, though my heart banged against my chest and the hairs on my arms prickled. "He's just a shy old man."

"Shy old man or shape-shifter. He could be watching us now. He could be that robin there, or a deer watching us quiet as can be from behind that mess of blackberries, or he could be that tree there, even. Coyote can be anything."

"Stories," I said.

"The Bible's full of stories," said Nora, and I recognized it as something Bertha had said in the past, at some now hazy coffee visit in our kitchen.

I watched the denim pull and stretch over Nora's bottom as she climbed up the path before me. The higher we climbed the drier it got, until we were in pine forest with nothing for underbrush. The hill leveled out a little, and Nora led me into a new meadow of fireweed and wildflowers, and there, in the middle of it, was a tiny cabin and garden plot. Even from there, I could see the neatness of it. The garden was planted in careful rows and the dirt around the house was swept out in a design of rays radiating from the house.

"What if he's in there?" I said again.

"Then we'll knock on the door like friendly neighbors and more likely than not he won't answer the door. He'll pretend he's not there. Or he'll run off. You ever seen him talk to anyone?"

I wiped the sweat from my face with the loose ends of my brother's shirt. "I don't know."

"Come on!" said Nora. She marched boldly across the meadow, knocking a path through fireweed and milkweed, black-eyed Susan and oxeye daisy, yarrow and thistle. I straggled along behind her, picking a few wildflowers as I went. This far up the mountain, the meadow was as much as two weeks behind the growth in the valley. The air was cooler, and the wind that swept off the top slope still had the bite of snow in it. I reached the little cabin with my heart thudding in my chest and my hands full of quickly wilting wildflowers. Nora was standing in the shade of the porch. The whole structure was even smaller than it had first appeared, like a child's playhouse with a high ceiling. Everything was swept clean. A little bucket of geraniums grew on a stump by the door. Nora gestured to me and we stooped into the window, cupping our hands over our eyes against the reflection.

"He's out," said Nora.

The cabin was just one tiny room with a cot, a small table, and one chair. A kerosene lamp and bowl sat on the table. At the foot of the bed stood a tiny three-shelf bookcase full of books. A pair of woolen pants, a white shirt, and a pair of long johns hung on pegs above the cot. There were no pictures, not even a calendar, on the walls. There was a small stump by the cot on which Coyote Jack had placed a milk jug of wildflowers, like the ones I held in my fist, in front of an old framed photograph of a young white woman.

"Who do you think that is?" I said.

"I don't know," said Nora.

"Could be his wife."

"Coyote Jack with a wife?"

"Could be. She could be dead. Or maybe she ran away. Maybe he came up here running from heartbreak."

"I can't see Coyote Jack with a woman of any kind," said Nora.

"Doesn't seem possible, does it? Maybe it's his mum, the Swede's wife. She used to live in our house, you know."

"I know. But she was a half-breed."

"Who would it be then?"

"Maybe it's somebody else's picture," said Nora. "Somebody he doesn't know. He's so lonely, he stole some strange lady's photograph so he could make believe someone loves him."

"I think you should be making up the stories," I said. "Not your granny."

There was a crashing in the bush. Nora and I turned and backed up to the little window, breathless and looking all around us. The crashing stopped and went on again, stopped, and a fawn stepped out of the woods. It high-stepped into the field and then called, mewing exactly like a kitten.

We let out our breaths.

"Jesus," said Nora.

"Let's get out of here," I said.

Nora led the way, stepping off the tiny porch already in a full run. The fawn leapt one way and another and then bounced back into the bush. I ran the whole way back down the mountain, clutching the jam jars in my pockets. Before I knew it, we'd crashed through the bush behind the church on the reserve. We didn't stop running until we reached Bertha's house.

The pregnant woman and the one with webbed fingers came out of one of the many rooms when they heard Nora and me run into the house. Nora's mother was sitting with Bertha at the table, sewing.

"Beth, dear!" said Bertha. "You come sit right down!"

I went to pull out the tiny jars of jam from my pocket and realized my lightning arm was still hanging on tight to the wildflowers I'd picked on Coyote Jack's plateau, so I handed Bertha those as well.

"Well, where did you get these?" said Bertha.

"Up near Coyote Jack's place," I said.

Nora's mother looked up angrily at the two of us. Nora pulled my sleeve to get my attention and shook her head.

"What are you, stupid?" Nora's mother said to Nora, in her gruff man-voice. "Going up there after all I've told you? What are you, dumb? Worthless little half-breed."

Nora didn't say anything. She stared out the window over the bed.

Bertha glanced over at Nora's mother and then went back to her sewing.

"You shouldn't go up there," said Bertha, quietly. "That man's not well."

"We didn't do anything," I said. "I mean, we didn't go inside his house or anything. We were just out walking."

"Well, I used to go out walking, too," said Bertha. "I'd walk and walk and walk, all through the bush and down Blood Road, and all over the plains with the horses. When I was just a young thing, not even sixteen. But that's what you did, you went out alone in the bush, both girls and boys, for a long time, weeks. That's where you met your guardian spirit, your power, something like your Christian people's angels."

Bertha smiled at Nora's mother, and the woman glared angrily back. Bertha sighed and went back to sewing. "But then I got old and started believing what I was told about going out," she said. "Mostly the men, my brothers and uncles. They said I had to be careful. There was always something out there to get me. Sometimes they said a bear. Sometimes my mother said a man, a bad man, would come after me and get me. I got scared. Then I didn't walk anymore. Now, of course, the young girls don't get their power from anywhere. They're afraid to go out searching for it."

"I'm not scared," said Nora.

"You should be," said her mother. I watched her and her odd extra finger for a while as she sewed.

"Look at me!" said Bertha. "I got old and fat and scared."

"You're not scared of anybody," I said. "You yell at my father even."

Bertha laughed at that. "I'm scared," she said. "Plenty scared. But that's no good. You don't be scared. Be smart. If somebody hurts you, you hurt back until they stop. Go out into the bush until you find your own trail. But my uncles, they were right about some of that. There is always something out there to get you. Know that, but don't be scared. Go hunt it down, so it don't get you."

"That kind of talk will get them killed," said Nora's mother.

"Tell Beth the stories about Coyote," said Nora. "She had one following today."

"Oh! There are so many!" said Bertha.

"The scary ones," said Nora. "The ones where he eats his wives."

Bertha looked over at Nora's mother. Nora's mother shook her head once. "Oh, those are just stories," said Bertha.

"Come on, tell her," said Nora.

Bertha picked up her sewing again. "Well, in the old times Coyote was a shape-shifter," she said. "He could be a fox, or mouse or man, or a deer, whatever he wanted to be."

I looked over at Nora, and she grinned.

"But he was still Coyote," said Bertha. "Always looking for trouble. He was greedy. Now, Coyote's son had two wives and Coyote wanted one of them. He did some magic and made a beautiful and strange bird appear at the top of a tree. 'Son,' he said. 'Go climb that tree and bring me that bird. I'm too old to climb.' Coyote's son did as he asked, but as the son climbed, Coyote made the tree higher and higher. Soon the son was tired and wanted to come back down, but Coyote called, 'You're almost there! Climb a little farther and bring me that bird!' So the son kept on climbing. Coyote made the tree higher and higher until it reached the sky. Then he pulled all his old wrinkly skin tight and tied it up in a bow behind him and pretended to be his own son. He tried to sleep with his son's two wives. But one of the wives wasn't fooled and she ran off. In the meantime, Coyote's son had reached the sky and found a strange world up there where the dead people lived. He recognized an old man he'd known when the old man was alive and he asked the old man to help him get back to earth. The old man tied a rope to a basket, and Coyote's son climbed into it and he lowered him back to earth. When Coyote's son reached the earth, he saw the wife his father had not been able to fool in a big crowd of people traveling to Kamloops. The wife saw him and recognized him and they went off to live together."

"What happened to the other woman?" I said. "The son's other wife."

"I don't know," said Bertha. "Coyote probably killed her. He killed all his wives sooner or later."

"How about Coyote?" I said. "What happened to him?"

"He went on to do other things," said Bertha.

"So what's the point?" I said.

"Point?" said Bertha.

"The point of the story," I said.

"There's no moral," said Bertha. "It's just a story. You take what you want from it. Did you know your ancestors, you white people, came from Coyote? You are his children. That's why you act like that. Always greedy. Got to have everything for yourselves. Always got your mouths open, yipping and yapping. Always chasing your tail, round and round. Rush, rush. Always telling fibs. Can't turn your back on Coyote's children. Well, that's not you, of course, Beth."

She grinned at me and I went shy. Nora shrugged and her mother went on shaking her head.

"So did Coyote die?" I said. "Did anybody get even and kill him?"

"Not then," said Bertha.

"How could he live?"

"He's Coyote."

"He's like a god?"

"Maybe more like a Devil," said Bertha. "But that's too simple. He's not a bad guy exactly. No good guys and bad guys. The world doesn't work like that."

The woman with the webbed fingers shook her head at Bertha and crossed her arms. Bertha looked at her as she talked.

"Of course the old men here wouldn't agree with that," said Bertha. "To them, Coyote gave us good things, like salmon. But he's a clown, a scary little clown, like that Hitler, always getting into trouble. Always beating his women. Stealing women. Killing women. But then Coyote also clears away the rules when they get too muddy. He knows what's at the root of things: a good meal, sleep, water to drink, a lover. Those are the things that matter. He doesn't know about shame, not until the end. Then he learns to be sorry. It's good sometimes to turn everything on its head. That's what Coyote does — makes everything crazy, breaks all the rules, puts on ladies' clothing and drinks until he sleeps. I won't have none of that in my house. But sometimes that's good, like them pills your mum gives you every week, eh? Them laxatives. Doing things different, and having a big laugh, cleans you out. Not good to be all stuffed up, living righteous all the time. That makes you sick too. Like that Mrs. Bell. She's one sick lady. Give her a laxative, eh?"

Everyone except Nora's mother laughed at that. She kept her head down and kept the smile off her face, though you could see it was a struggle.

"Anyhow, Coyote's not all bad," said Bertha. "He gave us night and day, the seasons. Just like his children, you white people, he gave us good things and lots that weren't so good. In the stories, in the end, Coyote learns to feel sorry for what he done. Maybe someday his kids will learn to feel sorry for what they done. Maybe someday they'll come around."

I lifted my cup to take a drink and the lightning arm went dead on me. The cup leapt out of my hand like a live thing and tumbled to the floor, spilling lukewarm coffee all over.

"Oh! You all right?" said Bertha.

Nora handed me a dry dishrag to sponge off my lap, and then wiped the floor with a mop. I cleaned myself up as best I could with my left hand. My right arm hung beside me without any life in it. I put the rag on the table and lifted the dead arm onto my lap and cradled it there.

"What you got happening there?" said Bertha.

"Beth was hit by lightning," said Nora. "Now that arm goes limp on her all the time."

Bertha came over to me and inspected my arm in the way she looked over a pair of men's work pants for holes to mend. She shook my arm and it wobbled like a rag doll's.

"Never seen a thing like that," she said.

"It comes back. It tingles, then it hurts, then I can use it again. It doesn't last long. But I never know when it's going to happen."

"Lightning, you say?" said Bertha.

She gave me back my dead arm and sat down again.

"Let me tell you about lightning," she said. "In the before times, Mosquito saw a young girl, no older than you. He said, 'She'll make a tender dinner.' So he went to the girl and sucked blood from her. When he was full, he flew up, way up into the sky, full of the girl's blood, up to where Lightning lives. Lightning said to Mosquito, 'Where did you get all that good red blood? I want some!' But Mosquito knew what would happen if he told Lightning where he'd got his blood. He didn't want Lightning to kill the young girl because he wanted to go back for more supper. So he said to Lightning, 'On the very tops of trees are little red buds. That's where I got my blood! I sucked it from the tops of the trees.' Lightning believed Mosquito. That's why lightning still strikes the tops of trees."

I giggled and Bertha sat back and went on sewing. Nora poured more coffee.

"You said something last time I was here," I said to Bertha. "About the children on our place, the homesteader's children, how they died. You said they died like Sarah Kemp."

Nora's mother looked up at Bertha and let her sewing drop in her lap.

"Yes, they died like that," said Bertha. "They went missing and then they were found all chewed up. Other children too, here, in the village, Indian kids. But those kids were never found. They're still walking out there, walking and walking."

"Mother!" said Nora's mother.

"I know, I know," said Bertha. "My daughter here thinks I'm full of stories, stories Christ people don't like. But I remember. The white men that searched said it was some animal gone crazy that got those kids. They shot a bear just like they shot one this spring and said it was that bear that got the kids. But it wasn't. The thing that got those kids walked these mountains for a long time after that."

"But they found the homesteader's children," I said.

"Yes, those children they found," said Bertha. "White children. Well, half-white. Killed near their own home. But none of them from the reserve, none of them who were killed in the bush. My father and brothers told me when they were hunting they sometimes came across a little child's footprints and they'd follow them but wouldn't find nothing. My brother came home saying he found little footprints just the year before he died. That was a long time after those children went missing."

Bertha leaned forward over the table at us, so close I could smell her sweet coffee and tobacco breath.

"But you know," she said. "It wasn't a bear. It was Coyote. He was walking here for a long time. Then my son, Billy's father, he took care of Coyote. He was Coyote's house, see? He was where Coyote went to rest. Coyote never made my son do any bad things like what he made those other men do. Once, when Coyote was resting inside him, my son took his own life — so Coyote would have to return to the spirit world with him — so we could walk in peace for a while. Didn't last long, 'cause Coyote just got born again, but it was a good time. My son gave us that as a gift."

A shiver went through Nora's body and a smile lifted her face. She clearly loved these stories, loved to be scared half to death. I was scared too, but I didn't like it. The stories weren't a welcome thing. I'd have to carry them now into the woods with me and they'd jump on me.

"I thought Billy's dad fell on a bottle," I said. "Bled to death."

"Yeah, he done that. But he did it on purpose."

"I don't get it," I said.

"Mother, enough!" said Nora's mother.

"Well, of course I'm an old woman full of stories, eh?" said Bertha. "What do I know?"

She threw an angry look over at Nora's mother. Nora's mother threw her sewing down and left the house. Nora, me, and the other women in the house watched her, but Bertha went on sewing as if nothing happened.

25

SOME HOT DAYS are like that. So hot everything goes liquid. The air over the cornfield shimmers, air so hot and wet you feel you're taking in another's hot, exhausted breath. Your skin's so slick with sweat, it's hard to tell where your body ends and the air begins. Smells that were forgotten come to the surface. The garlic in last night's soup rises up to the skin, irritating a mind that's already angered by heat. These are the days best spent submerged, in a cool blue room with the curtains closed, or in a cold bath with water drawn up to your chin, or better yet in a pool in a creek hidden by trees.

But instead my mother and I were driving the democrat down Blood Road, taking the cream to the train station in town. Blood Road was as dusty in summer as it was muddy and vexing in spring. Although the ruts were still there — created in spring when the horses and buggies ripped one way, then the other, through mud to avoid the turtles — at least a buggy didn't get stuck in summer, its wheels mired in a mess of turtle blood and horse shit. Now, in the summer, the ride was only a bumpy one. Great clouds of red dust welled up behind us.

I carried enough change in my pocket to purchase sanitary napkins, which I had run out of. I wore one of my mother's cloth napkins instead that day, a cloth that had once been my diaper. It was a shameful time. When I became a woman, my father had warned me to stay away from bulls and male dogs at that time of the month because he feared they would attack me. And so I kept my legs closed tight, and when we reached town, I went into G. Locke Drugs straightaway. That walk down the aisle towards Mr. Locke's raised counter took forever. The merchandise on the shelves, the little round tables and ornamental iron chairs where I'd sucked down a soda only twice in my life, seemed to recede away from the crack of my shoes against the flooring. I stared over Mr. Locke's head at the government war poster on the back wall, which said, COUGHS AND SNEEZES SPREAD DISEASES. I hated this chore, hated it more than shoveling the foul, sickly yellow shit of a sick calf from a stall.

"What can I do for you today, Beth?" said Mr. Locke. He smiled at me and waited.

Each time I made this purchase, I hesitated over how to ask. Bertha Moses called them "gunrags." Nora, copying something her mother had picked up from her Indian residential schoolteachers, called them "nappies." My mother didn't call them anything at all. This time, like every other time, I couldn't think of what to ask for, so I pointed at the row of plain brown paper packages behind Mr. Locke's head.

He turned, and said "Oh" quietly, and handed me a box.

An economy box cost eighty-five cents for forty-eight napkins, and I had exact change in my sweaty little hand. I exchanged money for the package and hurried back to the buggy, thankful that no one else was in the store, and hid the box under the seat.

The heat of the day overwhelmed my curiosity. I didn't go look in the shop windows, dreaming of things I couldn't own. I sat, sweated, and waited for my mother on the steps of the druggist. Storefronts and houses wavered in the hot currents of air. The few people on the street seemed to float like ghosts. The ghost of the old Swede floated down the street and saw me sitting on the steps. I tried not to watch him. He floated up to me and suddenly became solid.

"You tell your father he's crossed the line," he said. "You tell your father he better stop now, or there'll be hell to pay."

The heat was doing something to my head. I felt drowsy. His words echoed around in my ears like marbles in a jar. The Swede put his face close up and inspected me.

"You understand what I'm saying?" he said.

I nodded. He looked at me a while, shrugged, turned, and became a ghost again, and in ghostly fashion he disappeared behind the general store.

I whistled, nervously, and watched the albino crow sitting on the doctor's house, Goat's house. The crow was growing older, losing its juvenile salt-and-pepper feathers and becoming whiter each trip I took to town. Bread crumbs littered the street under the roof of the doctor's house and, as I watched, a little girl I didn't recognize stepped from the doctor's house and threw more bread onto the street. I stopped whistling. The little girl watched as the white crow swooped down, caught the bread, and flew up to the roof again. When a woman called from the house, the girl went back inside and closed the door behind her. I looked over at Blundell's Motel and stared at the window of the room where Ginger Rogers had slept, willing a face to appear until one did, looking back at me, a woman's face, I thought, masked by the reflection of trees in the glass of the window, or perhaps it was nothing more than a mix of shadow and light.

Then Goat was right there, at my shoulder.

"Something's got her," he said.

"What?"

Goat pointed down the empty street, in the direction of the few town houses belonging to the business owners and to the old widow, Mrs. Roddy, who thought Germans were tunneling under her home. Far down the road near the church, a scrawny dog crossed the street and disappeared behind the widow's house. Goat dropped his arm, and it hung loose like the arm of a rag doll. He kept on staring down the street.

"The dog, you mean?" I said. "Who are you talking about?"

Goat turned his whole body to look at me, stamping a small circle in the dust.

"Well, I've got to go." I stood up and dusted my skirt and stepped off the porch.

"Something's got her," he said again.

"Go away."

Goat didn't say anything more, but he didn't look away either. He looked straight at me as he'd never done before, and that got me scared of him all over again.

"What are you talking about? Go leave me alone. Go on. Git!"

I headed for the store, and when Goat began to follow, I picked up a rock and threw it at his feet.

"Git!" I said. "Go on home!"

He stopped following me and just stood there, in front of the druggist, drooping in the heat, staring after me as I walked over to our horses. I kept my back to him, conscious of his eyes on me, and whistled. When I didn't feel him staring anymore, I turned around. He'd gone off. I kept on whistling. My mother was taking her sweet time in the store, as she always did on days when we went into town without my father. People would talk to her then, when she was alone. Mrs. Bell left the general store and floated toward me, becoming solid as we met.

"Beth Weeks, why are you whistling?" she said.

"I don't know."

"A whistling girl and a crowing hen are sure to come to some bad end."

She kept on walking, not waiting for a reply. The skinny wild dog sniffed around the widow's porch steps, lifted its leg to them, then began digging under the boards of the bottom step. After a time my mother came out of the store, carrying her net bag with the few groceries she'd purchased inside it, and a lumpy flour bag.

"Mrs. Bell sent these," she said, holding open the flour bag. There were several jars of apricot jam in there. I took a jar out.

"Go ahead," said my mother.

I grinned at her, tapped the lid loose against the democrat, and opened the jar. I skimmed off the jam foam with my finger and slipped it into my mouth. I held the jar out for my mother, but she saw Mrs. Ferguson coming out of the store and declined. Mrs. Ferguson held up her head and walked right by my mother, as if her own husband had had nothing to do with the fight at the Dominion Day picnic, as if it were all my father's fault. Both my mother and I watched her walk away.

"Can I get some nylons?" I said.

"Nylons!" Mum turned to me. "You're not old enough for nylons. I don't even have nylons. Your father forbids that kind of wastefulness."

"You think the Blundells really have a mongoloid child in the motel?" I said.

"Where on earth did you get that idea?" said my mother.

I shrugged. "I saw a face. In the window. I think it was a woman's."

"There was talk," said my mother. "Years ago. But nothing came of it. Some said the Blundells kept a child, a slow child, like Arthur, locked away in a back room. The Blundells denied it all. They left the church over it."

"I thought I saw someone in that room. Where Ginger Rogers stayed."

"Well, maybe someone is staying there."

"Mr. Johansson came by. He was really mad. He said Dad better stop damaging his fence."

My mother sighed.

"He said he'd do something bad if Dad didn't stop."

"Bad? Like what?"

I shrugged.

As my mother loaded her groceries into the buggy and stepped up into the seat, the skinny stray disappeared around the back of the widow Roddy's house and reappeared in the shadows by the side of Blundell's Motel. The wild dog watched us — I could see his eyes shining as we turned the democrat and headed out of town — with one paw slightly raised and his nose pointing at us, in the hunting stance of a coyote.

26

SUMMER WAS SHORT in Turtle Valley. It was over before you believed it had begun. While the wheat still turned golden in the fields, the leaves of the poplar that was growing ever larger through the engine of my father's old Ford were turning brown and yellow. The sunflowers were ripening just as the first fall rains began. Nevertheless it was still a time of celebration, a time of harvest parties at the churches and in private homes, a time of picking and putting away, and that was a joy. In Turtle Valley, it was the fowl supper we looked forward to, a community dinner held in the United Church every farmwoman contributed to. It was a feast, even then, in wartime, a time of rationing. The excess food was the point of it all, a kind of prayer for bounty, an offering that might bring a better year next year. Always next year. The prayer of the farmer. Next year.

My mother's own particular offering was a dessert called Bird's Nest, appropriate enough for a supper called fowl. My mother's Bird's Nest recipe was pasted in her scrapbook alongside one of those ghost stories she clipped from magazines on the sly and never let me read. The recipe called for nothing but apples and a thin batter you could mistake for pancake if you didn't know better. My mother preferred greenings, but any large apple will do. Pare them and remove the cores in such a way that the apples are left whole. Arrange the apples in a deep pie dish, as many apples as you have guests. Then mix a batter with three eggs and enough sweet milk and flour to make it a little on the runny side. Pour it over the apples, filling the hole where the core was, and the deep dish besides. Bake the Bird's Nests in a hot oven until the apples are cooked and the batter is brown and serve them with a bit of butter and a sprinkle of brown sugar. Well, you can't get simpler than that. My mother and I made more than forty for that event.

We needn't have made so many. The church was nowhere near as full for that year's fowl supper as it had been for Sarah Kemp's funeral. The few people there crouched in small groups, shoulders hunched, heads down, barely picking at the food on their plates. The Swede was there, and that was bad because so was my father. Sarah Kemp's mother and grandmother were there, sitting alone at a table. Dan sat talking with a man I didn't recognize. Lily Bell, Parker, and the other kids who had stripped me in the Fraser house weren't there. I was relieved, at least, for that. My mother and father had come earlier, after taking the cream to town with Chief and the buggy, so my mother could help set up the church for the supper. I had ridden Cherry into town at dusk, after finishing up chores, so when I arrived almost everyone had filled his plate. I stood in line with the few other latecomers, listening to Ferguson gossip with Morley Boulee at the table behind me. Ferguson had avoided our family ever since he'd hit my father at the Dominion Day picnic, and he kept his back to me now.

"Well, the old widow's finally gone," said Mr. Boulee.

"Mrs. Roddy?" said Ferguson. "Yes, well, it's for the best. She'd lived a miserable life these last years. Never got over her husband's death. Bet she died thinking the Germans were coming to get her."

"Any word on what killed her?"

"Her heart is my guess," said Ferguson. "I don't suppose we'll ever know. She'd been laying there for quite a while. Something had started eating on her. Rats, I guess. It's a crime nobody noticed she was gone."

"She had no friends to notice, living like that."

Mr. Ferguson shook his head, and then Mrs. Halley, Sarah Kemp's grandmother, one arm dead at her side, stood up as I came close to her and shouted at me, "Sarah!"

Everyone turned to look. I put down my plate and ran outside and leaned against the building until I got my breath back. Twilight had come down and a gentle rain had begun to fall through the electric yard light in front of the church. We had no electricity at home, and I thought the light was a beautiful thing. Yet with the barbed wire on top of the fence to keep Goat away, it gave the churchyard the naked feel of a prison camp. Goat waddled out from behind Belcham's, started towards the church, saw me, and turned back to hide again behind the store. The albino crow swooped down to pick up a scrap on Main Street and flew over my head to land on the church roof. I rubbed my hands and moved a little down the wall of the church, so I was under the eaves, out of the rain.

The man who'd been talking to Dan came out of the church and leaned against the wall. He had the careless look of an unmarried man. He lit a cigarette and pretended I wasn't there. I folded my arms. An old man came out and talked to the bachelor. I realized they must be the Fowlers, father and son, who had recently moved to the Fraser property next to the school. The old man complained that his wife was taking too long to eat and he was getting hungry. I didn't understand. Then his wife came out, removed her teeth, and handed them to the old man.

"Food's getting cold," she said.

The old man brushed bits of food from the woman's teeth and put them in his mouth. He waved at the bachelor and went inside. The old woman put her hand over her mouth and followed.

I laughed. The bachelor laughed.

"He won't get teeth," said the bachelor. "Stupid old man."

I stopped laughing but carried the smile for a long time. The bachelor sniffed and ran his hand under his nose. I grew shy. The bachelor looked at his feet. He smoked. "Oh," he said, and offered me a cigarette.

"No."

He put the cigarettes in his pocket and threw the spent butt on the ground. "Stinky things," he said.

"It's okay."

"No," he said. He kicked the ground. After a while he lit another cigarette. "I heard you run with that half-breed," he said.

I looked up and looked away.

He said, "I know there aren't many men around, but there's no need for that. I'm here now. We could have some fun." As an afterthought, he said, "I've got money."

I understood he was calling me a whore and that I was being talked about around town. I ran over to Cherry, mounted her, and headed down the main street, driving my heels into the horse's flanks to get her galloping. I ran the horse to a sweat on the way home, replaying the scene with the bachelor over in my head — how strange things had gone, how I should have slapped his face, called him trash and laughed at his makeshift patchwork and buttonholes, the grass stains on the knees of his pants. He'd been so cocky, so self-sure that I would go running with him. I was so caught up in vengeful thoughts that I rode right by our driveway, bringing Cherry up at the start of our sheep pasture along Blood Road. I dismounted, and led her through the orchard gate. A wind carried the rank smell of the Swede's goat. A shadow skulked across the field, and I clapped to scare it off. The sheep bleated and headed for the barn, but one ewe didn't get up. There were dark pools all around the ewe, blood. But she wasn't dead. The blood was warm and she was breathing.

Coyotes go for the genitals and soft belly of a sick sheep. They nip like a dog at the legs and face until the sheep falls. Then they eat her alive. This ewe was still alive, and her genitals were eaten away. I pressed on with Cherry to the yard and tied her inside the barn as the homesteader's children knocked out a warning in their graves. I went into the house and took the .22 from the gun cupboard, loaded it, and headed back to the ewe. I aimed the gun behind the ewe's ear and fired, then shot the rifle into the air as a warning to the shadows. I slumped into the wet grass and cried for the sheep until the rain let up and the moon poked out of the clouds. A farmer's daughter, and I cried for the loss of one sheep.

When I reached home the second time, Nora was waiting outside my bedroom window. I threw down the gun and swung out at her. I don't know why, exactly. I was angry because of the bachelor's offer to buy me, and because of the sheep with her cunt eaten by coyotes. She took both my wrists and held me like a squawking chicken until the rage passed and I collapsed against the house.

Nora walked out into the yard. Her necklace jingled rhythmically, and the lights it sparked in the moonlight reflected off the house. She stamped out a circle in the dirt. Her movements were precise, as in a ritual, and the bell necklace sounded and shimmered to the beat. She sang quietly. I wondered if she hadn't bewitched me. But of course all lovers are bewitched.

"Some men beat their women, or don't allow them friends," she said. "Granny says it's all the same. That's why they want to pay for you. That way they own you."

She'd heard the rumors before me. Nora stamped her circle. The bells and their lights became their own music.

"I'm sorry," I said.

"We could go. We could leave."

When I shook my head, Nora stepped inside the circle and held out her arms. I stepped into the circle with her and wrapped my arms around her and we held each other until I heard my mother and father driving home.

27

I DIDN'T THINK I'd slept that night, the scene with the bachelor was playing so hard and so violent through my mind. Yet I woke to my father slamming into the house, reckless of the sleepers within. Though my mother must have been awake, he came into my room, came to my bed as a black faceless thing, with only the form of a man.

I removed myself into the forget-me-knots painted on the headboard of my bed, and watched from there, leaving all the fear and anger in my body. It was a moonless night. A few stars were winking just above the black trees. My room, though, was black, and my father was even blacker. He was a big black thing moving over my body, flattening me down to nothing, making me no more than a blanket on the bed. I felt nothing. I wasn't there. He didn't do that thing to me. That wisp of a black blanket under him wasn't me. The lightning arm moved, that was all. It pushed at the black shadow over it. My father took the lightning arm by the wrist and wrestled it down and made it part of the blanket he moved over, moved into. I watched him at it.

After a time the black thing stopped and got up off my blanket-body. It blocked the pale light of the window for a moment, then slid on, the shadow of a man crossing a wall. The lightning arm lifted up and felt the air, then fell, slack, to the bed. I didn't go back into my body or claim my lightning arm, not then, though my body rose up and went walking. I followed my body, because I couldn't do otherwise, through the parlor and past my father, who slept in his chair by the gramophone as if he'd never entered my room. Over him, her face reflecting the dim light from my bedroom window, my grandmother watched him grimly.

My lightning arm stirred vinegar and water, filled a wine bottle with the mix, and took the bottle to the outhouse to douche as my mother had instructed. I came back to myself there and when I left the outhouse I saw the eyes and feathers of the white crow from town glowing in the dark. He was sitting just outside the outhouse, looking at me. I said, "What do you want?"

The white crow tilted his head, shook himself, and hopped forward to peck at my white toes.

"Get out of here," I said.

I kicked at him, and he hopped back. I threw a rock.

"Git," I yelled. "Get out of here."

The crow hopped a few yards away. I charged at him, yelling and throwing rocks and he finally flew away. Once he was gone the night seemed to deaden all sound and weigh down on me. I wanted to break through the heaviness with my voice. I wanted to scream.

The sound was separate from me and had the power of many voices and made the sky expansive and huge. It woke every living thing and the forest began rustling. The scream in my throat stopped, but the scream went on. It was bestial and lonely, like nothing I've heard since. I ran back to the house, and my mother was at the door. She held the door open.

"What happened?" she asked.

"Something scared me," I said.

"What was it?"

"I don't know."

28

I WENT BACK to my room, but not to that bed or to those blankets. I huddled in the corner next to my vanity and hugged my lightning arm through the night. The pictures welled up and dissolved in the black: the slow fling of my father through glass, the pain on his face, the way my hand ached with the pushing. He crawled back through the broken window, dead now, a ghost with a form that enlarged and shifted and darkened into an animal shape crawling through broken glass, coming for me as I crouched in the corner.

The thudding in my chest woke me. Outside a haze backlit the trees on the benchland, though most of the sky was still black and speckled with stars. I stretched awkwardly out of the corner and dressed quickly, quietly. My father's black shape shifted in the chair as I passed him, but he didn't wake. I took down the .22 from the gun rack in the kitchen, put a box of shells in my skirt pocket, and eased open the screen door. Lucifer slid around my bare legs as I stepped off the porch and he followed me up to Blood Road and past the Swede's driveway, mewing, then gave up when I turned down the Indian path to the winter house.

The Indian trail was the half dark that slips into your blood and quickens it, sets it pounding. Every night creature watched; every crack or shifting branch was an unseen thing following. When I climbed down the ladder into the even deeper dark of the winter house, I was nearly scared out of my skin when my foot found a lump in the blankets and that lump let out a groan.

"What you doing here?" said Nora.

"What you doing here?" I said, louder than I meant to.

"Don't have to yell."

"Well?" I said.

"Don't ask."

"You neither."

I climbed under the blankets and Nora moved away from my cold hands. When her breathing said she was asleep again, I moved closer and held her arm, just above the place where she cut herself, and, chased by shadows but holding on to safety, I drifted off to sleep.

We didn't wake again until sunlight was shining directly down into the hole of the winter house, heating the wood of the chipped-log ladder and making us sweat.

Nora yawned and stretched and moved away from me. "You're all sticky!" she said.

"You're the sticky one!"

"We'll go swimming."

"You're crazy," I said. "There's snow on the mountain."

"Not here."

"Not yet. The water will be ice-cold."

"Don't be so chicken."

Nora pulled her jeans over her nakedness and slipped on the western shirt over the bells. I took longer dressing, put on my brother's jeans under my skirt, struggled into my brassiere, fiddled with the buttons on my blouse. Nora leaned against the chipped-wood ladder, grinning.

"You wear so much clothes, you'd think you were a suitcase," she said.

"Shut up."

"So you going to tell me what happened last night?"

"Nothing happened."

"Your dad?"

"Never mind," I said.

"My mum went into hysterics," she said. "Tore my stuff apart."

"What's she mad over this time?"

Nora shrugged.

"Remember how I asked you if you ever had something following?" I asked her. "In the bush?"

"Like Coyote Jack? Sometimes he follows. Spies on me. Dirty old man."

"No," I said. "Like something you can't see. But it leaves a trail in the grass, or it makes a noise behind you, like wind or roaring or something."

"Sure. That's the way it is in the bush. There's always something following. Especially at night. I go out walking in the night when I can get away just so I get spooked, so I think something's coming to get me. Makes me tingle all over, you know?"

I knew, but I didn't like it.

My lightning arm started going on me, shaking and making me clumsy. Nora saw that and hugged me from behind.

"Ah, don't worry about it," said Nora. "That's just you getting bush-scared. Everybody hears noises in the bush."

"I saw that white crow last night," I said. "That albino."

"Up here? In the valley?"

"It followed me back from town, from the fowl supper."

"Weird, eh?" said Nora. "Granny says it's some ghost come back from the spirit land." She started up the ladder. "So why'd you sleep in the winter house last night?"

"Why'd you?"

I followed her out of the winter house. Despite the turning leaves, the day was like summer, Indian summer. We followed the creek bed to where Dan and I had dammed the creek, where the pool was deepest, beside my old hollow stump. My father had never removed the dam, though he'd threatened to. Over the summer it had taken on a mossy weathered look, as if it had been there forever. I pulled off my brother's jeans, my skirt, my blouse, and brassiere, and laid them over the big hollow stump along with Nora's clothes and the gun. I stepped into water cold enough to make my teeth ache. Nora was off and running ahead of me, tinkling because, though naked, she still wore the bell necklace. She threw herself in, making a splash as big as when Dan threw the stumping powder into the creek. I held my lightning arm and watched Nora come up with her hair sleeked back, her necklace tinkling, and her breasts bobbing on the water.

"It's warm!" she said.

"It's nothing like warm."

Nora swung her arms up and sent a splash over my body that left me gasping and angry.

"Quit that!" I said.

"Can't take it?"

I kicked water at her, and she floated off on her back, laughing and tinkling. I let myself fall into the water and came up gasping at the cold. Nora laughed and splashed more water at me.

"I said stop it!"

"What's the matter with you today?"

"Nothing."

"You've been sulky all morning." And when I didn't answer, she said, "I seen Dennis looking at you."

"When?"

"I seen."

"You haven't seen anything."

"I seen."

"Maybe it's you that's following me," I said. "You're some spy, like them Germans. Or them Japs. Maybe you're a Jap spy."

She grinned and splashed me and I splashed her back and we got all boiled up in water, sunshine, and bells. Nora stopped splashing and fell back into the water. I bounced against the creek bottom. At the creek's deepest part, I could still feel the gravel and pebbles under my toes.

"Your mum say anything yet about going back to school?"

"Nope," I said. "Fieldwork's been so late this year and I've got to do all the chores. Anyhow, I'm not going back."

"It's already started," she said.

"I know." I kicked and shifted in the water so I was floating on my back.

"A lot of your aunts and cousins have webbed fingers and things," I said. "Like your mum and her extra finger. That's weird, all that stuff happening in one family."

"Granny says they're Coyote's daughters. If Coyote's inside some man when he's with a woman, you know, then the child that woman has by him is like that. Webbed fingers, or extra fingers, or weird birthmarks, or each eye a different color."

"You saying you're Coyote's daughter?" I said.

"Granny says that. My mother says my father was some white man working for the Fergusons, who caught her in the bush. She told my uncles and they went and beat the white man up. Then the Mounties came and put my uncles in jail."

"That's why she doesn't like you out walking."

Nora shrugged. "She doesn't like me doing anything. She'll hit me if I look at her cross-eyed."

"I've never seen her hit you," I said.

"She's got manners, eh? Won't hit me in front of company. She learned her good manners from those teachers at the school. Learned how to hit from them too. That's why I won't go near the residential school, won't go to church, though Mum hits me for that too. They want to teach me manners."

"I'm getting cold." I walked, shivering, from the water and Nora followed, shaking her hair like a dog, flinging sunlight in all directions. I picked up my skirt and dried myself with it, then dressed in my blouse and my brother's old jeans. Nora took up the gun and, sitting naked, aimed into the treetops and pretended to shoot.

"Give me that," I said.

I loaded the gun with the shells from the pocket of my jeans and shot off a few branches. The shots awakened the Swede's three-legged dog and set him off. His howls were answered by a coyote's yip farther down the valley, towards the reserve.

"You're getting good," said Nora.

"Been practicing."

"Dan's been practicing too, eh? I see him out with his gun. He'll be joining up soon."

"I guess. I wish he wouldn't."

"Then you'd be working with your dad, eh?" said Nora. "Doing fieldwork?"

I nodded and took aim at the trees again but didn't fire.

"Dennis wants to join up too," said Nora. "Granny won't let him. She says the army's no different than the residential school. They try to make a white out of you. She wants Dennis to stay here."

"She can't tell Dennis what to do."

"Sure she can. She's Granny."

I sighed and lowered the gun and leaned it against the hollow stump.

"See this?" I said.

"The stump?"

I pulled back the weeds and bramble and exposed the hole at its base. "This is my hiding place," I said. I took out the bottle of perfume, showed her, and put it back. "I hide in there myself sometimes."

"You hide in there?" said Nora. She pulled the weeds back farther and sat herself down in front of the opening. "I'm not sure I'd fit in here."

Seeing her moving herself into the hollow stump panicked me, made me angry.

"I don't want you in there," I said.

"Why?"

I couldn't explain, so I didn't say anything. Nora shimmied herself backwards into the hollow stump. The growth of grass, blackberry bramble, and forget-me-nots swept back into place when she pulled in her legs. If she'd kept quiet no one would ever know she was there.

"Can you see me?" she called.

"Please come out," I said. "I don't want you in there."

She pushed back some of the weeds and peeked out. "Why'd you show it to me, then?"

"I don't know."

"Jeez," she said. "Picky, picky."

I was sorry for my anger, but I couldn't shake it. Nora went sulky. She rinsed her body off in the water, her necklace tinkling as she did so, and plunked herself down on the creek shore, as naked as the smooth, round boulder she sat on.

"Come on, let's go walking," I said. "See what we find. Maybe shoot something for supper."

Nora shrugged and, a little while later, she said, "Let's go shoot out the windows in Coyote Jack's cabin."

"No," I said.

"Why not?" she said. "Who's going to care?"

"Forget it," I said.

"Somebody should take a gun to him," said Nora.

"He's just a stupid old man," I said.

Nora didn't answer that. Her face went dark and angry, so I looked in the direction of her gaze. Through the bush, the flax field shone like a bright lake. Dan and Filthy Billy harvested the oats with the binder. The horses' harnesses jingled, and Billy let his curses bounce off the sky.

"I don't know why your father keeps that mongoloid on," said Nora.

"Billy? He works hard. He does a good job."

Nora grunted and went on staring into the field.

"I seen how Dennis looks at you," she said. "I seen how you look at him."

"You haven't seen anything," I said.

Nora inflicted her two-woman eyes on me, held me with them.

"I seen," she said. "You think you're the only girl Dennis looks at, don't you?"

"I don't care if he looks at me." But the shame of the lie made me look down. "I got to get home," I said. "I haven't helped with chores at all today."

"Your daddy still thinks you stay in the house all day, eh, Daddy's girl?"

"I don't care what he thinks. Anyway, he's gone into town with Dennis."

"Maybe Dennis will buy you a present, eh? Maybe you'll be his girlfriend then, when he pays for it."

I turned on my heels, red-faced and confused by her insults, and, weighing the gun in my hands, cut through the bush into the alfalfa field.

Off towards the house, the flax, planted for a second time after the great storm, bloomed like a reflection of the sky. Before me a field of plumed corn stood as if it were a great army of soldiers on parade, and just beyond them Dan drove the horses to pull the binder, cutting a path through the bed of oats. He sat on a seat perched over the bull wheel, one reason we prayed daily for cloudless skies. The bull wheel was what powered the binder, and it was hell in mud. A good rain ended the day — even the week — in the field, and that could mean the year's crop, and all the work that had gone into it, was wasted. Billy sweated behind Dan and the horses, picking up the bundles of oats the binder dropped and throwing them up into stooks to wait on threshing.

I followed the trail that the binder had made through the oats. When I came on them, Dan called out "Ho!" and pulled up the horses. He wiped his face with his sleeve.

"Dad and Dennis back?" he called.

"Not that I know," I said.

Behind us, Billy stacked the bound sheaves of oats on end, one against the other, so they formed a tepee, a stook. The fabric of his shirt was wet through with sweat — almost transparent — and each time he bent and straightened the fabric molded around the muscles of his shoulders. Billy was no longer a boy. When he caught up to the binder, he stopped, stretched his back, and reached for one of two canteens wound around the base of the binder seat. He drank watching me. There was a bit of snakeskin tucked into the ribbon of his hat.

"You (shit) okay?" he said to me.

"Sure. Why shouldn't I be?"

He glanced up at Dan and shrugged.

"What's that in your hat?" I said.

"(Shit) Rattler."

"Why's it in your hat?"

"So I (shit) don't get a (fuck) headache."

"You been getting headaches?"

Billy shrugged and nodded, swore and took a swig off his canteen before handing it to me. I drank and watched a drop of sweat slide down his neck and over his collarbone.

"Bad ones?" said Dan.

Billy nodded again, and I gave him back the canteen. He poured water into his hand and tossed it onto the back of his neck.

"How's it going to help a headache?" I said.

Billy shrugged. "Ever (shit) seen a two (fuck) headed rattlesnake?"

"No," I said. "That's stupid."

"Not (shit) stupid," said Billy. "My uncle saw (shit) one himself. A head at each end. (Fuck) No rattle on that rattlesnake. But that same (shit) day, my uncle's best friend died."

"You saying the friend died because your uncle saw a snake?" said Dan.

Billy nodded and drank from his canteen.

"(Shit) It's a warning," he said.

"That's stupid," I said. "There is no such thing."

Billy shrugged and grinned. Dan poured water from his own canteen over his head and put his hat back on.

"We better get this done, eh?" he said. "Before Dad gets home. He'll fire us all if we don't. Hey, maybe that's not such a bad idea. Maybe we should sit here and do nothing, eh?"

But he giddyupped the horses anyway. Billy went back to stooking. I stepped into the army of corn and followed a row back to the flax field, where I picked a tender breath of blue flax to placate my mother. I didn't walk right up to the house. I couldn't. Instead I wandered across the yard and looked halfheartedly and unsuccessfully for Lucifer until I'd summoned the courage to enter the house.

My mother was making supper. She wouldn't look at me and began peeling away the leaves of a cabbage on the kitchen table. Her scrapbook was on the table next to her, open to the page that contained the photograph of Ginger Rogers and recipes for pancakes, angels on horseback, and quick Sally Lunn. Sally Lunn was a teacake that was sweet but not too sweet. My mother's recipe called for:

> *one half cup butter*
> *one cup sugar*
> *one or two eggs*
> *a pint and a little extra of sweet milk*
> *flour*
> *and two teaspoons of baking powder*

The recipe was one of my favorites and, without thinking, I put my finger to it. My mother batted the air over my hand, and when I ignored her and stubbornly kept my finger on the scrapbook page, she said, "Don't touch!"

"I'm not doing anything," I said.

"Did you hear what I said?"

I put the offending hand in my pocket and stared down at my mother's instructions. She creamed the butter and sugar together, added the eggs and milk and enough flour to make a cake batter. Then she added the baking powder and baked it in a quick oven. My mother served the teacakes hot for tea or breakfast, with butter. Tonight, though, we'd be eating pancakes.

"I had to do all the chores alone," she said. "I've done nothing but work the whole day. The cows haven't been milked this evening. God knows where they are by now."

"I'm sorry," I said.

"Where did you go? Who were you with?"

"I met up with Nora."

"Is that all?"

I didn't answer. I held out the bundle of blue flax, but she ignored me. She went on preparing cabbage for the early supper of a fieldwork day, removing the outer leaves, washing them, then filling a deep bowl with water and adding a tablespoon of salt. She would immerse the cabbage in water for an hour or so to rid it of insects. The insects would rise to the surface like the dead of a shipwreck, and my mother would skim them off before removing the cabbage. She would then wash the cabbage again and chop it into chunks for boiling.

"I had to lie this morning." She added salt to the water. "I told him you'd got up early this morning to do chores. Then I had to make up excuses when he went into the barn and saw you weren't there."

"You didn't have to lie," I said.

"Didn't I? What happened last night? Where did you go?"

"I felt sick. I went out to get air. I had a nightmare."

"You went out walking after a nightmare?"

I shrugged. She looked up at my face for the first time since I came in the house. "Your hair's wet."

"I saw Nora. We went swimming."

"Swimming? This time of year? You're lucky if you don't die of cold."

I held out the flowers again. "These are for you," I said.

She wiped her hands on her apron and took the blue flax, lifted them to her face, and breathed in. For a moment her face relaxed.

"Did you see Bertha?" she asked.

"No, just Nora."

"Does Nora say why Bertha isn't visiting anymore?"

"I didn't ask."

My mother put the flax into a canning jar filled with water and placed it on the kitchen table.

"Well," she said. "I expect it's your father."

She pinched a blue flax flower from the bunch and pressed it with her fingertip into the scrapbook next to the pancake recipe.

"There," she said. "Something to remember the day by, though Lord knows why I want to remember it."

She felt the edge of the photograph of Ginger Rogers, then put her hand to her mouth. The page also held her brief instructions for angels on horseback, and I touched my finger to it.

"We haven't had that for a long time," I said.

"I asked you not to touch that. How many times do I have to tell you?"

I pulled my hand away from the scrapbook and crossed my arms. My mother cradled her arm for a time and then tapped the recipe. "You get me some oysters and I'd make that in a minute," she said.

Angels on horseback were nothing but oysters wrapped in thin rashers of bacon, fried and served hot on buttered toast. But we were three hundred miles from the Pacific Ocean and there was a war on and oysters were a luxury we couldn't afford. Instead that night my mother and I made pancakes, fried ham, eggs, and boiled potatoes and cabbage. Pancakes in our house were an evening meal, never breakfast. The recipe on that page called for two cups of flour, three teaspoons of baking powder, one and a half cups of whole milk, two eggs, and four tablespoons of melted butter or lard.

The trick with pancakes is to beat all the ingredients together just enough to moisten — never overbeat — and to pour the batter onto the griddle from the tip of a spoon so you get nice round pancakes. A pancake is ready to turn when there are bubbles on top, but turn it only once. Otherwise the surface gets hard. The second side takes half as long to cook, so you must make sure that it doesn't burn. I kept my back to the table and my eyes on the pancakes as my father and the men scraped the dirt off their boots on the edge of the porch and came in for supper. My mother closed the scrapbook, firmly pressing the little flax blossom into the page with the angels on horseback, and dropped the scrapbook on the seat of her rocker.

"How was town?" she asked.

"People all over," said Dennis. "You'd think there was a carnival going on."

"It's the turning season," said my mother. "Everyone wants to stock up."

"Whatever it is, old Belcham's doing well for himself," said Dennis. "Hardly room to move in the store."

"You go in?" my mother asked my father.

My father shook his head.

"Goat's figured out a new way into the churchyard," said Dennis. "He was up there on the roof again, going at 'er."

"Shut up!" yelled my father.

The conversation went dead and the kitchen filled with the sound of pancakes sizzling. I flipped the cakes.

Eventually Dan said, "A coyote was chasing the sheep again today. I ran to get the gun, but he was gone. Can't wait to get trapping them again." He called over to me. "Hey, Beth, mixed up my special recipe today."

I glared at him and forced a smile. His "special recipe" was a scent for attracting coyotes, which he'd gotten from Bertha Moses. The scent led the coyote right into our traps and worked so well that my mother had written the recipe into her scrapbook. To make the scent, start with two one-quart glass jars. Fill one jar half full with dead field mice. Fill the other half full of chunks of brook trout, and leave both jars in the sun with the lids loosely closed to keep flies out. After a couple of weeks, mix the rotting contents of both jars together. Add two drops of skunk scent squeezed from the scent glands of a freshly killed skunk. Into this add a pinch of aniseed or a teaspoonful of aniseed oil and a handful of deer hair to thicken the mix. Lastly, add a quarter cup of coyote urine taken from the bladder of a female coyote killed while she's in heat. It's a good idea to wear gloves while preparing the recipe, which reduces to an oily gray sludge that stinks to heaven. A few drops of that on a stump brought the coyotes running into the snares that Dan and I set.

My mother placed plates, pancakes, and ham before the men and scraped back a chair for herself. I stood at the stove, cooking more pancakes, so I wouldn't have to look my father in the face.

"Don't know what's gotten into that Swede," said my father. "He was standing across the street when I came out of the blacksmith's, like he was waiting for me. But all he did was stare."

"I'd think he had a right to stare and more after that fight and all the damage we did to his fence," said Dan.

"Mr. Johansson warned me one day," I said, flipping pancakes. "He said he'd do something if you didn't stop taking down the fence."

"When was this?" said my father.

"A while ago."

"Why didn't you tell me?"

"You'd yell. You always yell."

"I don't yell!" he said, but his voice rose up to contradict him. "I wouldn't yell," he said again, quietly.

"You had no right to take down his fence," said Dan.

"I had every right! And who was taking it down right along with me?"

"And if I refused?"

"You like your nylons okay?" Dennis asked my mother.

"Nylons?" said my mother.

I turned to see my father shake his head at Dennis. Dennis looked into his plate. "I guess I spoiled the surprise," he said. "John got me to pick up some nylons for you today."

My father played with his food. "They weren't for Maud," he said quietly.

Billy's swearing swirled up into a little flurry and died down again.

"Well, who are they for?" said my mother.

My father glanced once, involuntarily, in my direction and said nothing. I was at once delighted and mortified. Nylons!

"You bought them for Beth?" she said. "She's not old enough for nylons. I don't have nylons. You said we couldn't afford nylons."

My father went on chewing his food. My mother's eyes watered up and her chin quivered. "You bought them for Beth?"

Dad ignored her. He cut his meat and ate, methodically, intently. He stared past Billy's shoulder at the gun rack on the wall. My mother pushed her plate angrily across the table so that it clinked against my father's and stood up. She muttered to her dead mother and threw dishes into the washbasin, filling the room with the noise of her anger. My father winced but he didn't get angry, not immediately. He clenched his teeth in between mouthfuls and, when her clanking reached high notes, he closed his eyes briefly.

"We'll get on the corn tomorrow," said Dennis over my mother's noise. "We're so late this year. Another week of rain like the last and we're done for."

Filthy Billy grew more agitated, scratching and shifting in his chair, until his swearing bubbled up like hiccups competing with my mother's muttering; the two of them seemed to be engaged in some insane conversation.

"Slokum saw the girl on the road with that breed again," my father said.

"Her name is Nora," I told the pancakes.

"What?"

"Her name's Nora!"

"Don't raise your voice to me!" He slammed his fist on the table. My mother briefly stopped her dishwashing and muttering and then went at it again. Billy jumped up and ran out the door, letting the screen door slap closed. I watched through the kitchen window as he made his way along the edge of the lake of flax to the oat field.

"Stay away from her," my father said to me.

"Dad," said Dan.

"I said stay away!"

Dennis stood, pushing away his half-finished plate.

"Sit!" said my father, then he lowered his voice. "Finish your food."

Dennis sat again. I piled the pancakes no one would eat onto a plate as my mother banged dishes in the washbowl next to me. My father turned in his chair and yelled at my mother. "What's the matter with you?"

My mother didn't answer or look at him. But now that she had a reaction from him, she took up the scrapbook and dropped into her chair by the stove and rocked and rocked, clutching the scrapbook to her chest, staring and muttering at someone only she could see. The words she said sometimes rose up so that I could almost catch them, then slipped down again.

My father smoothed his forehead and pushed his plate away. "Well," he said. "Let's get that binder fixed. We've got work to do tomorrow."

In a habit that remained from the good days, my father took three strides to leave the house — two into his boots and one out the door — fitting on his cap as he did so. Dennis gave my shoulder a squeeze and followed my father. Dan dallied a few minutes longer, sliding on his denim work jacket with a practiced unhurriedness, taking the time to tie up his boots. As he left he looked over at my mother, then shrugged and offered me his smile of apology.

My mother went on rocking beside the stove, with her back to the window, muttering to her dead mother.

"Mum?" I said. "Do you want some tea or something?"

She glanced up and, pouty as a small child, went on rocking. I reached out to touch her cheek, but she pulled her head away. I went into my room to change into my milking dress. Three pairs of nylons were lying there on the rumpled blankets I'd become the night before. I picked up the nylons and placed them on my parents' bed, on my mother's side. As I left the house I reached over my mother's head for my .22 and filled my pockets with shells.

Lucifer followed me through the orchard grass, parting a slim path beside mine. The sheep were wary and staring at the Swede's meadow, where a shadow moved through the new brush. Coyote. I aimed the .22, fired, and missed. Lucifer shot home, but the coyote skulked towards Blood Road, not in any particular hurry. After a time the sheep went back to their evening grazing.

There was enough day left for Billy to finish the oat field, but in the bush the trees sopped up what light there was. I searched the wooded areas for the cows, calling them. They were being tricksters this evening, standing very still when I called so I wouldn't hear the ringing of the lead cow's bell. I came out into an open area that surrounded one of the many sloughs, stopped, and listened carefully. I knew they would betray themselves sooner or later. Twilight descended. Mosquitoes sought me out and bit me. I brushed them off. Then there was a hand on my shoulder.

I jumped and turned. Filthy Billy was there, looking down at me with his pants legs bound to protect him from what chased him. He was freshly washed and smelled of soap.

"You okay?" he said.

"Okay?"

Billy licked his lips and looked around at the bush behind us and at the field of oat stubble stretching out towards the house. His eyes settled on the little black figures of my brother and Dennis working under my father's direction on the binder in front of the implement shed.

"He's coming," he said.

"Who? My father?"

I peered over at the flax field.

Billy didn't answer me. He kept looking over his shoulder, his eyes open wide, at something I couldn't see.

"What is it, Billy?" I said. "What're you looking at?'"

He took a few steps backwards, then turned and began running, looking over his shoulder. I looked at the direction he was looking and saw nothing at first. Then the sound came, of grass shooshing, and then the path, cutting a swath through the grass a foot wide and heading straight for me. I leapt out of the way and fell, but the path through the grass kept on going, past me, chasing Billy, pulling in its wake the overpowering stench of wet dog. Billy ran this way and that, but the path followed him, gained on him. He leapt out of its way, and fell into the long timothy grass, where I couldn't see him anymore. I ran to him, following the swath, and when I came on him, Filthy Billy let out a howl that had nothing human in it. His legs and arms jerked and his jaw clenched shut.

"Billy?" I said. "Billy!"

He went on convulsing. I left him and ran back to the yard, still carrying the gun. Dan, Dennis, and my father had worked up the smell of oil and sweat as they labored over the binder by the implement shed. I pulled on Dan's sleeve.

"Billy's having a fit," I cried.

"Billy?" said my father. "Where is he?"

I looked at the ground. "He's fallen. He's having a fit."

"Get your mother," said my father.

I kicked dirt. "She's having one of her spells."

"Spells? Well, ask her anyway. See if she'll tell you what to do. And bring me the medical book."

I did as he told me to and found my mother still rocking in her chair. I put the gun back on the rack over her head and called her.

"Mum," I said. "Mum!"

She turned my way but looked through me, at the gun rack on the wall.

"Billy's having a fit," I said. "What do we do?"

She went on rocking and looking through me as if she didn't hear me.

I said, "Is there anything in here?" and tried to pull the scrapbook from her, but she fought me for it. I gave up and went to the gun cupboard in the parlor where my father kept his books. The medical book my father told me to fetch was called *Everything Within,* a hodgepodge of information on how to build a house, store food, garden, sew, stay married, give first aid, take care of animals, type, give speeches, do bookkeeping, acquire poise and charm, play games and sports, travel, and so on. I stopped in front of my mother before leaving the house. I held her face with one hand so she would listen to me.

"Mum," I said. "Billy's down on the ground. He's shaking all over. He's having a fit."

"Fit?" she said, but her eyes looked as glazed as Billy's had, and I left her rocking.

When I reached the men out in the field, Billy was still on the ground, but his body wasn't jerking anymore. He lay on his side, breathing heavily like a snorting horse, his jaw clamped shut. My father and Dennis knelt on either side of him. Dennis held Billy's head, smoothing back his hair. My brother stood behind Dennis with his hands on his hips.

"What does the book say?" said my father. "Look under fits."

I looked in the index.

"All they've got is something on dogs' running fits."

"That's it?" said my father. "Read it anyway."

I held the big book awkwardly in the middle of the field and found the page.

"It says give a laxative and feed the dog lean meat and let the dog rest and be kind to it. It says a dog gets a running fit when he's upset."

"Jesus," said my father.

We stayed like that for a long time. I held the book, Dennis held Billy's head, and Dan stood over us, impatiently tramping the timothy hay around Billy.

"Well, what are we going to do?" said Dan. "We can't leave him here."

"Just give it time to pass," my father replied.

"Pass?" said Dan. "He's out cold."

"He'll be fine," said my father. "Or as fine as he ever is."

"I'll take Cherry into town and get the doctor," said Dan.

"No!" said my father. "I'm telling you he'll be fine."

"He could be dying," said Dan. "It could be anything." He turned and started walking away.

"Stay here!"

My father's raised voice jolted something in Billy. He opened his eyes and started swearing. The words were slurred at first.

"Billy," said my father. "You hear me Billy? Billy!"

Filthy Billy came round to his name, but he looked at each of us with a glaze of incomprehension in his eyes. He tried to speak, but all that came out was a jumble of swear words. My father and Dan sat him up, and Dennis put the canteen to his lips. He drank a little, sputtering. Then he drank a lot. A whole canteen's worth of water went down gulp after gulp.

"He's all right," said my father. "Aren't you, Billy?"

"He could have died," said Dan.

"Keep your goddamned mouth shut," said my father.

"What if I don't?" said Dan. "What you gonna do? What you gonna do?"

My father pushed Dan to the ground. There was surprise in his face as he watched Dan fall. My brother stood up, held on to his fists, and stared my father down for a while. Then he walked past him and headed for the house. Filthy Billy, Dennis, and I gaped after him.

"What're you just standing there for?" said my father to Dennis. "Get back to work."

"I'll take Billy up to the cabin," said Dennis.

"No (shit). I'm all right (fuck)," said Billy.

"Go on," said my father to me. "Get back in the house. See about your mother."

The cows had walked themselves home and wandered through the gate I'd left open. They stood waiting in their stalls as I passed the barn heading for the house.

My mother was still rocking in her chair but she was no longer muttering. She turned to me with a smile that wasn't hers at all. It frightened me.

She said, "Billy okay?"

"He's all right," I said, and placed the big medical book on the table.

"Good. Cows down?"

"They hid on me, then walked themselves home."

My mother nodded. "They can be tricksters."

I turned my back on my mother and poured myself tea.

"You seen Lucifer around?" I said.

She shook her head.

"Has Dad done something to him?"

She gave a little indifferent shrug that made me angry.

"I'll go milk the cows."

"I'll go with you," she said, but she made no move to get up.

"I can do it myself," I said.

I left the house and took my rancor into milking, gave it to the cows, and they handed it back tenfold. They banged over the milk buckets, spilling milk and bringing the cats — all but Lucifer — running. They hit me in the face with their tails and shifted from side to side so I had to move my stumping powder box again and again. They pawed at my hands with their back hooves, bruising me. The lead cow, the one with the bell around her neck, the one I called Betty, kicked out hard as I approached her from behind, leaving a bruise and swelling in my shin. The milking went on and on and my frustration grew until I was slapping the cows when they knocked over the buckets. When the last cow was finally milked, the sky had gone black, and the air was filled with smoke from woodstoves up and down the valley. Dennis and Billy had broken the blackout and lit their campfire. After I let the cows out into the back pasture, I leaned against the fence for a time watching Filthy Billy jump back and forth over his fire.

29

IN THE NIGHT I woke to hear cows bellowing and a bell ringing, as if a cow were running, but the sound neither came nor receded. A cow out? A cow with her head caught in the fence? I slid out of bed and into my brother's jeans, a sweater, and rubber boots. My mother's shape was still seated in the rocking chair in the kitchen, but she was slumped down, her chin on her chest, and she whistled in her sleep. I slipped by her and closed the kitchen door carefully behind me.

The night was dark, a dark like nothing you get now. No city is dark, of course, and even in the countryside these days the night sky is lit up by the dull orange of distant towns. I've heard some people living in cities their whole lives have never wondered over the Milky Way. Imagine! To live your life through never seeing the backbone of the sky. Then, of course, there were no city lights to obliterate the stars. There was electricity in town, but precious little of it, and none out on the farms in the valley. That dark was so dark you became the night when you stepped out into it. Only slowly, as your eyes adjusted, did you take on form.

I pulled my shape out of the dark as I followed the sound of the bell to the barn. As I approached, there was another sound like the soft hooting of an owl from a distance. The dark deepened when I stepped into the barn, and I took a moment to realize what I was seeing. In the hazy dark the lead cow, the one we put the bell on, stood in the spot where we milked her. The white on her body glowed a little. There were no other cows in the barn. Dan stood on a stumping powder box immediately behind her. His hands held the cow's pinbones and his face shone white in all the black of the barn. He pushed himself into the cow, and with each push the bell around her neck rang. He was making that other sound, the soft grunting. Dan turned sharply and some bit of light in his eye flashed in my direction. I turned on my heel and walked quickly back to the house.

The next morning at breakfast, Dan tried to wipe the midnight bell ringing out of the space between us with jokes and roughhousing. He slapped Dennis on the shoulder, grinning with his mouth full of egg. He kissed my mother on the cheek as Dennis did and tugged my apron undone. But I didn't give him anything. I didn't laugh at his jokes. Just like the others, he was filth and shame, the evil Mrs. Bell spoke of.

My mother was no help, no help at all. She sat in her rocking chair, rocking and rocking, hanging on to her scrapbook, staring off at nothing. I made breakfast by myself and laid it on the table for the men, refilled cups, and cleared away the dishes. My mother sat in her chair all that time, rocking, muttering, and my father didn't say a word about it. I brought her a cup of coffee sweetened with milk and half a teaspoon of sugar, the way she liked it. But my mother looked through me, like a stubborn child punishing the parent that punished her. I said, "You find the nylons okay?" I made a point of saying it, so my father would hear. But my mother ignored this too, only drawing her lips into a straight pink line, and my father went on eating as if he hadn't heard.

Dennis tried to slide his hand over my fingers as he handed me his breakfast plate. My father looked up just then, to see me shaking my head at Dennis. I turned away when I saw him watching, but I could feel his eyes on me.

I refilled the cups of all four men and took my apron off. As I tied my kerchief over my hair I said to my mother, "You coming?" She ignored me, so I said it again, and when I said it the third time, as I put on my boots, something broke inside and I found my mother's own words coming out my mouth. "Quit your sulking. We've got work to do!"

She looked up at me with eyes so big and hurt I wanted to slap her. "Come on!" I said.

My father said, "Don't talk to your mother that way." But he didn't raise his voice or look my way and I knew something had shifted.

"The cows aren't going to milk themselves," I said, to my mother, with her own words. "Get yourself ready."

She complied and, clumsy and slow-footed as a chastised child, followed me outside.

My mother and I let in the cows and set up our stumping powder boxes, rattled our pails into position, and settled into the shush-shush rhythm of the milk hitting the pails. I was off from my mother's rhythm, slower because of the weakness in my lightning arm, anxious from my father's hot, dark looks, sick with the image of my brother stepping on my stool to do his dirty business. I couldn't bring myself to lay my head on the cows. Their flanks were too hot, their stomach music disgusted me. The cows, picking up my case of nerves, rocked back and forth on their high-heel hooves, kicked, and slapped me with their filthy tails. The lead cow, the cow with the bell, would not stay still. She pawed my hands with her hooves as I milked, slapped me around the head with her tail, bawled, shook her head, and rang her bell, and that sent a ripple of nerves through the whole herd. They all started prancing and bawling like new mothers separated from their calves.

"There's been coyotes here in the night," my mother said, suddenly chatty. "You can feel it in them."

I didn't answer. I knew it hadn't been coyotes that had scared the cows. Then the rhythm of my mother's milking quickened, and she said, "My father gave me stockings too — silk stockings — while my mother went without."

I didn't say anything to that. At first I wasn't sure what she meant, and then I didn't want to think about it, because if she meant what I thought she meant then she knew, and the shadows that visited at night weren't just nightmares. I blocked it out of my head, pretended that she'd said nothing at all, and went on fighting my way to a full pail of milk, then another and another. When we were finally done I'd worked up a full sweat and my lightning arm was numb.

"Hope they settle down by tonight," said my mother, as she put her last pail to one side. She walked the cows down to the end of the pasture and let them out to roam over the benchland for the day, then went to feed the pigs.

I added a last pail of milk to those already covered with cheesecloth near the mouth of the barn. I stretched and took a step back, into an empty calf pen, so I could dry the sweat from my face with the edge of my skirt without surprising Dennis or Billy with a view of my bare thighs. I needn't have stepped back. Dennis came into the barn and caught me like that, with my face in my skirt.

"Hey," he said. "Nice legs!"

I pushed my skirt down, horrified that he'd seen, and looked around nervously for my father.

"He's still in the house," said Dennis.

He stepped into the calf stall with me and I stepped back against the wall. The stall was only three by six feet, set off in the darkness of the corner of the barn, filled with the dusty homes of spiders. All the stalls were empty now. The calves were in a small pasture behind the pigpen until winter was truly on us. Dennis clutched the low walls that encompassed the stall and moved towards me, slowly, blocking the way out. The smell of him was woodsmoke, bacon, and coffee, and under that the sweet stench of his sweat. His hands on my arms were nothing like velvet.

"Don't," I whispered. "What if he sees?"

He moved into the shadow and wrapped himself around my waist and kissed me, so long and deep that I felt that part of him growing up against me. The surprise wasn't that my lightning arm wrapped itself around Dennis, nor that my other arm followed suit, nor that I kissed Dennis back. I'd planned all this out in the daydreams that took over my nights. The surprise was that pleasure could push so far past fear as to make me reckless.

I didn't hear their footsteps any more than I'd heard Dennis's. All I heard was Dennis breathing against my cheek, his little piglike grunts so much like what I'd heard coming from my brother as he stood behind the cow the night before. Past Dennis's shoulder I opened my eyes on my father and Dan as they walked into the barn. I pushed Dennis off, and my father saw us for the first time. Behind him, all around him, sunlight reflected off the dusty air. He squinted at us and said, "You!" Then he moved into the shadow of the calf stall and a darkness slid under his eyes. Dennis stood back against the barn wall, blinking and looking perplexed, as if stunned by sudden sunlight.

"You!" my father said again, and as he said it he grabbed Dennis's shirt by the shoulders.

"What the hell?" he said, and said it again, over and over, each time pushing Dennis into the wall. Once he got a grip on my father's arms, Dennis gave one great push and tossed my father over the low wall into the next calf stall. Dust billowed up in the barn air, reflecting sunlight like flecks of glass. My brother had been trying to pull my father off Dennis and he now leapt over the stall wall and stood between them, holding my father at the chest. My father pointed at Dennis.

"You get out of here now!" he yelled. "Take your things and get out!"

"Don't be stupid," said Dan. "We need him."

"Get out!" said my father.

"He's not going anywhere," said Dan. "We've got the corn to do yet, then the flax."

"I won't have him here."

"Calm down, just calm down."

"There's no harm done," said Dennis. "It was just a kiss."

"You get out," said my father. "Don't you ever come near my daughter again. Get out! Now!"

"Then I'm out of here, too," said Dan, and he nodded for Dennis to leave. Dennis headed out the door, giving me a wink as he left. My father roared ridiculously at that and finally broke free of my brother's hold. Dan chased my father into the house as my mother came running up the barn aisle.

"What's going on?" she called.

I said, "Oh!" and began to cry.

She took me in her arms. She said, "What's wrong, Beth, dear, what happened?" But as she spoke, a gunshot sounded from within the house, and then we were there, at the kitchen door, uncertain of how we'd gotten there, panic at our throats. My brother was just rising from the floor with a gun in his hands. My father lay on the kitchen floor. Neither of them was hurt. My father didn't try to reclaim the gun. The kitchen table was askew, and two of the chairs had been knocked over. There was a bullet hole in the roof. My brother unloaded the gun and placed it back in the gun rack.

"I'm leaving," Dan said. "This is it. I'm going."

My father heaved himself up.

"You try to leave, and so help me God I'll track you down and shoot you."

"So shoot me," said my brother. "By the time you find me there'll be plenty of other people shooting at me."

My father held his head. "Jesus."

I backed away then and ran from the house. My mother called after me, "Beth, where are you going? What's happened?"

I ran down the sheep pasture to Dennis and Billy's cabin, chased by the ghost in the grass and the sound of the homesteader's children knocking rocks in their graves. Dennis was stuffing clothes into a duffel bag when I pushed into the cabin. He was alone in there. Billy was already back out coiling haycocks in the alfalfa field.

"Well," he said.

"Oh, I'm so sorry."

"You're sorry," he said. "Jeez, that was my fault."

He came up close to me, grinning. "Maybe we can pick up where we left off, eh?"

"No." I stepped away. "I've got to get out. He'll do anything when he gets like this."

"Yeah, well, I didn't think."

"What are you going to do?"

"I don't know. Go back to Granny's for now, I guess. Dan's talking about leaving. He means it this time. He'll go. He'll join up. Maybe I'll go too."

"But what about Mum and me, if he's gone. If you're gone."

"Billy's here. He watches, you know. He'll be around. He's not crazy, like everybody thinks."

"I know that," I said.

I leaned down to look through the little window as Dennis collected the rest of his things. Dan banged out of the house and marched up the driveway, heading towards Blood Road, carrying a small bag. He wasn't carrying his gun this time. Not a minute later, my father slammed from the house and went the other direction, through the orchard. The sheep rose up and away from him like a spooked flock of birds. Unseen by my father, a coyote skulked through the long grass behind him, then disappeared into the growth in the Swede's pasture. My father took up his ax and started where he'd left off on the Swede's fence. From that distance, I heard the ax chop on his upswing, so the sound appeared to lead the motion. The Swede's goat came up to the fence and challenged him, butting at the fence. My father knocked the goat between the horns with the ax handle, foolishly, and the goat took that as a challenge and went after my father again. My father picked up a stout branch from the Swede's wrecked fence, leaned over the wire fence, and knocked the goat across the side of the head, hard enough so that the goat tottered and staggered away. My father took up his ax and went back to dismantling the fence. He would chop and saw and tear down the Swede's fence all that day and into the night until the whole fence was down and our sheep were grazing in the Swede's weedy meadowland along with the goats.

Dennis came up behind me and put his hands on my shoulders. "What you looking at anyhow?"

"He's at the fence again."

"That's some war them two got going," said Dennis. "You know what Billy says? He says your daddy met Coyote in the mountains, last year when that bear attacked your camp. Coyote got hold of him then. Made John act like a wild man. He gets some crazy ideas, that Billy. Well, I guess he gets them from Granny. The way John's been acting, maybe they're right." He chuckled, then slid his hands down my arms and put his face in my hair. "You going to be my girlfriend now?"

"I don't know," I said, still watching my father. Then I pulled away from him and headed for the door. "I've got to get out of here," I said. "I've got to stay away for a few days. He'll come after me when he's tired of that fence."

"Where you going to stay?" he said.

"I've got a place. Maybe I'll see you at Bertha's."

"Listen, I'll get one of my cousins to come by and let your mother know you're okay. She'll go crazy if she don't know. As long as you're not staying out in the open. Granny's right. There's something picking off kids. Promise me you won't stay out in the open."

"I promise," I said.

"No walking at night, in the bush, eh?"

"All right, all right."

I left Dennis holding his one sack of belongings and I ran away from the cabin and the farm. I took the long way around to Blood Road, following Turtle Creek, past the hollow stump, now tatty red with dying leaves, up to the benchland, then across the back of the harvested oat field to the road. I ran as if I were being chased, across Blood Road, into the bush, down the Indian trail that ran parallel to the road, and reached the winter house out of breath and hurting. It took a moment for my breath to calm enough to hear the ringing that accompanied it, a rope of bells jingling.

"Nora?" I said.

"Down the hole!"

I blinked into the hole of the winter house to see her face appear in the circle of light surrounding the chipped-log ladder.

"What you doing here?" she said.

"How about you?"

"I asked first."

"My father, he, well, he's gone insane. Forgetting all about harvest and tearing down Johansson's fence in daylight. I'm hiding out for a day or two."

"You okay?"

"Okay as I can be."

"What did you bring?"

"I didn't bring anything."

"How you going to hide out if you didn't bring anything to eat?"

"There wasn't any time."

"I'll get something from Granny, then. We've got to eat something."

"No. I don't want her to know. If Mum comes she'll know where I am. You got to tell her you haven't seen me."

"If your mum comes looking, Granny will guess here anyway."

"There's a chance she won't. Dennis is going to get one of your cousins to let Mum know I'm okay. I'll go back tonight when it's dark and get something from the root cellar."

"Dennis said he'd do that?"

"Dad fired him today."

"Fired him! He must have done something, eh? To get fired during harvest. What did he do?"

I climbed down the ladder into the hole. "I don't want to talk about it."

"Why not?"

"I just don't."

"He touch you?"

"I don't want to talk about it."

"If he did something to you, I'll beat him up," she said. "I'll knife him."

"Yeah, sure," I said.

Nora crossed her arms and leaned against the dirt wall of the winter house, sulky. "You like him better than me," she said.

"Do not. Don't be so silly."

Nora jumped up. "Let's go," she said. "Now! Those factories in Vancouver will hire any woman who shows up on the doorstep. We could be making airplanes or guns. We'll be making money for sure. We could get a place of our own. No underground dirt house. A real house, with windows."

"Nobody's going to hire fifteen-year-old girls," I said.

"You're just about sixteen. We'll say we're eighteen. You can get a red dress. We'll wear make-up. Nobody will know. You can wear this!"

She pulled a Tangee lipstick from her breast pocket, the kind that changed from orange to red when you put it on, color changed by the warmth of your skin. She handed it to me.

"Where did you get this?" I said.

"My mother bought it for me."

I tried to look her in the eye, and she looked away.

"She did not," I said. "You stole it."

"What does it matter where I got it. Try it on. Here let me."

She kneeled in front of me, took the lipstick from my hand, and slowly, carefully, applied it to my lips. Then she kissed me, smearing lipstick on her and me both. She fell back on the blankets and laughed.

"We could go anywhere," she said. "We could jump the train and just go!"

"I don't know. We don't have any money."

"I know where Granny's got a bundle socked away."

"I'm not going to steal from Bertha," I said.

"Why not? Okay, then from my uncle, or one of the old men. They just drink their money anyway."

"No," I said. "I'm not going to steal."

"Don't get so high and mighty. You're planning on stealing tonight, from your mum's root cellar."

"That's not the same," I said.

"We could go tonight even."

"I'm not ready to go," I said.

"What're you staying for? A crazy father? Mother who talks to herself?"

I cuddled my lightning arm against my knee and rocked.

"Or are you staying for Dennis?"

"I'm not staying for Dennis."

"Who then? Filthy Billy?"

She laughed, but she threw the lipstick at the wall.

30

THE DARK TUGGED at my clothing, yanked on my hair, held my wrists with its long snaggy hand. I knew the paths so well that, as a child, I'd closed my eyes and walked them blind. But all paths change in the dark, snake off to do some night creeping of their own. It wasn't until I stumbled out onto the grass behind the house that I smelled the smoke, or saw the fire flicking out into the night sky. Even then I thought at first my eyes were fooling me, that I was seeing Dennis and Filthy Billy's fire near the cabin, but somehow in the wrong spot. Then I realized: the flax field was on fire! A shadow of a man appeared to run through the flames with a torch, lighting the grass along the field's edge. He threw the torch up and it streaked back down, sparking a trail like a meteor, landing a little farther out into the field. The shadow ran across the yard, disappeared against the barn, and reappeared again in the sheep pasture, heading through the orchard. The Swede.

I leaned against the side of the house with my heart at my throat and my stomach ludicrously growling for food, watching the Swede run, uncertain, at first, of what I should do. Finally sense got hold of me, and I ran up to my parents' bedroom window and banged on the glass. I shouted, "Fire! Fire!"

My father pulled the blanket away from the window and loomed up in the glass, so ghostly in his nightshirt that I stepped back in fright and ran around to the front of the house. The door was open, but the screen was shut. My mother had been sitting in the rocker next to the kitchen stove, rocking and rocking, holding the scrapbook to her breast, so engrossed in listening to her dead mother that she hadn't heard the Swede or the fire. Alerted by my shouts, she was holding the blanket away from the kitchen window, clutching her scrapbook. I opened the screen door.

"Beth!" she said. "Oh, Beth!"

I took a step back when she came to hug me. My father came into the kitchen then, still dressed in his nightshirt but with his field denims underneath.

"Where the hell were you?" he said.

"The Swede set the field on fire," I said, and stepped off the porch. "I'll get Billy!"

But Billy was already there, leaving the barn with our milk pails — five clanking to each hand — heading for the pump.

"You fill these," he said, setting them down by the pump. "I'll get the shovels."

When I looked back at the house, my mother and father were standing on the porch yelling at each other. My mother had hold of my father's shirtsleeve and no matter how he twisted and turned she wouldn't let go.

"You will stay here!" cried my mother. "You will help put this fire out!"

"Let go of me! That Swede!"

"That Swede nothing. There'll be nothing to come back to if we can't hold the fire. Don't be a fool, for heaven's sake!"

Billy marched up to my father, forced a shovel into his hand, and directed him on how best to put out the fire, and my father let him. He stood there with his mouth a little open, listening to Billy instructing him. *Instructing him!* My mother let go of my father's shirtsleeve, and we all did as Billy told us. I pumped water into our milk pails until my lightning arm went numb, then I pumped with my left arm. My mother carried and poured, carried and poured. I watched, as I pumped water, the black silhouettes of Billy and my father shovel blackness onto the bright orange flames, sending sparks showering into the sky.

The torch the Swede had sent spinning into the sky fell on a rich wet crop of flax and sputtered out. He'd had better luck lighting the dead grass around the flax field, but once the fire met the dirt of the field and the green flax crop, it licked back on itself. When it became obvious that the fire in the flax field wasn't anything a woman and a fool couldn't take care of, my father threw down the shovel and started marching my way. He disappeared for a time as he stepped away from the fire. I went on pumping water, searching for his man shape in the black, convinced he was coming for me. But when my father disentangled himself from the night, he walked right past me, ignoring me, making me wait, fearful, for whatever punishment he was concocting. He went on walking into the house, then out again, carrying a square black shape I knew was the tin of kerosene, and another that I knew was a gun. He went on walking across the orchard and into the Swede's pasture that was speckled with our sleeping sheep. My mother came for more water, setting the milk pails down beside me.

"He's gone to Mr. Johansson's," I said.

My mother sighed.

"He took the kerosene," I said. "And the gun."

"Oh, Lord," she said.

"We should do something."

"What can we do?"

Fire lit up her face, reflected in her eyes. She ran a hand over her mouth, leaving a long black streak there.

"Help Billy mop up the fire," she said. "It's in hand now. I'll get a coat and ride Cherry down to Boulee's. We can't stop him alone."

I went on pumping water and sloshing it clumsily to the fire, even when the gunshot echoed from over the Swede's way, and fire lit up the tree line that hid the Swede's house and barn from view. Filthy Billy stopped shoveling dirt when the gunshot sounded, and tried to offer me some comfort by placing his sooty hand on my shoulder. But I went on pumping and carting water even as a horse and buggy, a wagon, and one car cut the darkness down Blood Road and passed our driveway for the Swede's.

ALL HELL BREAKING LOOSE, and I decided to make cake. Honey cake, a pound cake, my mother's own recipe. I stole my mother's scrapbook from her rocking chair and left my sooty fingerprints on the page called "Honey Cake," so like it or not I could never forget that night. Filthy Billy sat at the kitchen table, not scratching, not swearing, just watching, as I spread the scrapbook out on the table in front of him, cleaned my hands, and made cake. Outside, over the trees that curtained the Swede's yard from view, fires of hell stormed up into the black. I knew it, but I didn't want to know it. So I made cake. Billy read out the ingredients slowly, painfully, as I collected them:

> two and a quarter cups flour
> two and a quarter teaspoons baking powder
> a quarter teaspoon salt
> three quarters cup butter
> three quarters cup honey
> three eggs
> three quarters teaspoon vanilla
> three quarters teaspoon lemon essence

I mixed the flour, baking powder, and salt together and in a separate bowl I creamed the butter and beat the honey, eggs, and vanilla into it before adding the dry ingredients a little at a time so the mix was smooth. Then it was just a matter of stirring in the lemon flavoring. It was a nothing-to-it-cake, as rich as sin, heavenly to a hungry, worried belly. I poured the batter into a greased loaf pan and set it in the oven. The fire in the kitchen stove had burned down from neglect, and I stoked it up some, but a slow oven is what a pound cake needs.

Billy shimmied his chair up to the stove and propped his feet on the lid of the warm reservoir in the way my mother forbade. Though he had sworn little as he fought the fire, he cursed softly now. I sat next to him in my mother's rocker, leafing through her scrapbook, waiting for the cake to bake, waiting for the sound of my mother's or father's footsteps, or word of the fire over the Swede's way, or what the gun-shot meant, waiting for dawn.

The stiff pages of the scrapbook crackled as I turned them. The smell each page contained wafted up and was replaced by the next. Vanilla. Allspice. Lily of the valley. Rose. This was the first time in a long while I'd had the scrapbook to myself, and I pleasured in the bits of our lives that my mother had managed to salvage and save. A yellow violet, taken from the bouquet that had been on our table the last day Mrs. Bell visited, was pressed between the recipes for raspberry buns and daffodil cake. And on the page with the queen's photograph, my mother had pressed a single blue flax flower. Beside this she had written the date of the big storm when the flax rained down on us. There were additions I hadn't seen before: a recipe for laundry and hand soap, made from lye, grease, resin, and soft water, that my mother had cut from some magazine, and a newspaper clipping announcing the fowl dinner that was glued next to the recipe for Bird's Nest.

I flipped quickly past the pages with reminders of the bad days: the newspaper clippings warning of bear attacks and Sarah Kemp's funeral notice, the bit of ribbon from those that adorned the horses' halters on the day of the Boulees' picnic, a newspaper story about a child who had gone missing on the reserve, the widow Roddy's death notice, and a little square cut from a pair of nylons and glued to a page. I stopped on the photograph of Ginger Rogers, and on the space between the cure for death by lightning and the butterfly with its wing torn away, where my mother had written my name and the date lightning had left my arm something close to useless.

"You should (shit) leave that alone," said Billy.

"What?" I said.

He nodded at the scrapbook. "That's (fuck) your mother's private place."

"Ah, come on."

"No, you should put that (shit) away. Everybody needs a place to sort things out (fuck). You've got to know (shit) nobody's going to snoop around in it."

"There's nothing in it. Nothing I can't see. Not like a diary."

"Doesn't (shit) matter what's in it. (Fuck) Excuse me."

I grunted and leafed through the crinkly pages some more just to prove that Billy had no place telling me what to do. Then I tossed the scrapbook on the kitchen table.

"You got a place like that?" I said. "A private place?"

Billy hummed yes. "My father's stone (shit), where he died. (Fuck) Sorry. That's my place."

He rearranged his feet away from the heat of the stove and looked up at the ceiling. "You (shit) got a place?" he said.

I didn't answer him, and he didn't repeat himself. I checked on the pound cake and then took up rocking in my mother's chair.

"You talked to Dennis?" I said.

Billy looked uncomfortable for a moment, then said, "Yeah (shit), we talked."

"He joining up?"

"Granny's trying (shit) to talk him out (fuck) of it."

"What's he going to do?"

"Don't know."

After a time, I said, "You seen Lucifer?"

Billy looked a question at me.

"My black cat."

He shook his head.

"He's gone missing," I said. "I think my father might have done something."

"A tom?" said Billy. "(Shit) Excuse me. They wander."

"Everybody's leaving," I said. "Everybody all at once."

"Not everybody," he said, and put his hand on mine. I didn't move away. His hand was sooty. My hands were the only clean places on me. Black marks covered both of Billy's cheeks. He tapped the end of his nose, so I would touch mine, and I found a streak of black soot mixed with white flour there.

I said, "That was something, you taking over, with the fire. Telling my father what to do. He doesn't let anybody tell him what to do."

"He was (shit) surprised. (Fuck) Sorry. He's easier (shit) on me than Dennis 'cause (fuck) he thinks I'm slow."

"You been tricking him? The swearing, I mean?"

"That's (shit) no trick," said Billy. "I feel bad (shit), you know. (Fuck) It's dirty."

"I don't mind," I said. "It's kind of funny. Mum won't let you in the house when Mrs. Bell visits. I wish she would. That would get rid of Mrs. Bell for sure."

"Maybe I'll sneak (shit) in next time she visits, cuss (fuck) until Mrs. Bell (shit) leaves."

He laughed again, a sweet high laugh that caught me up and took me with him. I turned my hand over and held his and we sat there like an old couple past the clumsiness of romance, me rocking, him with his feet warming on the stove. The smell of cake filled the kitchen.

Nora opened the screen door and caught us like that. I pulled my hand from Billy's and slid it into my pocket. Nora laughed when she saw us and clapped her hands together.

"Look at you!" she said.

Billy took his feet off the stove and slumped in the chair. I opened the oven and tested the cake, to hide my embarrassment.

"What're you doing here?" I said, and took the cake out, though it was still moist in the center. "You'll catch hell when Dad gets home."

"He isn't coming home," said Nora. "They've taken him away."

"Who? What do you mean?"

"Some men," she said. "I think they were Mounties. Their outfits were different. They came in a car and took him away."

"My mother?"

"She's the one that set it up, got them to take him away."

"What are you talking about? How do you know all this?"

When I hadn't come back to the winter house, Nora had headed out on Blood Road to track me down and see that I was all right. But then she'd seen the fire glowing at the Swede's place and that had drawn her into his yard. Her eyes lit up with the telling of it.

"The place was filled up with people running around and yelling," she said. "Horses coming and going, dogs barking. The barn was burning, sparks up higher than the trees!"

"We (shit) heard a gunshot," said Billy.

"Yeah, the Swede. When I got there, Mr. Ferguson and Mr. Boulee and some others, they put the Swede's body in the back of a buggy and drove him off. Must've been dead. Your dad looked really creepy, all soot-black under the eyes, crazy. Your mum was standing there, crying, telling him to keep quiet. But it's like he didn't hear her. Some other guys I never seen before handcuffed him and put him in the car."

"The Swede's (fuck) not dead," said Billy. "(Shit) Sorry. He was (shit) likely drunk."

"How'd you know?" said Nora. "You weren't there." She turned to me. "Boulee said your dad was setting the woodpile against the house on fire when they got there — your mother and the Boulees and the Fergusons — and the Swede was on the floor inside the house. The barn was already burning. They put out the fire in the woodpile and then tried to fight the barn fire, but it was going real good. That was when Mr. Ferguson took your mum's horse over to the reserve and woke Granny up, so she'd get some of the men over to help put out the barn fire."

Her face lit up as though she were still facing the fire, watching it. Filthy Billy stared into his coffee cup and shook his head.

"They took your father away." She grinned. "He's gone!"

I got up and made coffee to hide the tears welling up.

"Hey, what's the matter?"

I shrugged my shoulders.

"Come on, what's come over you? He'll get it for murder. They'll lock him up!"

"He's still her (shit) father."

"He's a monster," said Nora. "A creep. Johansson wasn't much better."

"Where's my mother?"

"She went with the men — in the car, to put your father away."

I took up the scrapbook and sank back into my mother's rocker.

"Beth, don't you see?" said Nora. "We can go! We can get out of here now, right now. We can take some money and just go. Nobody's going to know until we're so far away they can't find us."

"Maybe you should go," I said. "I've got to do chores. Nobody's here to take care of things."

"Aw, come on!" she said. "This is our chance."

Billy stood up and held open the screen door. Light was crawling up the sky. The lead cow's bell jingled as she walked from the pasture into the barn and took up her stall.

"(Shit) I think (fuck) you should go," said Billy.

"Shut up," she said.

"Please, Nora, I've got things to do," I said. "We haven't slept and we've got chores yet. I don't want you here when Mum comes back."

"Jeez," said Nora.

She slapped out onto the porch, and I followed her out to the yard. I walked to the fence line and looked over the fire damage as Nora stormed and kicked up the driveway to Blood Road. Dawn was sending its first feeble light over the hills, but that was enough to see what needed to be seen. The Swede's attempt at violence had turned into nothing but a favor. We often burned the grass in the pastures ourselves come fall, so it would grow back lush the next spring. He'd done it for us, cleaning up the weedy grass along the field's edge. A few of the fence posts were scorched, but no real harm had been done. Filthy Billy came up behind me and put his hands on my shoulders. The comfort of him made me suddenly weep.

"He's coming," said Billy.

I looked up at him and he nodded in the direction of the wood that had once been the Swede's living fence, stacked in the orchard pasture. As we watched the sheep suddenly scattered in two directions. Down the midst of them a path opened up in the grass and sped through the orchard straight for us.

"That's Coyote," he said. "That's him walking."

I stepped back into Billy, and he held me for a moment with his face in my hair. Then he gave my shoulders a squeeze and stepped back. He took hold of the seat of the binder and the bull wheel as if bracing himself. The thing left the grass and ran across the yard lifting the dust and leaving red footprints as the only indication that anything at all was there. The footprints ran right at Billy and seemed to slam into him. Billy buckled under the impact, falling to his knees. He grunted and shook, and I was afraid he'd go into convulsions again, but he didn't. He sat up again and began cursing louder than he had all night.

I said, "Billy?"

He looked up at me and, still cussing, nodded that he was all right. After a time he stood and leaned against the binder.

"I'll (fuck, shit) start on the (fuck) corn," he said. "(Shit) I'll just fill my (shit) canteen. Excuse me."

Billy unwound the canteen from the base of the binder seat and walked across the yard to the pump. He walked in the footsteps of the thing that followed and as he did the red footprints disappeared.

The cows had already entered the barn and lined themselves up. I stepped through the chores, shaken by the events of the night, thankful for the mind-dulling salve of habit. As I was throwing the chop to the pigs, my mother walked into the yard, leading Cherry. When she saw me, she let go of the reins and crumpled to the ground. I ran to her and helped her up.

"What happened?" I asked.

"They've taken your father away," she said.

"Is Mr. Johansson dead?"

She looked confused. "Dead?" she said. "No! He was drunk. On beet wine. *Our* beet wine. He stole the wine we made last year from the root cellar. He must have stolen other things too. There's been jars going missing."

I blushed at that, but she didn't notice.

"We heard a gunshot," I said.

"I don't know what your father was up to. I don't think he knew. All I know is no one was hurt. I'm thankful for that."

I helped her inside and she took up her scrapbook from the kitchen table and sat in her rocking chair. I put on the kettle for tea.

"What's going to happen?" I said. "With Dad?"

"I don't know," she said, and that was the last thing she said out loud until lunch. She closed her eyes and muttered to her dead mother and didn't let up, even as she dozed, until I put a dinner plate down in front of her place and sat at my own place across from Billy. She ate the meal heartily, as a man eats, hunched over the plate, scraping the food into her mouth. My dead grandmother had taken over the rocker; it went on rocking all through dinner. My mother came back to life after the meal, though her eyes glistened with sleeplessness. She slapped both palms on the table.

"Well!" she said. "We'll have to get Dennis back here. Any word from Dan?"

"No," I said. I expected her to sink back into one of her muttering spells, but she did nothing of the kind.

"I guess that's for the best," she said. "He's been biting at the bit to join up for a long time. It had to happen soon or later."

"What's going to happen to Dad?"

My mother looked away, poured herself more tea. After a time, she said, "We won't talk of that. Do you understand? You don't talk to anyone about that."

"Why not? What's happened?"

"I said we won't talk about it. Finish your plate."

I exchanged a look with Billy, and played with my food.

"I don't know what's going to happen," she said. "He won't be home for a long time."

She wiped her hands on a napkin and gave me a little smile. "Well, no school for you this fall. I'll need you here. I expect you won't be disappointed at that."

I shook my head.

"Billy," said my mother, "when you get a chance, please ask Dennis if he'll come back, and if he would please stay on after harvest. Do you think he will?"

Billy shrugged and nodded. "(Fuck) It'll (shit) make Granny happy," he said. "Probably he will (shit). Excuse me."

"Good. There's work for you right through the winter if you want it."

Billy grinned and swore and nodded.

"But you will stay away from Dennis, young lady," she said to me. "Understand me? I'll have enough work to keep you two very busy."

I felt my face grow hot. Billy's swearing quieted down to nothing for a minute and then flared up again so that he nearly choked on his food. My mother stood up and poured him a glass of water.

"We're going into town tomorrow," she said.

"(Shit) You think that's a (fuck) good idea?" said Billy.

"The cream's got to go in and there's things we need."

The meal made us all drowsy and we made up for the sleepless night there in the warm kitchen. My mother dozed in her rocking chair, and Billy and I propped our chairs together against the wall near the stove. We slept much longer than any of us had intended, and when I woke, still serenaded by my mother's sleeping whistle, I was surprised to find night was creeping over the window and Billy's sooty-black hand was hanging on to mine.

32

THE ROAD THROUGH TOWN had gone muddy from the first fall rain and was littered with yellow and red leaves. Blue plums hung on the trees in the churchyard like Christmas ornaments. Old men with time on their hands had dug several fresh graves in the churchyard as they always did this time of year, before the ground frost set in, so the graves would be ready for that winter's dead. These were shallow graves, dug to just below ground frost level and filled with leaves. In the winter when a grave was needed, the leaves would be removed and the rest of the earth in the grave would be dug out. The leaves kept the soil in the graves from freezing. When filled with leaves, the graves looked more like beds, deep soft pools that tempted you to jump in.

I bounced down that muddy road in the democrat with my mother and the cream cans, angrily watching for signs of gossip, and watching for it I saw it. Mr. and Mrs. Slokum, farmers with property next to the Boulees, left the blacksmith's laughing, but when they saw us pulling up to the train station to unload the cream, they ducked back into the shop. As we drove the buggy back to Belcham's, several faces peered out at us from the one fly-specked window of the blacksmith's shop.

Some others, though, who had helped my mother the night before, were friendlier than they had been in months. Mr. Boulee waved at us from the steps of the druggist's, and Ferguson, who had beat up my father at the Dominion Day picnic, came up to my mother, as she tied Chief and Cherry to the poplar by the store, with his hat in his hands. He kicked at the mud.

"You need any help on that farm, you just let me know," he said.

My mother nodded but kept her arms folded across her chest.

"I didn't mean it to come to that," said Mr. Ferguson.

"Then you shouldn't have spoken out about him that way," said my mother.

"It seemed the best thing to do at the time," said Ferguson. "He's been so odd this last year. What if he'd done something to you, or the girl? What then? I couldn't live with that."

I looked off at Blundell's Motel and the white crow that sat over the haunted room.

"What's done is done," said my mother.

"Look, I didn't come to argue my case," said Ferguson. "I came to say I'm sorry about it all. And if there's anything I can do, if there's anything Mrs. Ferguson and me can do, you just call on us."

My mother unfolded her arms, and said, "Oh, Bob, how did all this happen? We used to be such good friends."

Mr. Ferguson shrugged and the sorry sack slipped off him like an old coat. He straightened himself out and looked full into my mother's face for the first time.

"That's all I come to say," he said.

"Well," said my mother. "Send my regards to Mrs. Ferguson. Perhaps you can both come up for coffee. Some time soon."

"You heard anything from that boy of yours?" he said.

"No, not yet."

"Well, I expect he's getting his training. It's likely the best thing for him. Louie Moses said he saw Dan hopping the freight for Vernon."

"Yes," said my mother. "I heard that."

"Some time soon, then," he said, and put his hat back on. He nodded at us both and headed for the blacksmith's shop.

I followed my mother into the general store with my head down. The old men who had dug themselves graves at the churchyard were sitting around the stove. They watched us as we came in and when my mother went to the far end of the store to the post office wicket, I turned and caught them whispering and gesturing at us. I stared at them until they stopped whispering and looked at their boots, then walked past them, with my head up, out of the store.

The town was quiet. Nobody on the street now but me, Cherry, Mrs.

Bell's horse over by the church, and the albino crow that sat on the roof of Blundell's Motel, preening its dirty white feathers. A dispute over a strip of land half a world away had taken up all the young men and many of the young women besides. I walked across the mud to the motel and the room where Ginger Rogers had spent a night the year before. The window in the room was small and crossed like the windows in our house, no fancier than that. Poplar leaves had gathered around the steps to the door. As I walked up to the building, the sun came out for a moment and a face jumped into the window and scared me half to death. I put my hand up to the glass and saw my own face reflected there. I cupped my hands against it in the glass and looked for ghosts or some hint of the glamorous life of Ginger Rogers. Some graffiti maybe, a message cut into the cedar wall with a knife, "Ginger Rogers was here," or a thread from an exquisite gown overlooked in a year of cleaning. There was the picture of Ginger Rogers standing between the elderly Blundells, framed in a locked glass box on the inside wall near the door so no one would steal it, and that was something, to see that surprising glamour strung up between two such ordinary faces.

I wiped my fingerprints from the window with the sleeve of my sweater and crossed my arms against the cold. Over at the plum tree in the churchyard, Mrs. Bell untied her mare and stepped the horse and buggy back a few steps before setting her eyes on our democrat in front of the store.

I turned a little, preparing to take a quick-heeled walk in the other direction, just as my mother left the store on the arm of the schoolteacher, Mrs. Boulee. My mother and Mrs. Boulee exchanged a few quiet words and embraced around their packages. Mrs. Bell stopped in the center of the street when she saw that, her boots up to the ankle in mud, then turned on her heel and got into her buggy. She drove by as Mrs. Boulee went back into the store and my mother got into the democrat, and though my mother waved, Mrs. Bell kept her hands on the reins and her eyes on the muddy, rutted road.

W H E N T H E M E N C A M E in for supper I was at the stove throwing together a quick meal of pancakes and sausage, and my mother was at the kitchen table pasting the newspaper story of the Swede's barn fire into her scrapbook. Dennis took off his hat, kicked off his boots at the door, and sat at our supper table grinning as if the events of the last week had never happened; Filthy Billy came in after him, slow-footed and weary, carrying the certainty that they had.

"Glad to have you back at our table," my mother said to Dennis.

"Least I could do," he said. Dennis didn't look at me all supper long, but talked to my mother instead, about her plans for the manure pile. Did she want the manure spread over the north field near the bench-land, where the alfalfa had grown so thick that year? Should they get the flax off in the morning? And would she leave the sheep where they were in the orchard pasture this year, and what should he feed them, the alfalfa or timothy? How often and when did she want the barn cleaned out? Each morning, or in the afternoon? Billy smiled at me now and again, but said nothing more than whispered curses.

"I'd like you and Billy to finish off Mr. Johansson's fence and help rebuild his barn," said my mother.

Dennis nodded and chewed his food.

"But I'd like you to keep it between yourselves."

"Why?"

"It doesn't matter why. I just don't want anyone to know."

Dennis nodded. "So John don't find out, eh? Let him think he won the war."

She didn't say anything to that. She wiped her mouth and began clearing away the dishes.

"I was figuring we should have a Halloween party," said Dennis.

"A party?" said my mother. "Doesn't seem fitting right now."

"When is a party not fitting?" said Dennis. "We'll get Granny and the girls over here and we'll get a fire going. This place could use some good times."

"It would be good to see Bertha," said my mother. "I haven't seen her for so long. I'm glad she convinced you to stay."

"She's been wanting to see you," said Dennis. "She said so herself. What say we do that, have that party?"

"I suppose," said my mother.

After supper I went out to the orchard, stepping between the sheep and the Swede's goats resting together in their little bedding ground, and climbed into the cradle of an egg plum tree. The moon crept over the hills, illuminating the rushing clouds, and appeared to be held in the hands of the plum tree. The moon had a halo of deep blue, a sure sign of rain. I ate plums right from the tree, without manners, so juice ran down my face and arms. There was still a little warmth from the day at the center of the plums, but the juice made my fingers cold, and I pulled my sleeves over my hands and hugged myself. The smells in the air alternated with the direction of the wind. The smell of frost and snow was there, then gone. The rank scent of the Swede's rutting goat rolled up and faded. Then a strong wind came up, bringing the pungent, smoky air from countless woodstoves and rocking a few plums from the tree. After a time I became aware of Nora's presence, the smell of her violet talc. She leaned against the tree quietly for a long time.

"Sorry I had to tell you to go," I said.

"Sorry I got so mad," she said.

"That's okay."

"It's cold," she said, and when I didn't answer she said, "What're you thinking?"

"I was watching the moon."

"You can feel winter coming. You should go in. There'll always be a moon."

"Not like this one," I said.

After a time she said, "Granny says the moon is a woman and the woman gives birth to herself over and over."

"You can't give birth to yourself."

Nora shifted against the trunk, shaking plums to the ground. She picked a few up and ate them.

"Dennis came back, eh?" she said. "You should have seen him, all hell-bent to enlist. He was going to catch up with Dan. Then Granny got after him. Told him, How could he leave you and your mum alone with no one to help? What kind of man was he, running out like that? On and on she goes, 'til Dennis says okay, okay, he's going to stay. Granny gets her way when she sets her mind to it. I don't think he'll stay when your dad comes back though."

"Mum says there's work for Dennis all winter if he wants it."

"She'll have him work here even after what happened?"

"Nothing happened!" I said.

A little rain of plums fell to the ground. Nora filled her pockets with them.

"Well, whatever. You better stay away from him. He'll lose his job if you don't."

I shook a branch over her head and more plums rained down on her.

"Hey!"

"Mum's having a Halloween party here," I said. "Tell Bertha and everyone to come."

"Your mum? A party? After all that?"

I didn't answer.

"Big changes, eh?"

"What did Dennis tell you happened?" I asked.

"He wouldn't tell me nothing. So I figured something did. He tells lies about girls if nothing happened and says nothing if it did."

"What girls?" I said.

"Jealous?"

"No!" I said, and yet another flurry of plums fell to the ground.

"Mind if I take a few of these to the winter house?" said Nora.

"You sleeping there again?"

"Things are getting ugly with Mum." She took out her knife and began carving into the trunk of the plum tree.

"Don't do that," I said. "You'll kill it."

Nora stopped carving and leaned against the tree. She used the knife to clean the dirt from under her fingernails.

"Put that thing away. It gives me the creeps."

Nora went on cleaning the dirt from under her nails for a few moments longer, then closed the knife and slid it in her back pocket.

"I love you, Beth Weeks," she said.

"I know it," I said.

34

THE DAY of Halloween, excited by the possibility of a party, a house full of people after all these months, my mother made gingersnaps. She had scribbled baking instructions on the back of one of her own mother's letters, a letter about nothing at all, a garden that needed tending and how there was no one around to do it; a dog that had given birth to a litter of nine pups and no homes for them; weather wetter and colder than old bones could stand. But the recipe, that was pure magic. My mother ran her buttered finger down the page, leaving a streak and a fingerprint that made the paper permanently transparent.

The gingersnaps called for:

> *one half cup butter*
> *one half cup sugar*
> *one half cup black treacle*
> *one cup flour*
> *half a teaspoon, or a little more, ginger*
> *half a teaspoon baking soda*

My mother heated up the butter and, once it was melted, she added all the other ingredients, stirring until the batter was mixed, then removed it from the stove, covered it, and left it sitting for a time. Later she plucked pieces the size of walnuts from the batter, pressed them down lightly on a greased cookie sheet, and baked them in a slow oven. As they were baking, the gingersnaps spread out into wide lacy circles. When the cookies were cooled enough to handle, we rolled them up into cones and filled them with whipped cream.

She and I were doing just that when Dennis stumbled into the kitchen, smelling of booze and grinning like a lunatic. My mother saw the drunk on him but didn't say anything. She went on filling the lacy cones as he sat himself down and put his feet up on the stove next to us in the way she hated.

"Well!" said Dennis. When we ignored him and went right on with what we were doing, he laughed too loud, then went into a fit of coughing. My mother glanced at him, wiped her hands, poured coffee, and slammed the mug on the table so hard that coffee spilled onto her hand and the oilcloth. Dennis let out a racket somewhere between a laugh and a cough, drank the coffee all at once, and held his cup out for more. I poured him another cup and he drank that one down too, and another. He wasn't hiding anything that day. He looked at me with desire so frank it made my stomach rock. I didn't like the smell of him. I didn't like his rudeness. I turned my back to him and felt him watching as I filled gingersnaps. My mother saw the look on his face and knew it. She told him, "Get your feet off the stove."

"I ain't hurting nothing," he said.

"I don't like it," she said.

But Dennis didn't take his feet down, only adjusted them for comfort. My mother started banging around the dirty pots and dishes.

"I went to town today," he said.

"I see that," said my mother.

"Ferguson tells me Doc finally put Goat away, at least for a time. Going to get him castrated."

"I haven't seen him around," I said. "I wondered."

"Doc put him in Essondale," said Dennis, and he watched my mother, "with all the mentals."

My mother quit fussing over the dirty dishes, put both hands on the counter, and pushed as if she were holding the cupboard down so it wouldn't go spinning off. Dennis laughed.

"Hey," he said. "Bet John and Goat can get together in that place and pal around, eh? Think they can do that?"

"Is that where he is?" I said. I looked at my mother, and when she wouldn't look me in the eye I turned to Dennis. He laughed and went on laughing as my mother pushed his feet off the stove, throwing him off balance. He let out a whoop when he hit the floor.

"I've had enough of this," said my mother. "Get out. Go home and sober up."

"Okay, okay," said Dennis. He heaved himself clumsily off the floor and drank the last of his coffee.

"Out!" said my mother.

"I'm going," said Dennis. He rubbed his face with both hands and seemed to sober up some. "I'm sorry," he said. "It's the booze talking. I'll get a good fire going for tonight, eh? You and Granny and everybody come over later and we'll have a good time. Tell some stories, eh?"

My mother sighed. "Yes. But you sober up. I don't like the drink any more than John does."

"Oh, he liked a drink well enough," said Dennis.

"He won't have a drunk working for him and neither will I," said my mother.

Dennis held both hands up. "Okay. All right." He left the house without saying anything more. I watched him walk unsteadily across the black grass the Swede had burned, and over the muddy fields that had held the flax and corn.

"Is that where Dad is?" I said again. "In that place with Goat?"

"I don't want to talk about it," said Mum. Then, a minute later, she said, "Yes. I don't want anyone to know. Do you understand?"

"It looks like everybody knows already," I said. "Except me."

"They're guessing. They don't have to know."

I turned back to filling the sweet gingersnaps, but as I did a flash of red in the trees near the road caught my eye. The Swede limped on his cane down our driveway, dressed in a neat red jack shirt, not his usual dirty denim jacket, and carrying a jack-o'-lantern under his arm. His dog limped behind him, sniffing and peeing on this and that.

"Mr. Johansson!" I said.

"I know," said my mother. "I invited him over."

"You invited him?"

"We have some things to discuss. Get some more coffee going. And I don't want you talking or interfering. You stay in the kitchen while he's here. Understand?"

I stared after her as she wiped her hands and placed several ginger-snaps on a plate and set them on the parlor table. I went on tiptoes to watch the Swede round the trees before our house. He slid his cane under the arm in which he carried the jack-o'-lantern and patted his hair into place with his free hand before knocking on the door. He presented the carved pumpkin to my mother, and looked around the kitchen as he propped his cane against the bench.

"Looks the same," he said. "Been a long time."

"Too long," said my mother.

"Hear from Dan?"

"Not yet. I expect it'll be some time."

The Swede looked down at his boots so the brim of his hat covered his face.

"Does he know about John?"

"Not that I know."

"You've heard from Dad?" I asked.

My mother stared a warning at me and then turned her back to me to talk to the Swede. I watched her carefully, trying to catch her eye, but she wouldn't look at me. She set the pumpkin on the kitchen table so it leered at me.

"Any word how long?" said the Swede.

"Not yet," replied my mother. "Come into the parlor. We've been making gingersnaps."

The Swede ignored me as he and my mother passed into the parlor. I put coffee on and leaned against the kitchen cupboard waiting for it to boil. From there I could see my mother's back and the tip of the Swede's wide-brimmed hat. My mother believed a man who wore a hat in the house was beyond rude, but she had spoken politely to him. I strained to hear what they were saying now, but my mother led the tone of the conversation, speaking in almost a whisper.

When the coffee boiled, I collected cups and spoons and served in the parlor.

"I'd rather we kept this to ourselves," my mother was saying. "You understand it's better if John doesn't know, if he thinks you have given in and given up the land."

As he did with almost any request, the Swede spit off to the left, onto my mother's clean floor, and considered, working the idea around in his mouth. He placed a lump of sugar in his mouth and sucked his coffee through the sugar lump, not from his cup, but from the saucer. My mother looked on with disapproval but said nothing.

"Well, it's no skin off my back," he said.

"Does it seem fair to you?" said my mother.

"'Spose. Long as you're paying for it. But it's a bad time of year for digging fence posts."

"We have to do it quickly before the ground frost sets in. There's not much work left on the fence. Dennis and Billy can help you with that this week. Then they can start work on your barn. My only concern is that the settlement seems fair to you, so there's no resentment, so we can put this to rest once and for all."

"No, that seems fair," said the Swede.

I lingered over the table, placing the coffeepot just so, adding cream to a jug almost full, checking that sugar bowl with the bird on its lid. My mother gave me a stern look and nodded at the kitchen, and so I went back to leaning against the cupboard. I sulked and licked the whipped cream from the inside of a gingersnap cone, listening to the Swede's rumble and my mother's whisper.

My mother's scrapbook was still open on the table. I stepped quietly forward and, very carefully, so the stiff paper wouldn't make a sound, I turned the pages to the newspaper story about the Swede's barn fire. There was nothing in the story about my father, no hint that the fire was a case of arson. My mother shifted in her chair in the next room so I let the scrapbook fall back to the gingersnap recipe and went over to the window to stare out at the Swede's dog sniffing around the rock pile that marked the homesteader's graves. All at once the dog sat up unsteadily on his back haunches with his front paws in the air, as if begging for food. He went on sitting like that, staring at nothing, pawing the air in front of him, begging. Then the birds began to land on the roof and, sure enough, Bertha Moses and several of her daughters and granddaughters were fluttering and glittering down the driveway, followed by a huge black flock of crows. A few blue-winged jays scolded them from a tree nearby. Nora trailed behind them all. She saw me in the window and waved.

I called out, "They're here!" and the conversation between my mother and the Swede broke off in a scraping of chairs. The Swede walked into the kitchen followed by my mother.

"It's just between you and me, then," Mum was saying, and the Swede nodded his big-brimmed hat at her.

She picked up the scrapbook from the table and placed it on the top shelf of the kitchen cupboard. "Are you staying?" she asked. The Swede shrugged and nodded again. "Then take off that hat. There are ladies present."

The Swede went pink, took off the hat, and hung it over the head of his cane as Bertha Moses and her family trooped through the door. One by one, they tweaked and teased the Swede as they came in. Nora found her way through the crunch of bodies and pushed up next to me. She took my hand behind her back. The daughter who had come to our house pregnant in the spring came this time carrying a baby wrapped in flannel. She unwrapped the child for my mother as she came through the door. The baby had purple-red patches across both cheeks, birthmarks, and a thick head of black hair. She looked like a puppy.

"Oh!" said my mother, and then, to cover her alarm at the child's appearance, she said, "A girl?"

The daughter nodded.

Bertha patted my mother's arm. "Don't worry. It will pass," she said. "All my girls were born with those marks, some on their faces, some on their backs, some on their hands. They fade away and then they become beauties, eh?"

"Such black hair!" said my mother. "Well, come in, come in."

Bertha sat at the head of the table, in the place my father usually sat, and her daughters and granddaughters all found places to stand or lean against. The woman with the baby took over my mother's rocking chair.

I put out the big plate of gingersnap cones filled with cream. The women were shy about reaching for the treats so I had to take the plate around and offer one to each of them.

"It's been a long time," said my mother.

"Too long, eh?" said Bertha. "Haven't seen you all summer."

"How have you been?"

"It's been a tough year," said Bertha. "Too many things going on. I'm getting old."

"The Lord doesn't give us more than we can bear," said my mother.

Bertha raised her eyebrows and looked up over her shoulder at Nora's mother. The Swede cleared his throat.

"How's John?" said Bertha.

"He's fine." My mother turned her back on the Swede and the women and put the pot back on the stove. "He's got a job at the mill. He's living up there, in the camp. He'll be there 'til spring."

"You don't have to lie to me," said Bertha. "I know where he is. It's all right, Maudie."

"I'm not lying. He's at the mill."

"There's no shame in it," said Bertha. "That place will keep him from making more trouble."

My mother said nothing to that. She pressed her lips together and started making hot chocolate in a big aluminum pot. The Swede put his hat on. Bertha went on sitting like a queen at the head of the table, in my father's place, with her arms stretched out before her and both hands palm down on the table. She looked grim. Nobody said anything for a long time.

Finally the Swede stood and made for the door. He said, "Well, I'll be going then," but didn't wait for the chorus of goodbyes from my mother and Bertha and the other women.

The house had grown dark, and I lit the lamps. Nora grinned at me and played with her necklace so the room filled with bells as the daughters and granddaughters murmured among themselves.

Billy stuck his head in the door and swore at us all.

"Billy boy!" said Bertha. "My grandson!"

Billy grinned at her but didn't say anything to any of us. The swearing filled his mouth. But he held open the door and nodded at the fire burning over by his cabin.

"Billy and Dennis have a bonfire going for us tonight," said my mother.

"Ah!" said Bertha. "Got to have a fire to chase away the dead tonight, eh?"

All the women put their coats on and made their way out the door. I took my father's gun down off the rack and filled my pockets with shells. Billy carried the kettle of hot chocolate and we all made our way over to the hired hands' cabin, crunching over the frost-crusted mud of the fields.

As we came to the cabin, it was obvious that Dennis was drunker than before. He leapt crazily, clumsily, in a circle around the fire, tripping and righting himself, singing out and stopping to drink from the bottle in his hand. Billy was as sober as he ever was. He fed the fire and teased up the flames. We all found logs to sit on, or places to stand. Bertha and my mother sat together on a log. Nora and I sat side by side on two stumps. Dennis stumbled by us, leering, so close we had to move our feet out of his way.

The daughter with the webbed fingers and the one with the dog-baby exchanged a look. The one with the webbed fingers shook her head in disgust and nodded at Dennis. "Coyote's come took him," she said. "Stupid man, shouldn't have got drunk, not now. He knows better too."

"What's all that about?" I whispered to Nora.

Bertha overheard me, and said, "Coyote goes for the weak ones, just like the coyotes you get in your traps. Booze makes you weak. So does a knock on the head." She gave her forehead a light tap with her fist. "So does too much time alone in the bush. Anything like that, what makes you crazy, that makes it easy for Coyote to come in and take you over. Then he makes you do things, stupid things. Like this silly moose."

She pointed at Dennis as he danced around the fire with his bottle. Long shadows stretched out behind him, distorted monsters against the trees. He tripped over a log and went sprawling. The bottle leapt from his hand and crashed against the side of the cabin. Nora laughed, but the daughter with the baby and the one with the webbed fingers shook their heads and stared angrily at Dennis as he crawled around on his belly like a lizard.

"Look at him!" said Bertha. "That's what Coyote does. He'll make you do any nutty thing."

Bertha looked around at her daughters and gave a little wave. "But nobody wants to hear that," she said. "The priest comes and tells me to quit telling those stories, that they're no good, they're scaring people. Then the old men on the reserve, they don't like me talking either. They say I'm making fun of what's sacred. Coyote's like a god, eh? But the things Coyote does, well, he does us women no good."

Nora's mother shook her head at Bertha, and Bertha sat back and sighed. Dennis had passed out as Bertha spoke and was now snoring loudly on his back. A little whirlwind spun a circle around him and then swept through us all, leaving a chill, before disappearing into the black field behind us. Filthy Billy sat up straight and very still, listening.

"Coyote," he said, and as he said it a coyote howled and yipped close by, in the orchard where the sheep had bedded down for the night. I reached for my gun, and Billy and I jumped up and marched back across the frozen field towards the orchard pasture.

"What Granny (shit) says is true," said Billy.

"What's that?" I asked.

"Coyote (fuck) goes for the weak ones. (Shit) He goes for Coyote Jack, your father. Now he's out (shit) walking, trying on Dennis. (Fuck) You be careful when Coyote's in Dennis."

"Yeah, yeah."

Billy shrugged and took my hand and I let him. His hand was warm and mine was so cold. We didn't say anything else until we reached the bedding ground. Once there, he gave my hand a squeeze and let it fall. The sheep were standing and wary. When they heard us approach, one called out and that started a chorus of bleating. The lead ewe ran to us with her bell jingling and sniffed my hands.

"None down," said Billy.

"That's something."

Beyond the bedding ground we could see nothing but black. But there was a sound. Just wind through the trees at first, and then it became more, a rushing, air through a tunnel or water plunging. The sheep split and ran in two directions, opening up a path between them that ran straight for us. The sound became water rushing at us, deafening. I shot the gun off into the air twice because there was nothing to aim at. Billy held his ears against the rushing sound and slid to his knees.

"Oh, Jesus," he said. "Sweet Jesus."

And the sound was on us, engulfing us, the rush of a huge heart beating. Billy fell over and went into convulsions. I dropped the gun, knelt beside him, held his head, and smoothed back his hair. There was nothing of Billy in his face. His body jerked like animal flesh, like the body of a calf or a chicken just slaughtered, just a bundle of unthinking nerves. The rushing sound collapsed down on us and the convulsions stopped. I rocked him until he began to move his mouth and his eyes fluttered open. Almost immediately he began cursing loudly.

Nora crept out of the black and knelt beside us. "What's the matter with him?" she said.

"Nothing," I said. "One of his fits. He's all right now."

"We heard shots."

"I thought I heard something in the bush."

"Sounded like a big wind blew up," said Nora.

"You heard it?"

"Yeah, just over this way. Didn't touch us."

Filthy Billy came back to himself slowly. A nervous tic started jumping under his eye. He put his hand over it and the tic stopped.

"You okay?" I said.

"(Shit) I'm all right."

"Why don't you and me go off someplace," Nora said to me. "So many people around."

She looked at Billy like he had no right to be there. I helped him up off the ground and wiped the dirt from his pant legs.

"Want to go back to the fire?" I said.

Billy nodded and swore, apologized, and swore again, and we made our way back to the fire with Nora trailing behind. When everyone at the campfire looked at us, I said, "It was nothing," and the women turned back to my mother as I helped Billy sit on a log. I sat next to him and Nora sat on a stump off by herself. My mother was talking spirits.

"Anyway, we'd sit around a table and join hands," she said. "My sisters and me, and try to contact the dead. That's what we'd do for fun in the evenings. Everybody held seances. They were like parties, social things to do. There were books on how to do it. What to wear — you should wear white — and how to eat before — you must eat lightly — and how to hold your hands just so, palms against the table and hands spread out so just our little fingers were touching those of the person next to us. The room was dark except for one candle off in some corner. Sometimes we'd sing hymns, can you believe that? Singing hymns and trying to contact the dead. Oh! Mrs. Bell would be frantic if she knew I had done that!"

"Mrs. Bell!" said Bertha. "It doesn't take much to get her flapping."

"Did you see anything?" said Nora. "Were there ghosts?"

"There were raps under the table once," said Mum. "And I thought I heard a voice. But it could have been my sisters playing a trick. I thought I saw a ghost in my room, at the foot of my bed when I was a girl, no older than Beth. I was sure of it then."

I looked down at Billy's boots. I wished my mother would quit talking about these things. I had heard all of it before and everyone knew my mother talked to the dead.

"And now?" said Bertha.

"I think so still. But memory, you can never be sure, can you? My mother always said she would contact me from the other side, and she did. She's still with me. We talk. She advises me."

"You're a lucky woman to have your mother talking to you still," said Bertha. "My mother only comes in my dreams."

"Nothing lucky about that," Nora's mother said, in her man-voice. "Followed around by your dead mother. I couldn't stand it. She should let go of you. Go off where she belongs."

"Well, you would say that," said Bertha. "The way you treat me, the way you treat your own daughter, you're raising her like a white girl. No respect for children anymore. No respect for old people. Used to be people had children to help them, take care of them when they grew old. Now they have children because they got drunk and forgot themselves."

Nora stared at her feet drawing circles in the dirt, smiling nervously.

"She's my daughter, and I'll raise her like I want," said Nora's mother.

"You're doing no raising at all," said Bertha. "You're squashing her down."

"You shut up!" said Nora's mother. "Dirty old squaw. Don't you tell me how to live my life."

"You should listen to Mum," said one of Bertha's other daughters, the one with webbed fingers. "You'll learn things. She's been there, where you haven't been yet."

"She's got nothing to teach me," said Nora's mum. "All the old ways are dead. She's got to learn that."

The baby started to cry. Her mother stood up with her and walked around the fire. "Old Alfred Johnny says listen to your ancestors," she told Nora's mother. "Hear what they've got to say. Even those who've passed over. They guide us."

"That's witchcraft," said Nora's mother. "The only ghost you should listen to is the Holy Ghost."

"You lived too long with the white men," said the daughter with the webbed fingers, and all the women, Bertha too, laughed at that. Nora's mother stared at her feet. Her anger rolled off her in waves, and Bertha turned her back to it. My mother didn't laugh with the other women, or say any more about her mother. She drank from her cup of cocoa and stared into the fire. Billy, still sitting up, was dozing in and out of sleep. The party went quiet and soon after a wind smelling of snow came down from the mountain bringing a cold with it that the fire couldn't ward off, and just like that winter was on us.

35

AND WHEN WINTER CAME to Turtle Valley it came quickly, without hesitation. I woke the morning of All Saints' Day to a new clean brightness that put a shine to everything in my room and made the whole outside world seem settled and quiet. Snow! The house was quiet too. My mother had already been out doing chores for hours. She'd let me sleep in. I bundled up quickly and went outside.

The world was as transformed as it had been that day when blue flax rained down, except the world was white this time and getting whiter. White capped the barn roof, the house, my father's old Ford, and clung to the stick arms of the tree stretching through it. I stood quietly in the yard for a time listening to how the snow deadened every sound. There were no saws cutting in the distance, or harness bells ringing, or voices echoing off the hills. The quiet filled my ears. Then, slowly, I began to hear the noises that made up the silence. The shush of snow kissing the ground, the raw calls of crows, the crack of expanding wood, and my mother talking sweetness to the calves as she fed them from the bucket of skim milk.

There was the knock of hammers too. Dennis and Billy were over in the orchard, putting up the last bit of the new wire and post fence. The Swede's old billy was eyeing them as they worked. They'd put up a board gate that morning, leading from our orchard pasture to the Swede's.

I waved at them as I kicked my way through the snow in the orchard and opened the gate into the Swede's meadow. As I closed the gate, I saw Coyote Jack standing at the edge of the meadow near the bush, watching me. Here, in daylight, in the fresh, clean snow, Bertha and Billy's stories meant nothing: Coyote Jack was just a shy sad man watching everybody live from the outside. He turned and vanished. I looked over at Dennis and Billy to see if they'd seen Coyote Jack, but they were working with their heads down.

I stood in the meadow for a while longer until I heard the bell ringing, one bell. Thinking it was a sheep that Dennis and Billy had missed, I followed the ringing down Turtle Creek well past the Swede's outhouse. Behind the reserve the creek widened and dropped into a gully — Watson's Gully, named after Bertha's first husband. The Y in the creek sent water one way to the reserve, another to Bertha's house.

The bell was one of our sheep bells, I was sure of it, and that meant trouble. A sheep off alone in coyote country always means trouble. I trudged up a low rise at the mouth of the gully so I could take a look down into it. The sight was something. Everything was white, whiter than white, silver and sparkling. A patch of deep blue water opened at the crotch of the Y of Turtle Creek and it was there that I found the source of that ringing: a patch of red so brilliant in all that white, it could blind you with loveliness, and it was one of our sheep, all right. She was dead, lying down there with her belly as open and scarlet as a whore's mouth, and he was eating on her, that coyote, eating on her belly and into her breastbone, so each bite he took, each push of his nozzle into the warm bloody cavern of her body, rang the bell at her neck and threw the ringing up into the walls of the gully. He knew I was there watching him, but he also knew that I was unarmed and too far off. After a time he shifted the ewe, pulled her body a little farther onto the bank, and stopped the ringing altogether.

36

I SPENT THE MONTH of November trapping coyotes on the trapline that had been my brother's. I knew trapping. I'd gone out trapping coyotes with Dan every year since I had turned eleven and I loved it. It was a chance to get away from the house, to get out of chores, to have my brother to myself. I'd learned all the trapping tricks my brother knew; he'd learned them from Billy and Dennis, who in turn had learned them from Bertha and their aunts on the traplines behind the reserve.

Coyotes are smart, so you've got to be smarter. When trapping coyotes you must keep in mind that each coyote is very much an individual, with habits of his own, and that what will work on one coyote may not work on another. You've got to understand a coyote to trap him — to stop him from eating your livestock. You've got to know his habits.

Coyotes like open country, pasturelands with clumps of bush, the very landscape farmers created for them. Most times they eat voles and mice, but they'll eat anything they can get their teeth into. They'll get drunk on the fermented fruit rotting under snow in an orchard, steal chickens from the coop, gnaw on squash left in the field, and when they're really hungry they'll take down a lamb or calf.

They sleep days in clumps of bush, holes in rocks, or burrows they dig for themselves, and then go out skulking at night. They are creatures of habit, with regular routes that they travel. Like dogs, they mark their territory with their scent by urinating on clumps of grass, snags, bleached carcasses, and the old bedding grounds of sheep. Where they urinate, they scratch the dirt or snow and these are the places to hide traps, where they stop and sniff. They like woods, bushes, shadows.

You know a coyote trail by the footprints and by the scat you find on it. A coyote's trail is a straight line and looks for all the world like the trail left by someone jumping a pogo stick. Coyote scat is made of hair and bone, and you find it at the center of the trail, often at a cross-roads, where two trails meet. I put out traps at these crossroads, on snags, old carcasses, and clumps of grass. I used the scent made from mice and fish that my brother had concocted, putting a few drops against a stump or tree about a foot off the ground. I then hid my traps at various distances around the scent.

In open country I killed a porcupine, fool hen, or rabbit and put it in the center of any small clump of bush I could find, and then set snares on the coyote trails leading into it. In the bush I fixed snares on very young trees, about ten inches off the ground, on any trail frequented by coyotes. When a coyote passed by, the snare caught it by the neck and the coyote choked to death.

My mother or Billy skinned and cleaned the coyotes by the implement shed and stretched the skins inside out on frames shaped like ironing boards. Once they were dry, my mother packed them in boxes and shipped them by train down to the fur buyers, Little Brothers, in Vancouver, the same place we got the trapping supplies, the snare wire that came in a hundred-foot coil. As my bedroom wall was right behind the kitchen stove, my mother hung the skins to dry on my wall. They smelled wild and raw.

"You're not going to join up," I said.

"Nah," said Billy. "Missing (shit) Dan?"

"Yeah. I got mad at him sometimes. But he made me feel safe. He took care of me, sometimes, when Dad went crazy. He taught me stuff. He hasn't even written."

"He'll be (fuck) all right," said Billy.

We were out walking the trapline in mid-November. I had tried to go out again by myself, but my mother made Filthy Billy go along, with his gun, to protect me from some crazy bear or wild man, to chaperon me, to make sure Dennis and I didn't meet up in the bush. I was bundled up in a couple of sweaters, and, under my skirt, long johns, and old wool trousers with their long cuffs stuffed into my boots. Billy wore my brother's tin coat over layers of sweaters. The stiff material in the coat made a scuffing sound when he walked.

This was Christmas tree country, and every year hundreds of thousands of trees were shipped from the district by train, bound for export in the United States. The trees where we walked were full and stately, decorated with snow and the empty nests of birds.

As we walked into a clearing, a deer stepped out of the bush, very close to us. Billy held out his hand and when the deer took a step back, Billy reached down slowly, so slowly, and plucked a leaf of dry grass poking up through the snow. He put that grass between his hands and blew through it, making a mewing sound just like the sound of the fawn Nora and I had seen at Coyote Jack's cabin. The deer put her head up and took a step forward, confused by the sound of a fawn crying. Billy blew his mewing whistle again and held out his hand. The deer took a few more cautious steps forward, sniffed his hand, then bounded off as if it were on springs. It disappeared into the bush.

I was delighted. "She wasn't afraid of you," I said.

"Aw (shit). Excuse me. Anybody can do that."

"Yeah, sure," I said, then called "Fox and goose!" and gave Billy a slap on the shoulder, so he was fox. We both put our guns down and went running off, stamping a circle in the snow. We made an X in the circle, and the game of tag began. I was the goose and Billy chased me, but we had to stay on the paths we created in the snow, on the circle or the X, or we lost the game. Billy was catching up to me so I stood dead center in the circle, the safe place, where he, the fox, couldn't come and eat me. We stood there for a minute, facing each other, giggling and excited, our breath clouding the air. I took off as the deer had done, and Billy lost his footing and fell and took a moment to catch up to me again. Then suddenly Nora was there, chasing behind us, being fox, and both Billy and I were silly geese. We ran, laughing and throwing snow, accompanied by Nora's bells, until Billy stood his ground in the center of the circle and I joined him, so close in that little safe spot that our noses touched. We giggled at each other, enclosing ourselves in breath, so Nora couldn't get us. We stood there too long, maybe, giggled too loud, stood too close. Whatever it was, it made Nora mad and she pushed the both of us to the ground. Instead of getting mad, Billy and I giggled louder and made snow angels there, in the middle of the circle, in the safe place, and that just seemed to get Nora even hotter.

"Let's go!" she said to me. And when I didn't answer, and went on making a snow angel, she said, "You going to stay here or come with me?"

I was giddy. I giggled and flapped my arms in the snow and didn't answer her. Billy flapped right along beside me as Nora stomped off through the snow and disappeared down one of the bush trails. Billy and I stood up, laughing, knocked the snow from our clothes, and looked down at our snow angels that were holding hands.

37

THE DAY of the Christmas pageant at the school, an event my mother had no intention of going to, she and I rigged up Cherry to the cutter and took a run into town with the cream to do our Christmas shopping. In past years we had driven down to the school at night to endure an evening of nervous children reciting poems they didn't understand and getting words hopelessly confused on the songs they sang. In the end Santa always turned up and handed out gifts of oranges, hard candy, dolls, trains, slippers, and cheap perfume. Though these gifts were rare things indeed, it was the anticipation of the evening itself I craved: the spectacle of a frosty night — gas lamps shining through the schoolhouse windows onto the snow-covered playgrounds and winking off the icy sled runs; the nervous waiting, first to see who would make the mistakes that embarrassed us all, second for the costumed man (usually Morley Boulee) who handed out glory and excess to children who had had neither all year; and lastly that ride home down Blood Road, the bells on the harnesses of the horses, the rise and dip in the road that made our stomachs sink and our spirits soar just to go over it.

My mother and I wouldn't make that journey tonight, not this year, not with all the talk going on, so we cut down Blood Road during the day instead. We were accompanied by a heaviness where my father usually sat and wasn't sitting, and a heaviness in the back where Dan wasn't that made this trip into town weigh on us, take longer, wear colder. But there was that other thing too: a lightness jingling with the bells on the harnesses, a spring in the step of Cherry that bounced through bone and flesh and into our hearts, making them thump a little faster. Christmas. I loved it and my mother loved it and we would celebrate it despite Dan's absence, my father's crimes, and the town's gossip.

People were in town. The pageant that night was putting a light into everyone's step, making them hungry for plum pudding, Christmas cake, and eggnog. Folks leapt across the muddy road onto the snow banks that were our sidewalks. Candles lit up the shop windows and the tables in the Promise Cafe. Someone had decorated the two trees growing on either side of the church steps. Goat was back too, sitting on the steps in front of Blundell's Motel, just sitting, though, just sitting.

While I fingered red velvet and lusted after the jars of hard candy in Bouchard and Belcham's, my mother went straight to the back of the store to the post office wicket, her heart set on news of Dan and fearing news of my father. She left the wicket with my aunt Lou's annual Christmas box under her arm and a letter from Dan.

"He's just finished training in Vernon," said Mum. "He won't be home for Christmas. He'll write when he knows more."

My mother turned the page over to see if there was anything on the other side, but there wasn't.

"That's all?" I said.

"He says he loves you and me. He doesn't say anything about your father. He said it was hard in the training camp and that he's sorry it took so long for him to write. He says they kept him busy."

I took the letter from my mother and read it for myself. It was written in my brother's big, looped childish hand. I had always teased him for his messy handwriting and had often written his letters for him. The thought of him made me cry.

My mother put an arm around me and patted my shoulder. "He'll be just fine," she said. "We should be proud of him. A soldier! Think of it! Our Danny, in uniform!"

That only made me cry harder. My mother looked around the store, at the old men sitting at the stove chewing snuff and trying not to stare at us, at the customers at the front counter.

"There, there," she said. "Enough of this. Not here."

I turned my back on the rest of the store and blew my nose into the hanky my mother offered.

"Look!" she said. "We've got Auntie Lou's package!"

Aunt Lou's packages were the same each year: chocolates, cookies, and handiwork. They held few surprises but never failed to delight us. My mother gave me the package, and I tucked it under my arm and blew my nose again just as Goat's father, Dr. Poulin, came up to us. He was a tall man with red ears that stuck out and he was so skinny that his face was that of a monkey. The handsomely tailored suit he wore couldn't hide his homeliness. Nevertheless he was well liked in the town. He would still work for a side of beef or a freshly butchered lamb.

My mother said, "I see Arthur's home."

"For the holidays, yes."

"That's good for him."

"I stopped in on John when I picked up Arthur," he said.

"Please," said my mother, glancing at the old men. "Not here."

Dr. Poulin lowered his voice to a whisper. The old men leaned forward in their seats but didn't look at us.

"He says you haven't come to see him," the doctor whispered. "He wants to see you."

"I can't," said my mother.

"Surely at Christmas."

"No," said my mother. "I can't."

She pushed past Dr. Poulin and began collecting items from her shopping list. Dr. Poulin followed and leaned over her, talking quietly. Now that their backs were to them, the old men watched my mother and the doctor.

My mother said, "Please, leave me alone!" and the doctor backed away from her. She glanced briefly at the old men. She was on the verge of crying. The old men looked at their boots or spit into the spittoon. The doctor left her then and went over to the post office wicket to do his business.

I went outside and leaned against the wall of the store, under the porch, holding on to the panic in my stomach. Across the street, Goat still sat on the steps of the room where Ginger Rogers had slept. He was only sitting, not fidgeting or being rude, so still I thought he might be sleeping. A light dusting of snow was over his shoulders. I left the porch and walked over to him. In front of him the body of the dirty white crow lay in the muddy snow, its gnarled feet clawing out at the air. Goat stared at the crow, not moving, not fidgeting, just shivering. The snow went on collecting on his shoulders and the knitted toque he wore.

I said, "Goat?" but he didn't answer or look up. I touched his shoulder and when he didn't respond, I gave him a nudge. He breathed in deeply, quickly, like a sleeper disturbed, but he didn't look up.

"Goat," I said again, and put my hand under his chin so he would look at me. "You see my father in that place? You see John Weeks?"

He looked up at me, but his eyes were as dead as those of the crow. His face was cold. He shivered a little.

"Oh, Goat," I said. "Come on now."

I took him by the arm and pulled him off the stoop. He stood up heavily and shuffled after me, kicking the body of the crow deeper into the mud and snow. I pulled him by the arm across the street and over to Bouchard and Belcham's. At the steps before the store Goat stopped with his toes against the wooden sidewalk, and I had to urge him onto it and onto every step. Once inside the door, some small light came back on within him; he looked around as if he'd never been there. He went on gazing like a surprised child as I pulled him over to the stove where the old men who had dug their own graves sat around, waiting. Goat's father looked over at us once as we came in, to see that everything was all right, and went on with his business at the post office wicket.

"What you got there?" said Mr. Aitken, one of the old men at the store.

"He was near frozen," I said. "Sitting in front of Blundell's."

"Waiting on Ginger, I suspect," said one of the other old men.

They all laughed.

"Doc should have kept him in that hospital," said Mr. Aitken, in a low voice.

One of the other old men nudged him and nodded once at me. Mr. Aitken said, "What?" and then, "Oh."

I left Goat to thaw out with the old men and went back outside to wait for my mother in the buggy, though my feet were going so cold I could barely feel them. I pulled the old buggy quilt over my lap and sought out the tin of coals with my feet. It was still warm and after a time my feet began to tingle and ache with the heat. Under the blanket I put my hands between my thighs, as I knew I shouldn't, to warm them. My mother took her sweet time choosing a few items that would ward off the loneliness of Christmas. In past years on Christmas Eve, my father had cooked barley sugar, the only recipe in the scrapbook that came from him, but only if the weather was clear. Barley sugar candy was nothing but brown sugar, water, lemon juice, and luck, because it was a lucky thing to have a clear day in late December in Turtle Valley. If the day was cloudy, the candy went cloudy. If the day was clear and sunny, free of moisture, then the candy turned out clear and golden, as lovely as amber. But there would be no barley sugar this Christmas. The sky was cloudy, threatening snow, and my father was hidden away in a place so terrible and shameful my mother wouldn't talk of it. Dan was gone and his letter said he wouldn't be home for Christmas. There was little worth celebrating. Nevertheless, my mother left Bouchard and Belcham's with both arms full and that sweet smile of apology on her face. When she handed me the packages and sat in the cutter beside me, she smelled of the warm pipe smoke of the old men.

"Goat's quieted right down," said my mother. "He's nothing like he was before."

"He killed that white crow," I said.

"Killed it? Are you sure?"

"It was dead. He had it and it was dead."

"Maybe he just found it. It's been so cold."

"Maybe," I said.

When we reached home there was a little time yet before milking and chores, so I stole out for a walk, hoping to see Nora, with the excuse of checking traps. I took my usual route up to the trapline, across the field, and to the benchland so I wouldn't raise my mother's suspicions. Just before the benchland a red trail appeared in the snow. I noticed it suddenly, the trail of blood weaving a pretty pattern, a dance and splatter of red on white. I followed it, stunned, slowly at first, and then at a trot that was the best I could do through the snow. The trail of blood led over the field and into the bush, then into a clearing, where Filthy Billy stood with his back to me and his head down.

"Billy!" I shouted. "Billy! You okay?"

Filthy Billy turned and, as he did, the trail of blood disappeared, becoming a mere shadow in the snow.

"Yeah," he said. "(Shit) Fine. Excuse me. Why? (Fuck) What's up?"

"I thought I saw blood," I said, coming up to him.

"Blood?"

"I thought I did. I followed it here, to you, but it's gone. I don't know what I saw."

"You (shit) saw blood all right," said Billy. "That was (shit) my father's blood, the trail Johansson (shit) followed when he found him dead. This (fuck) is where my father died. (Shit) This here spot."

He pointed down at a boulder sticking up from the snow. The area around it was littered with bits of paper, wooden matchsticks, unlit and wet cigarettes, foil gum wrappers, sequins and beads, things small and shiny that would attract hoarding magpies for miles around.

"This is where my father (fuck) fought Coyote and took him back to the spirit world. (Shit) This is where my father died to (shit) save us."

"There you go again," I said. "Talking crazy."

"No. That thing you (shit) got following you — that follows me. (Fuck) You don't have to name it Coyote. (Shit) You call it demon or ghost, but it's the same thing. Coyote (shit) won't kill me. I'm his house. (Fuck) But he'll kill you. He kills (shit) all his wives. He'll take over (shit) somebody's body and kill like he's killed Sarah Kemp. He doesn't use me that way. (Fuck) I'm his house. I'm his safe place. But sometimes (shit), like now, he takes off. Those are good times. But those times (fuck) scare me too because he puts on some other body, like (shit) putting on a coat, like he did to that Parker kid, or Coyote Jack, or your father. While he's in there, there's no telling (shit) what he'll do. I chase him down, find out (fuck) who he's in, and try to stop whatever he's up to. But (shit) I'm tiring out. I can't keep up."

"This is nuts," I said.

"No," he said. "You know it's not. (Shit) He wants you for his wife."

"If you think Coyote Jack killed Sarah Kemp, why didn't you tell the police? Why didn't you say something before?"

Billy laughed and shook his head. "Who'd believe me? (Shit) Everybody thinks I'm a crazy man. (Fuck) Maybe I am. But I didn't (shit) want you to think that." He kicked the snow near the boulder that marked his father's death. "Police wouldn't do nothing anyhow. What could they (fuck) do? My father took Coyote with him when (shit) he killed himself. (Fuck) That's the only way, and even then Coyote comes back. Granny says he comes (fuck) back riding a newborn soul."

"You're not thinking of that."

"I don't know," he said. "I don't (shit) know no other way."

"Billy, no!"

"I don't want (shit) any of this. Half the time I don't (fuck) believe it. But he's already killing. I'm not brave like (shit) my father, if that's what it was. Maybe he was just an old drunk. (Fuck) Maybe Granny's wrong."

Billy dug into his pocket and threw several cigarette butts on the rock that marked his father's death.

"What're you doing?" I said.

"Granny (shit) says he smoked," said Billy.

I laughed. "You see Nora around?"

"When I left (shit) Granny's this morning, she was heading to Granny's old (fuck) winter house."

"I'll see you then," I said.

"Wait." He dug deeper into his pocket and pulled out a bell. He rang it and put it in my hand.

"I (fuck) seen you like these things," he said.

I rang the bell, grinned at him, and turned to walk back across the field. I felt him watching me, but when I turned and waved, he was gone.

I headed down Blood Road to the winter house. Nora was there, outside, collecting dead sticks off the trees for kindling. We climbed inside the winter house and Nora started a fire. We took off our wet clothes, hung them on sticks pounded into the dirt walls, and wrapped ourselves in the big quilt we'd left there. Our skin was gooseflesh.

"Beth, you got no blood in you," said Nora.

I was as white as the snow outside. Nora was brown, though not as brown as she got come summer. Her black hair shone red in the firelight.

"Billy thinks I got Coyote following me," I said.

"Coyotes will follow anything," she said. "They're as curious as dogs."

"No, he means Coyote, that spirit thing your granny talks about."

"Granny's full of stories," she said.

"I know, I know."

"He's got you scared, eh?"

"Something's been following me. I keep trying to tell you. All summer and now too. When I set traps, something's in the bush."

"Old Coyote Jack spying on a pretty girl," she said.

"There's something else," I said. "I hear this wind, and then there's something there, something I can't see. I don't know. Billy says it's Coyote looking for a bride. He says Coyote killed Sarah Kemp. He took her for his bride and then killed her."

"You're listening to some mongoloid's stories?" she said.

"Billy's not a mongoloid. He's as smart as you and me, and a lot nicer than you."

Nora shifted herself closer to the fire and went sullen for a time. Then she seemed to brighten.

"Well," she said. "Maybe you do have Coyote following. Remember he's a shape-shifter. Takes any form he wants. Takes your body over too, if he wants. Mum says he's like the Devil."

She laughed when she saw the fear in my face, then she touched my face and kissed me. There was scuffing and sniffing above us. We looked up and saw the pointed face of a coyote. Then he was gone.

Nora was delighted. "Look at that!" she said and laughed. "Coyote Jack. He's spying on us, dirty old man." She tried to scare me further. "There's no place safe from a shape-shifter," she said.

When I didn't laugh, she took my hands. I pulled away from her, stood, and put on my clothes. Then I sat with my back against the dirt wall.

Nora became cranky over my fear. She stood and dressed.

"Where you going?" I said.

"Home," she said.

I didn't want to be left there alone, not with some coyote sniffing around. I kicked dirt over the fire as Nora headed up the ladder. When I finished and climbed up after her, Nora had already disappeared into the bush.

On the way home I took a trail that ended up in the orchard pasture, hoping to find newborn lambs steaming in the snow next to their mothers. When I reached the orchard, however, the sheep were wary. They were huddled in a clump near the barn, all except a ewe near the Swede's fence line, who bleated and circled her lamb. The noise of my walking had just scared off a coyote. The tracks were there, and the coyote had torn off the jaw of the lamb. I wished I'd been a few moments later; the coyote would have finished the job. Instead I had to.

I picked up the lamb by its hind legs — one good knock on the head would kill it — and swung the lamb as hard as I could against a fence post, then lay its body gently on the snow. I took off my mitten and rubbed my face.

Coyote Jack, scruffy in his tattered blanket coat, stood at the edge of the bush. When I went to wave, as I would to any neighbor, Coyote Jack disappeared.

Another ewe had given birth to a lamb near the barn. The ewe turned and turned around a little bundle that steamed in the snow, nudging it with her nose, bleating in hope of some response. The afterbirth still dangled from the ewe's rump, creating a circle of blood in the snow around the newborn lamb. The lamb had been left too long out in the snow. Its legs were straight and stiff like a dead thing but its heart still beat and breath rose from its little nose. I picked the lamb up from the snow and tucked its body against my own inside my jacket. The lamb shivered in waves against my chest. She was still for a moment, then shivered suddenly, convulsively, as if fear had just caught up with her. I hugged her close and ran with her through the slushy snow, back to the house. As I stepped from my boots, my mother brought a towel and took the lamb from me.

"She's gone stiff," I said. "A coyote got to another one."

"I've brought worse round," she said.

As I washed the blood from my hands, my mother opened the oven door, tested the heat with her hand, and then placed the lamb, wrapped in the towel, in the oven, and reached to the top of her cupboard for her bottle of medicinal rum. I squatted down next to the stove and slid my thumb into the side of the lamb's mouth to open it while my mother placed a teaspoon of rum in the lamb's mouth.

"That will fix what ails you," she said.

The lamb swallowed fitfully and a stream of rum ran down the side of her mouth, dripping down to the oven floor, filling the kitchen with the sweet, warming scent. I stripped off my brother's jacket and my blouse right in the kitchen, and slid on one of my mother's sweaters, pulled up a chair, and warmed myself by the open oven door. The sweater smelled of my mother and the powder she wore, and combined with the light lamb smell and the warmth of the rum. My mother brought me a cup of tea and pulled up a chair next to me.

"Ah," she said, and breathed deep. "Peaceful. There's life for you, that little thing."

I put my feet up on my mother's cupboard counter and instead of complaining my mother followed suit.

"We'll have to check in the night for lambs," she said. "You go once again before bed, then I'll wake in the night and have a go."

"They're all in the heifer pasture," I said. "They've got snow if they're thirsty."

"Anything in the traps?" she said.

I blushed and turned my face to the window. "No," I said.

"Odd," she said. "Those coyotes are smart ones."

The lamb lifted her head and stirred a little. "There you are," said my mother. She knelt next to the stove and slipped her hand into the towel and rubbed the lamb's tiny legs. "She'll be just fine," said my mother. "Warm her up and get her back to her mum. Get the first milk in her. That's the best chance they have."

The lamb bunted against my mother's hand, as she would against the ewe's teats. My mother sat back to drink her tea and the lamb took a few faltering steps around the open oven, looking for her, and fell back over onto the towel. There's nothing as magic as a lamb just born. She's tiny, as light as nothing, covered in wool of the tiniest curl, so tiny you can't believe it's a sheep you're looking at, not even after years of lambing seasons. Look at this wee animated thing, suddenly up in the air as if all four legs were springs, then suddenly fallen, knees tucked under her, bunting and sniffing at every passing shadow, so trusting she'll suck the finger of the man who will butcher her.

38

CHRISTMAS EVE, the moon was full; it cut in and out of the clouds, bruising them blue and yellow, teasing the stubble in the fields with silver light and then hiding again. I stood at the kitchen window, and my mother sat in the rocker, leafing through her scrapbook, hoping for something that would excite us out of loneliness and into some celebrating.

My heart wasn't in it. I missed Dan and, though I still feared him, I missed my father. In past years we spent Christmas Eve dressing up and eating a late supper of pork pie, carrots, turnips, Hubbard squash, and Christmas cake for dessert. The Christmas before, my father had won the school's turkey raffle and the day before the turkey was to be butchered, it escaped the chicken coop, where the chickens had tormented him, pecking everything that was red on him, and flew up to roost on the barn roof. We spent Christmas dinner eating an unlucky chicken and listening to the turkey gobble. Dan and my father never did get that turkey off the barn roof. Sometime Christmas night it flew off, and we never saw it again. Bertha said some of the hunters off the reserve had caught sight of it that winter and tried to bag it for supper, but then Bertha was always telling stories like that. Christmas Eve was a time for decorating the tree and, if my father was out doing a few extra chores for Christmas Day, for singing Christmas carols. If he was inside we didn't sing; the sound of our voices, even my mother's sweet soprano, made his head ache.

Now, with my brother soldiering and my father locked away with crazies and idiots, we didn't have the strength for singing or eating. For supper we had sandwiches made from a ham cooked two days before, and a slice each of the Christmas cake my mother had made in late November and iced that night with almond icing. Dennis had taken off to spend the day at Bertha Moses's, but Billy had eaten supper with us. He'd brought a Christmas tree with him, the bushiest he could find, a stout young pine that now leaned against the wall of the house outside on the porch. None of us spoke. When he was done eating, Billy had given us a little bow and walked over to Bertha Moses's, leaving my mother rocking and me staring out the window. Without bodies to dampen the sound, the room felt hollow. Our voices bounced against the walls. My mother's rocking echoed too, creating a creak that set me on edge.

"Snapdragons!" she said, scaring me half to death.

Snapdragons were nothing but raisins heated on a tin plate and then doused with whiskey or brandy and set on fire. When we were children, Dan and I had grabbed for the raisins through the blue flames, but this year my mother and I only turned down the lamps and watched the raisins burn. Loneliness had made us both tired, without appetite. Nevertheless, once the raisins burned to nothing and my mother tossed them onto the snow outside, she tried again at celebrating.

"The tree!" she said.

We brought the tree into the house and set it standing upright in a corner of the kitchen, with the aid of string nailed to the wall, in a box of sand and dirt. We decorated it with bits of fabric and shiny paper, wool, and the few glass balls we owned. When we were finished, my mother opened Aunt Lou's Christmas box. It was smaller this year, on account of the rationing, but it held the usual assortment of English chocolates and cream-filled cookies and samples of handwork — crochet doilies and embroidered handkerchiefs. We filled stockings and hung them on each other's bedposts.

After that we went to bed because neither of us could think of what else to do. I stared at the coyotes that Billy had skinned and my mother had stretched on frames like ironing boards and hung on my bedroom wall, their inside-out skins shining in the moonlight, their dark eyeholes watching me. Outside a coyote howled. When one coyote howls, he sounds like many coyotes, a chorus in himself. He howls at the moon and jumps up when he howls, cries for the joy of it. His cries, and yipes fill the night. I became breathless in my terror of the coyotes. I waited for them to attack. It was a long time before I slept. The coyotes entered my dreams; they growled at me. Their weight made the floorboards groan. A darkness crossed the window and fell on my chest. When I cried out, the coyotes put their claws over my mouth. They lifted my nightgown. They rubbed their wet tails between my legs and over my belly. They told me to keep quiet. I hid my dream self in the darkest corner of my room and watched the shadows of the coyotes suck the breath from my body. When they had their fill, the shadows sighed deeply, came together, and took the form of my father. He lifted his weight from my body and left the room. At dawn I woke to the sound of my mother stoking the fire and Nora climbing through the window.

"It's all right," she whispered.

I relaxed and made room for her. She held me and stroked my back.

"What're you doing here?" I said. "It's Christmas morning, don't you know?"

"Caught lots of coyotes, eh?" she said, looking at the coyote skins hanging on the walls.

"I hate them. They smell. They scare me half to death. They came into my dreams last night."

Nora rocked me and sang quietly, and my spirit began to fill again. I woke as if from sleep, and was surprised to find her there, singing. When Nora finished the song, she combed my hair with her fingers, as my mother used to when I was a small child. I became aware of my mother, listening at the door. After a moment she moved away.

Nora fingered the fat Christmas stocking hanging from the end of my bed. She said, "Your mother loves you."

I didn't answer.

"You hear when your father's coming back?"

"No," I said. "Mum won't talk about it. She tries to act like nobody knows where he is. Everybody knows."

Nora said, "At least your mother doesn't yell. My mother yells. Boy, does she yell."

We laughed and Nora tickled me. I fought her and we fell from the bed. Her necklace tinkled and flashed. She let me up and we sat against the bed. She took my hand.

"You have hair like Rita Hayworth," she said.

We looked at each other for a long time, until my mother called out, "Breakfast!"

I got up quickly, ahead of Nora. She caught my ankle and made me trip. I grabbed the loop of her jeans as she ran to the door and the room filled with light from her bells. We tumbled into the kitchen red-faced and giggling. My mother gave me a look and we quieted down and sat like proper ladies while my mother poured us both tea and set a plate in front of us. When we were done eating, my mother and I emptied the contents of our stockings — oranges, candy, trinkets, and little books — onto the kitchen table.

"Aren't you spending Christmas with your family?" said my mother.

"They're coming here," said Nora. "Granny, Mum, and everybody."

"Here?" said Mum. "When?"

"Sometime this morning."

"Oh, Lord!" said Mum. "We've got so much to do! I hadn't planned much of a Christmas dinner. Just for the two of us."

"Granny's bringing a porcupine," said Nora. "She said we could say it's chicken."

My mother laughed at that.

"And my aunts are bringing things. Billy and Dennis are coming here to help with chores. There they are now."

Nora pointed out the kitchen window. Billy and Dennis were walking down the road in the morning twilight in their field denims, jack shirts, hats, and gloves. They didn't stop at the house, but went straight to the barn and started feeding. My mother and I dressed in our milk clothes and rushed out to help them.

It was important to feed the animals extra on Christmas Day, to make sure their bedding was dry, their water troughs were clean. It was as important as the Christmas stockings or the excess of Christmas dinner. With Dennis and Billy's help, we finished chores quickly and set about making our contributions for Christmas dinner. Mum laid the scrapbook out on the kitchen table and searched out her special Christmas Day recipes. She decided on a Christmas stew of:

one pound beef
one pound of mutton
the front quarters of a hare
a cleaned fool hen
four onions
a turnip
peppercorns and salt to taste
four apples

She chopped all the ingredients in small pieces and placed them in four quarts of water. The stew would simmer for five hours or more, and, an hour before serving, my mother would add a few peeled and sliced potatoes.

We swept and cleaned the kitchen, and Billy brought in boughs of pine and white cedar and then disappeared again. We decorated the kitchen with the boughs and put out candles, plates, cutlery, and cups. My mother threw a small handful of dried lavender into the kitchen stove for a fragrant fire.

By the time the arrival of birds signaled Bertha's arrival, we had cleaned ourselves into excitement. My mother tucked her scrapbook away into the top shelf of the cupboard, and both she and I leapt for the door like schoolgirls.

Bertha brought the promised porcupine, still warm from her oven, and a kettle of soup made from dried turtle meat. After her came the daughter with webbed fingers, carrying bread, and after her, the one with the birthmark across her forehead, carrying a bowl that smelled of cinnamon and apples, and Nora's mother, carrying a bowl of fluffed potatoes mixed with turnip. Each of them carried something: a bowl, a covered frypan or saucepan, a fryer, a parcel, a gift. Dennis and the Swede came in with them, and the Swede ate with his hat on, sitting on the bench by the door. His stocking feet moved around each other like two mating mink.

The food filled the table in the kitchen, left no room for sitting, and so we ate standing, leaning against the counter, squatting against the wall. The parlor was dark and cold without heat and, despite the crowd in the kitchen, no one went in there. The kitchen was the one warm room in the house. During the meal, the daughter with webbed fingers pointed out the window at a figure slinking through the trees along the driveway.

"Coyote Jack," she said.

My mother turned to the Swede. "He isn't spending Christmas with you?"

"Never does," said the Swede. "I try, you know. I go up to the cabin, try to talk to him. But he won't talk. He locks the door or he runs off. Imagine! A son scared of his own father. This year I dropped off some flour and sugar and tried to talk to him, but he threatened me with a gun. I don't know what possessed him."

"No one should spend Christmas alone," said Bertha.

My mother flushed red but said nothing.

The Swede shrugged.

"Beth, see if you can wave him in," said my mother.

I did as she asked but went no farther than the porch. Coyote Jack stood by the side of the barn near the pile of rocks that marked the graves of his mother and young aunts and uncles. When I waved him to come in, he slunk farther into the shadows. Then he was gone.

I went on standing on the porch for a time. The air was a refreshment from the warm, crowded stuffiness of the house. Billy was walking across the field, carrying something, and I waited on him. Nora came outside and hugged me from behind.

"What're you doing out here?" she said.

"Nothing."

"You should come inside. You're cold."

I didn't say anything to that. I stayed where I was and she let go of me and stood beside me with her hands in her coat pockets, watching with me as Billy walked across the yard. He was all cleaned up. His suit was brushed down, and he wasn't wearing his rattlesnake hat. His hair was slicked back with bear grease and he was freshly shaved. When he stepped up onto the porch, his strange blue-brown eyes sparkled, and he smelled of something sweet, something too sweet, something familiar. It took me a moment to remember the smell: it was my old bottle of violet perfume. He must have found it in the stump and worn it as after-shave. It made me smile.

Billy grinned at me and handed me the bundle he carried.

"What's this?" I said.

"Merry Christmas!" he said. "(Fuck) Excuse me!"

The burlap bundle was tied at the top with string. The bottom was wet. I pulled the string, and the burlap fell away, and I found myself holding the whole plant, dirt, roots, and all, of a buttercup. The wonder of it was that the plant was flowering delicate yellow petals. It was a beautiful thing, and surrounded by all that snow it was magical.

"Where did you find this?" I said.

Billy shrugged and grinned. "(Shit) In the snow," he said. "I found it (fuck) a week ago, and I said that's what I'm giving Beth for Christmas (shit) because that's how (shit) she makes me feel. She's the bright spot in the snow. (Fuck) That's Beth, I said."

"Billy!" I said. "It's beautiful!"

I gave him a peck on the cheek. Nora went off by herself and leaned against the wall at the far end of the porch, but I ignored her sulking and took Billy and the plant inside.

"Look what Billy found!" I said, and placed the flowering buttercup on a plate in the center of the table.

All the presents came out then. My mother and I cleared the mess off the table and onto the counter and everyone exchanged and unwrapped their presents at once around the table. The presents were wrapped in bits of cloth, sugar and flour bags, the pages of magazines, and tied with wool and strips of fabric. My mother gave me a bar of sweet-smelling soap. Bertha gave me a little pouch made of that precious red velvet. Dennis gave me a wink and a package of nylons that embarrassed me. I squirreled them away in my room before my mother or anyone else could see them.

Dennis and the Swede started outdoing each other in stories and off-color jokes that made my mother laugh despite herself. Conversations filled the house and finally spread into the parlor, warming it. One of the women put on a record and others took turns cranking the gramophone. Enrico Caruso filled my father's empty chair and made it seem as if he was with us. My mother pulled out the dusty board games and cards she'd brought with her from the old country, from under her marriage bed, and the Swede and Dennis played chess while the women played tiddlywinks, checkers, snap, and old maid. The women giggled, chatted, drank coffee, and ate cake so long that the flock of crows gave up waiting and lifted off the roof in a great black cloud that darkened the sky for a moment before disappearing over the benchland.

Nora never came back inside. When the crows lifted off the roof, I poured coffee for her and took it outside, but she was no longer on the porch. I stepped out onto the yard and called her, but she didn't answer. Billy came outside then and sat with me on the porch steps as I had often sat with my brother. We shared Nora's coffee to keep warm. Coyote Jack slid up to the edge of the bush behind the barn, and Billy pointed him out to me. As soon as he did, Coyote Jack disappeared.

"He keeps turning up," I said. "I don't know what he wants. Scares me half to death sometimes."

"He's (shit) sweet on you," said Billy.

"Oh no, not him!" I said.

"Sure," he said. "Dennis (shit) wants you for his girlfriend too, and Nora (fuck). Others, I bet."

He didn't look at me, and I didn't look at him, but our hands found each other and that was enough to hold on to for a time. Neither of us said anything more until the door started creaking open and both of us pulled our hands back into our laps. Dennis and the Swede came outside laughing at something the Swede had said. I dusted off my skirt, went inside to join the women, and left the men alone to smoke their Christmas cigarettes.

39

THE HOUSE was still full of Bertha's progeny when I tucked Dennis's gift under my sweater and slipped out to find Nora, under the pretense of checking traps. Dennis gave me a long look as I closed the door, but he didn't follow. Billy was winning a game of chess over the Swede. I ran to the winter house but didn't find Nora there. I dropped the nylons Dennis had cursed me with down the hole of the winter house and listened until I heard bells. I followed them until I found Nora sitting on a log in the center of a clearing. She had cut herself again. A rivulet of blood dripped from her arm onto the snow. She didn't look up.

"Pretty, isn't it?" she said.

"Stop that!" I cried. "There's nothing pretty about it."

"It's so red." She sucked the blood from the cut on her arm. "So salty. You'd think you were drinking the ocean."

"Stop," I said. "You're making me sick."

Nora looked up at me. She'd been crying. Her lips were smeared with the blood from her arm. She licked them clean.

"How's the party?"

"Still going. Why'd you leave?"

Nora shrugged and wiped the blood from her hands with some snow. She rolled her shirtsleeve back down and warmed her hands between her thighs.

"Bertha gave me a little bag made of that red velvet," I said.

"I saw her making it," said Nora. "I've got something for you too."

She stood up and dug into her front jean pocket and pulled out a string of bells just long enough for a bracelet. She dropped it in my hands.

"You like it?" she said.

"I love it!"

"You like it better than Billy's present?"

"It's beautiful," I said. "I'll wear it always."

Nora tied the bracelet around the wrist on my lightning arm, and I shook it. The tinkling notes bounced off the trees and filled the patch of woods. A few birds twittered back.

"You'll hear me coming and going," I said.

"I'll keep track of you," said Nora.

"Look, I've got to get back," I said. "Mum's keeping her eye on me pretty good these days."

"Dennis is still there, isn't he? In the kitchen with her?"

"I don't think it's Dennis she's worried about," I said.

"What then?"

"I don't know. Why don't you come back?"

"Nah," said Nora. "Too crowded."

Nora watched her feet stamp out a circle in the snow. I touched her face and tried kissing her, but she pulled back. I turned to go, and she said, "Wait."

She pushed me up against a young poplar so the tree waved our location to the whole valley. She kissed me with all of her body and went on kissing me even when I tried to pull away, kissed me until I didn't want to go anymore. Then she stopped, leaving me pumped with desire, sweating in it.

"See you later," she said gruffly, and walked off through the snow, not once looking back, not once waving. I watched her going through my own hot breath.

As I headed back home, following one of the coyote trails on which I had set my snares, Coyote Jack was suddenly there, crouched down at the edge of the bush, watching me.

I raised my hand to wave at him, but thought better of it. He knew I was there. I turned and fled the way I'd come, and after a time something caught up to me and ran parallel in the bush. I didn't think. I ran with my heart in my throat. Then he was there again in the path in front of me. His hair was plastered to his head, a line of spittle ran down his chin, and his shirt was wet with perspiration. He looked laughable, a clown. I turned once again towards home and his footsteps crunched behind me. He threw me down in the snow and fumbled with his clothes.

Suddenly he got up. He twisted, batted the air, and screamed, and the scream became a howl. His body flitted back and forth between man and coyote, then the coyote dropped on all fours and cowered away from me. He bristled and growled. I stood slowly and clapped my hands, as I would to scare off any wild animal. The coyote turned and trotted off and disappeared into the bush. I slumped back into the snow, exhausted by fear, staring at Coyote Jack's clothes sitting in a heap in front of me. A movement made me look up, and there was Jack standing at the edge of the path, covering his puckered genitals with one hand. He gestured for me to go. I stood, backed away, and ran.

When I reached home, the house was empty. Off in the distance near the benchland, Mum was calling to the cows. I went to my room and closed the door behind me. Standing with my back against the door in the warmth of my room, I could almost believe I hadn't seen the thing. The coyotes on the walls smelled. I stared at them. After a time Nora came to the window. She opened it but didn't come in.

"I thought you weren't coming," I said.

"I saw Granny and everybody walking home," she said. "I thought we could spend some time together, alone."

"I saw it," I said. "I saw Coyote Jack change. He pushed me down. He changed. I saw him change. Into a coyote. Billy's right."

Nora watched my face but didn't say anything.

"You don't believe me!"

"I believe Coyote Jack came after you. He followed me a few days ago. Came too close. I threw a rock at him and he took off."

"You don't understand. He changed. You've got to be careful."

"You want to leave?" she said. "We could leave. Today."

"I can't go. What would my mother think?"

"You're old enough to decide for yourself," she said. "We'll go to Vancouver. We'll say we're sisters."

I laughed a little because we looked so unalike.

"We'll become nurses," she said. "Or get jobs in the factories. We'll take care of each other."

"No," I said, and when I said it Nora became suddenly angry.

"You don't love me," she said.

"Sure I do."

"No. Nobody loves me."

Nora closed the window before I could say anything more and ran around the side of the house to follow the trail beside the root cellar. I closed my eyes and when I opened them again, he was there, at the window. I screamed and backed against the wall, knocking against the coyote skins. Outside the window, Coyote Jack held up his hand in a wave or a threat.

40

SOMETHING IN ME TURNED. I got angry, angrier than I've ever
been in my life. I yelled at him and ran at the window.

"Get away!" I said. "Get the hell out of here!"

Coyote Jack disappeared as soon as I went for the window, but I
went on yelling at him anyway, and kept on yelling as I took down my
brother's rifle, loaded it, and pocketed a box of shells. I yelled as I
threw a halter on Cherry and jumped on her, bareback. She pranced
sideways across the yard, and I had to kick her to get her up the road. I
whipped her side with the reins until she was galloping and went on
whipping her as we followed Blood Road, then the old Indian trail,
ducking branches. I rode her all the way to Coyote Jack's cabin, and
left her standing there free. I carried the gun as my brother carried it
and pounded on the door to Coyote Jack's cabin. He didn't come to the
door. I pushed it open and there he was, sitting on a little neatly made
cot, with his head in his hands. He looked up as I came in. I pointed the
gun at him.

"You stay away from me," I said. "So help me God I'll shoot you."

Coyote Jack held out his hands, palms up, and looked at me. That
was the first and only time I ever got a really good look at him. He was
a little man and had keen blue eyes rimmed in red and watery — the
eyes of an old man, though he was the Swede's son and couldn't have
been more than forty-five.

"You have no idea," said Coyote Jack. "I try to stop it. I try to keep
to myself."

I lowered the gun a little.

"Bertha says you've got some ghost thing riding you," I said. "I didn't believe it before. But I don't want any part of it. You understand me? You quit following me. You stay away."

Coyote Jack covered his face with both hands and sobbed. I'd seen my father cry over music, but even then only a few tears had rolled down his face. This man sobbed, his shoulders heaved, and he cried out. It made me so angry I wanted to shoot him there, as he sat on his cot. Instead I backed up to the door, still pointing the gun at him.

I said, "Stay away. Just stay away!"

He didn't look up. He went on sobbing. I closed the door behind me and found that Cherry had taken off on me. It was only then that I became afraid again — the anger had carried me. I ran home convinced that Coyote Jack would come after me, appear on the trail as he had done before, take some form, and eat me as I was now convinced he'd eaten Sarah Kemp.

It was that night, Christmas night, that Coyote Jack hung himself, I'm sure of it, though it was a week before anyone thought to go looking for him. Scared to death and chased by shadows, I had run from Coyote Jack's cabin all the way down the mountain and down Blood Road and across the field to the hired hands' cabin. Home wasn't safe. Billy seemed the only safety offered to me. So I had run to him. He was there all right, tying up his pant legs for the night, but so was Dennis. It was Dennis who opened the door when I knocked. He was wearing only a pair of wool trousers and a sleeveless undershirt so thin I could see his dark nipples through it. A man didn't show his chest then any more than a woman would now. Dennis might as well have been standing there naked.

"Well, my girlfriend's here," he said. "Sure your mum don't mind?"

"I've come to see Billy," I said.

"Billy?"

I waved for Billy to come outside and turned my back on Dennis's nakedness. Billy threw on a jack shirt and his rattlesnake hat and met me outside over by the fire. I sat on the log I'd sat on at Halloween and hugged myself. The first wave of panic was wearing off, leaving me cold. Billy sat next to me, so our arms were touching. We huddled together like that as I told him what I thought I'd seen, as night closed in on us.

"That wasn't (fuck) smart — chasing him up there," said Billy.

"What am I going to do?" I said.

"I figure (shit) you're safe for tonight," said Billy. "He's not so different (fuck) from them coyotes you catch in your snares. (Shit) He's okay if it's him doing the (shit) chasing, but if he gets chased, then he gets scared (fuck) and stays away, for a while anyway. You'll be okay tonight, but (shit) we got to do something soon."

My mother was still milking when I reached the barn. I took up my stumping powder box and started in on the cow beside her.

When she saw me come in the barn, she said, "Thank God! Cherry came back by herself. I'd thought you'd been hurt."

"I fell off in the bush," I said. "She took off on me. Something spooked her."

"Where were you?" she said.

"Just out riding."

"I didn't see you go."

"Do I have to tell you everything?" I said.

"I'd just like to know," she said. "In case something happens."

I grunted, but my mother didn't say any more.

After I'd finished separating the cream and cleaning out the machine, I took my brother's rifle down from the rack by the stove. Mum was sitting in her rocker, gluing Bertha Moses's Christmas card to a new page in the scrapbook.

"Where are you going with that?" she said.

"Cleaning it," I said.

I took the gun and a second lamp to my room and lit both lamps so there were no shadows but the ones under my bed. I loaded the gun, locked my bedroom window, and fastened a blanket over it. I tucked my chair under the doorknob to keep anyone from coming in. Then I sat on my bed with my back against the wall and the gun in my hands and waited.

41

BILLY CAME IN for breakfast on Boxing Day wearing a bloom I'd never seen on a soul before or since. He didn't say a word, not even a cuss word, but a grin stayed on his face for the whole meal. He shook his head at some thought he'd had and laughed out loud. Sleepy and relieved that no nightmares had visited me, I grinned back at him and that only got him laughing more. Dennis chewed his food and turned from Billy to me, from me to Billy, and then raised his eyebrows at my mother.

"What's so funny?" she said.

"Nothing," I said. "Nothing at all."

Dennis caught my eye and looked a question at me, but my mother saw that and started talking about what needed to be done for the day. She had Dennis out of the house and cleaning calf stalls before Billy had even finished his eggs. She went out there with Dennis herself and gave him a list of jobs that would keep him busy from now 'til the new year.

After she'd gone outside, Billy took my hand, and said, "He's gone."

"Who?" I said.

"Coyote. He didn't come last night. He didn't take me over. I think you scared him off. Maybe for good."

"Coyote Jack?"

"No, no. Coyote. Last night he didn't come. Listen! I'm not swearing! He's gone!"

"I don't know."

"You got to believe me. You saw Coyote riding Coyote Jack, shifting him around. That's what Coyote does. He made me his house, but now he's gone!"

"I don't know what I saw," I said. "It feels like a nightmare. The whole thing, one long nightmare."

"Well, all I know is last night I got the first good night's sleep in a long while."

Whatever it was that had haunted Billy and tried to track me down didn't turn up again that winter, and neither did Coyote Jack. No one saw him lurking around the edges of their fields or trying to steal a chicken from their coops, or inching open the doors to their root cellars for a taste of strawberry jam. It was New Year's Eve before the Swede finally got suspicious enough to go up to Coyote Jack's cabin, and what he found then hanging from a beam was half eaten by maggots. It was these strange facts — rot on a body in all that cold, maggots at a time of year you couldn't find a fly if you wanted to — that the Swede came back to, over and again, when he sat in our kitchen on New Year's Eve, shaking and drinking my mother's medicinal rum.

"I thought he might want to share a drink with me," he said. "A drink with the old man, to bring in the year. And there he was hanging from the ceiling. He must've been there for a week or more. But rotting, can you believe it? Frozen solid and rotting. Full of maggots this time of year. I never seen the likes. I can't believe it. I can't believe it."

More than a week after the Swede found his son dead and raising a stink, Coyote Jack was buried by the church he'd never once set foot in, in the grave next to Sarah Kemp. The only ones there were the Swede, Bertha Moses and her girls, me and Mum, and the old men who sat around the stove in Bouchard and Belcham's. The old men came because they remembered Coyote Jack when he was a boy, and it was their job to fill in the graves. Because of the rot in the body, Coyote Jack had been shipped by train to the nearest crematorium in Kamloops. Cremations were so rare then that nobody knew what to do with the urn containing his ashes, so it was buried in one of the leaf-filled graves that had been dug by the old men in the fall. Those same old men lowered the urn into the leaves in the grave next to Sarah Kemp's and then filled in the grave, leaves and all, with dirt.

When everyone else went back into church for the lunch that followed, Billy and I stayed behind and watched the old men shovel dirt into Coyote Jack's grave.

"You think he would have killed himself," I said, "if I hadn't gone up there?"

"Don't go blaming yourself for that," said Billy. "He's been crazy a long time."

"I don't know."

"You've got nothing to be scared of no more," said Billy. "Nothing."

"You think that Coyote thing is gone for good?"

"I don't know. I think maybe he rode on Coyote Jack's back into the spirit land. Or maybe he found somebody else to live with. I keep waiting on him, scared, you know, thinking he might come back. But I woke up Boxing Day and I didn't smell him no more. That dog smell was gone. Now the swearing is gone. The tics and scratching are going. Every day what's left of him fades away. I'm thinking maybe nothing's chasing you no more."

I kicked at the frozen dirt and held myself.

"You still don't believe any of this, do you?" said Billy. "After everything you seen."

"I don't know," I said.

"You see it with your own eyes and you don't believe it."

"I'm not sure what I saw."

"Well, I guess it don't matter much anymore."

We left the old men to cover the remains of our nightmare and went inside to eat. When I saw that Nora wasn't in the building, I took my plate and went outside to find her. As soon as I stepped out onto the front steps of the church again, I heard her bell necklace. I followed the sound of bells quietly, thinking to sneak up on her, and turned the corner on the back of the church that was pretty much hidden by bushes. Nora was in those bushes all right. Dennis was holding her there. His face was buried in her neck. Her western shirt was undone, and Dennis was cupping her breast and moving his hips against her. Nora's eyes were closed as I stumbled on them, but she opened them slowly, luxuriantly, as she had opened them to look at me on the blanket in the winter house. When she saw me, her eyes opened wide.

I turned and ran back into the church as Nora pulled away from Dennis and pulled her blouse closed. She called after me, "Beth, wait!"

But I wouldn't wait for her. I found myself standing in the church with everything circling around me. Billy came up and took my arm. "You all right?" he asked.

"I've got to leave," I said.

Nora was sitting on the outside steps and Dennis was standing with her when we came out, but I ignored them both and kept my back to them as we drove out of town. Once home, Billy let me alone and I ran straight for my room and closed the door. Some time later, Nora came after me, too quick, so quick I didn't have time to guard myself. She banged on the window and started talking, though I refused to open it and turned my back on her.

"He said he could help me get out of here," she called. "He's talking about leaving again, joining up, or getting a factory job. I thought maybe we could go with him. Get away. He says he's got some friends in Vancouver. He said he could get us some money."

"You took money?" I said.

"Not yet."

"He's family."

"He's a cousin. Cousins marry."

I opened the window and she climbed in. "You going to marry him?" I asked.

"No, no. I want us to go someplace, you and me. It seemed like the only way I could go someplace. He said he would help."

"If you messed around with him."

"If he and I was friends," she said.

"Friends?" I said.

"Look at you! Stepping out with a mongoloid."

My lightning arm struck out and slapped her square across the face. She breathed in sharp and held her cheek. I could see the water stinging her eyes. I looked down at the palm of my hand. It was red, I could see that, but it didn't hurt. I didn't feel anything. I slumped down onto the floor, holding the dead lightning arm. It slowly tingled back to life.

After a while, I said, "I'm sorry."

"That was wrong. What I said. I didn't mean that."

"Billy's not stupid," I said. "He's smarter about a lot of things than Dennis."

"Tell me you wouldn't have gone with Dennis if you had the chance."

"I wouldn't."

"Look me in the eye and tell me."

I turned and looked her in the blue eye and then the green. "I wouldn't," I said.

She looked away quickly and leaned back against the wall. "You're lying," she said. "I saw you kiss him."

"You watching me all the time?" I said.

"Some of the time."

"You got no right."

"You go walking in the bush and there's lots of things watching," she said. "You want privacy, stay home."

"I have no privacy here either, and you know it."

Nora grunted. We sat stone silent for a while longer and then the idea grabbed hold of me.

"You went after Dennis, didn't you?" I said. "You went after him so I wouldn't get him first. You were scared he and me would go out and you'd be out of the picture."

"That's crap!" she said.

"You knew he liked me. You were jealous."

"I got nothing to be jealous about," she said. "You're just some girl. I don't need you. I don't need nobody. Plenty of boys after me."

"Fine. Go off with Dennis. He's nothing but a bum Indian. You neither. You fit together. Hope you're very happy together."

"Fine."

"Fine."

She crossed her arms, and when I found myself crossing mine, I held my hands in my lap instead. After a time, I said, "You like him better than me?"

"He smells like a goat," she said. "They all smell like goats."

"They all act like Goat," I said. "Only got one thing in their heads."

"Sometimes I only got one thing in my head," she said.

I looked at her sideways. She smiled at me with her head down and ran her finger along my leg. I shook my head. She put her hand back in her lap.

"I don't want Dennis," she said. "I want you and me to go away. Get factory jobs."

"So how come you went with him?" I said.

"To get you back."

"So you were jealous."

"I wasn't jealous."

"Well, what are you?" I said.

"Mad."

She harrumphed. I saw I'd crossed my arms just like her despite myself. I stood up. "I've got to do chores," I said, and left the house. As I brought the cows into the barn, Dennis ran across the field from the cabin and caught up to me out of breath.

"I'm sorry about what happened," he said. "Really." When I kept on ignoring him, he said, "I thought you weren't interested no more. I mean I never got a minute alone with you."

"Yeah, well."

"You don't have to live here," said Dennis. "There's other places. Nora says you're talking about leaving."

"Nora told you that?"

"I'm leaving," said Dennis. "I've been making plans. I've been saving money."

"If you go, how are we going to run the farm?"

"I promised Granny I'd stick around 'til your father gets out of that place, and I will. I wouldn't leave your mum like that. But we don't have to be around when your dad gets home. We can get out of here, for good."

"I have no money," I said.

"We could work that out," said Dennis. "We could be friends."

"Friends! Just leave me alone!"

I thought I was marching back to the house, but I hit Blood Road before realizing where I was. I stood there breathing hard for a long time, until I saw Nora coming down the road from the reserve. So I waited on her. She carried the red carpetbag stuffed so full it wouldn't close. When she saw me, she stopped and looked as if she were thinking of cutting off through the bush, but she didn't. She kept on coming.

"Where are you going?" I said.

"Does it matter?"

"It matters."

Nora pushed back the sleeves of her jacket and showed me both arms. She had cut herself yet again. Blood dripped onto the snow on the road.

"This place is going to kill me," she said. "Nothing here but this."

"You're not leaving 'cause of me," I said.

Nora shrugged. "Some of it's you," she said. "But mostly Mum's gone crazy. I guess she seen a little of what you saw at the church."

"Where you going to go?"

"Vancouver, maybe Calgary. I'll see which train I can get on. I'll find work there. I got a little money from my uncles."

"They know about it?"

"They know they've got empty wallets," said Nora.

"Jeez, Nora," I said.

"You going to come with me?"

I shook my head and looked at the carpetbag she carried.

"What're you staying here for?" she said. "Your father's coming back. You know he is."

"It's home," I said. "I don't know anything else."

"You're never going to if you don't step out."

"I got things to do here first," I said. "I'll go when I'm ready. Anyway, Mum needs me now."

Nora fingered the bell necklace.

"I got to go," she said. "Before she sends someone out to find me."

"You write?"

"Sure, I'll write. I'll find a place. Then maybe you can come."

"Maybe," I said.

She touched my hair and smoothed her hand down my face, then adjusted the bundle on her shoulder and started walking down the road. She turned once and waved. I couldn't believe then that she wouldn't be back the next day. Spots of blood dropped from her arm to the snow, creating a trail behind her, and when she was so far down the road I could no longer hear her bells, the Swede's three-legged dog jumped from the bush and followed her.

Filthy Billy slid out from the bush around the swamp and pushed through the snow to reach me. He put his hand on my shoulder and we watched together as Nora disappeared down Blood Road.

"She'll get into some trouble," said Billy.

"Maybe," I said.

"She got money?"

"I don't know."

"You going to leave too?"

"No," I said, and his grip on me got stronger.

42

SPRING CAME on Turtle Valley like a change of mind. One day, we were tugging rocks from their concave beds in the frozen field and throwing them on the stoneboat. The next, weeds were breaking through that same field, birds were challenging each other with their voices for nesting places, and the painted turtles were straining across Blood Road. When spring hit Turtle Valley you felt it in your step. A load was lifted off. Moving got easier. It was like an old body had sloughed off and left a new, sleeker skin, like those black lizards in our yard that shed themselves. That spring it hit Billy most of all. Once he shed his winter clothes, I don't think I saw him once without a smile. Of course he wasn't swearing anymore or scratching, but that had been gone for a while before spring hit. It was something else. His skin shone in the way leaves do after a good rain. It was as if he'd been remade, as if that old Billy had been sloughed off and he'd grown a new skin. His laughter made him a pleasure to be around, a joy to talk to. Then again, maybe it was I who had done the changing, like those lizards, got a fresh pair of eye skins to look through, so I could see him better. Whatever the case, he was different. Nobody, not even Dennis, called him Filthy anymore.

"Beautiful day," said Billy.

Billy and I were cleaning out the chicken coop, loading a year's worth of poop onto the stoneboat to spread it on the field. Dennis was already out harrowing the field. It seemed like only yesterday that we'd been racing against the snow to bring in the flax. My clothes stank, Billy stank, the air stank of chicken manure, and I wasn't thinking of it as a beautiful day until he'd said it, but when he did, I had to admit it was. We both leaned on our shovels in the middle of that stinking chicken coop and looked around us. Clear sky as high and purposeful as a cathedral. Grass poking up through the brown. Chickens were scattered all over the yard, chasing the black lizards. The robins were back, singing at us from the trees around the house, waiting for us to get out of the coop so they could get at the worms. One didn't wait. He swooped down, pecked a worm out of the mess near our feet, and flitted up over the chicken wire, taking the worm with him.

A day like that, a day when the world was shedding its skin and growing a new one so fast you could see it happening, my mother had kept me busy with the jobs of making paper and cleaning the chicken coop, and without telling me what she was up to had gone into town with the cream to pick up my father. I didn't know that then, as I cleaned the coop with Billy and admired the day, didn't expect a thing.

"How about you beg off going to church with your mother Sunday," said Billy. "You and me, we'll pack a picnic, hike up over the mountain, see if we can't find a wild horse yet."

"And Dennis?" I said.

"He don't need to know where we're going," he said.

I looked over at Billy. He wasn't looking at me as he did his asking. He turned his back a little to me and watched the robins. He was wearing his denims, trousers and shirt, and he'd replaced the rattle-snake skin for a red bandana around the band of his hat. His sleeves were rolled up past his elbow, so I could see the tender skin at the crook of his arm.

"I'd like that," I said. "I'll make a pound cake."

He grinned, but he didn't turn to look at me. He watched the robin that had flown into the coop. It was sitting on the roof, still fighting to eat the worm.

"Hear your mum got a letter from Dan, eh?" said Billy. "Says he's got an army placement on the coast."

"I miss him," I said. "I wish he'd come home. I wish he'd never left."

"He'll be just fine," said Billy. "Just fine."

"Wish he'd write me," I said.

"He isn't much of a writer," said Billy. "Not like you. You know that."

I grunted because when Dan had needed a letter written I had often done it for him, and because that spring I had acquired an urge to write everything down, set it down so I wouldn't lose it. That morning, before cleaning the coop, I had made paper for my own scrapbook because my mother had refused to buy me one when I pleaded with her. My scrapbook wouldn't be a collection of odds and ends as my mother's was. It would be a book of words, my words. Billy was right about my mother's scrapbook. Everyone needed a private place, a safe place in which to sort things out. I had come to understand that my mother didn't put her words in her scrapbook because she had spoken them all to her dead mother, and would keep on speaking them to her. It was craziness, talking to a dead woman, but she spoke the words, got them out of her mouth, and that was what mattered. As Billy said, if you could only get things out of yourself — speak them, or write them down, or paste bits of them into a scrapbook — then you could sort things out. I only had Billy, now that Nora was gone, to speak my thoughts to. But there are some things you can't tell the man who courts you, just as there were some things I could never let Nora know. Nora hadn't written. Bertha hadn't heard from her and never would. She had disappeared as surely as if she had stepped off the earth. Perhaps she had. Whatever the case, now that she was gone, I was determined to put my words down on paper, so I would never gabble to a dead woman as my mother did.

So I made my own scrapbook. My mother had written out instructions on how to make paper in her scrapbook, on a sample of paper she made from old letters and rose petals. I needed a screen (my mother used an old picture frame with wire mesh stretched across it and nailed in place), couching cloths (squares of cotton a foot or more across), and something to make the paper pulp with, and in. My mother made paper from anything with a lot of fiber in it — potato plants, corn husks, flowers, bits of fabric. But most often she remade new paper out of old, from salvaged wrapping, newspapers, letters, and catalogues, as I had that morning, before I cleaned out the chicken coop with Billy.

I tore the paper into strips and soaked them in water, and then mashed the paper back into the pulp it had started out as, with a potato masher. When my mother used plant matter — like the dry stalks of potato plants — she boiled it first, until it was soft, and then mashed it. I placed the pulp mess into the washtub in which we took baths, which was half filled with water. I dipped the screen down into the bath and brought it up from the water, flat, so the paper pulp caught on the wire mesh and the water drained through it. This pulp became the paper.

But I had to dry it first. To do that, I made a mound of folded newspapers and wet it thoroughly with water. Over this, I placed one of those dampened couching cloths. I took that screen filled with paper pulp, turned it over the mound, and kind of rolled the paper off the screen and onto the cotton.

The paper now looked like a layer of porridge. I smoothed another damp couching cloth over that mess and went on stacking sheets of pulp and couching cloth until I had ten or so sheets. I took this wet stack outside to the porch, put it down on the porch floor, and placed a flat board over it and stood on that, to drive the excess water out. After I had squashed the water from the paper, I spread the sheets out on a blanket on the grass to dry in the sun as Billy and I cleaned out the coop. Once they were almost dry, but still a little damp, I would iron the pieces of paper smooth.

As Billy and I left the robin to his worm, and turned back to the chore at hand, I saw my mother and father driving down Blood Road. My mother drove slowly because of the turtles that spooked the horses. My father was nothing but a slumped black figure in the buggy beside my mother, but I knew him at that distance.

Billy and I were waiting for them in the yard as they drove in. When my mother jumped down to tie the horses, my father went on sitting in the buggy and only stared at his feet. Despite the warmth of the day, the buggy blanket covered his lap.

I called, "Dad!" but my mother intercepted.

"Move slowly, talk quietly," she said. "Don't expect much."

He looked up, and I saw recognition there, but he went back to staring at his feet. Billy held my arm, held me back from my father. Then he went up to him himself, approached slowly and deliberately, as I'd seen him approach that deer. When he reached the buggy he kept a bit of distance from my father and talked softly. Whatever he said got a brief smile.

Spring hadn't touched my father, hadn't changed him for the better. He came out of that place looking worse than he had when he went in. He'd lost weight. The clothes he'd worn the night he burned the Swede's barn were loose on him. He was pale from too many months cooped up inside, and his hands were as smooth as a city man's. He was tired, weak. He needed help from my mother and Billy to walk from the buggy to the house.

My mother sat my father down in his chair in the parlor and brought the ottoman close so he could rest his feet, and that's where he stayed for the next three days. He slept there at night and sat there through the day listening to the same Caruso record over and over. He seemed to have lost his ability to shed a tear, or else the music had lost meaning for him. He stared at the wall, or flipped through one of the big war books my mother had placed on the table beside him. He took the plates of food we brought him but ate little. Although he talked to Billy, whispered to him, he said little to my mother, and nothing to me for the whole of those three days.

The day my father returned Dennis disappeared. He packed his few things, said goodbye to Billy and Bertha, but left without saying a thing to my mother and me. Even Bertha couldn't talk him out of leaving this time.

"He wouldn't come to the house," Billy told me. "Afraid of your dad, I guess. And I think he kind of knew, I mean, about you and me. He's going to hop a freight to Vernon. Join up. See the world, eh?"

When Billy later told my mother that Dennis was gone, she and I were milking the cows.

"Well, that's best for him," said my mother. "We could use his help, but I'm sure we'll manage."

"He said to say goodbye," said Billy. "And to say thanks. He said don't worry about this last week's pay. He says he owes you that for leaving without notice."

"That was kind of him," she said. "But when you hear from him, let me know and I'll forward the money."

My mother stood up from her milking stool and wiped her hands. "Do me a favor, Billy. Tell John that Dennis is gone again. You have a way with him. While you're at it, tell him about that tractor we're looking to buy. And the cow you had to shoot last month. It was one of his favorites."

Billy did this for my mother, and more. He became the bearer of bad news, a translator between my mother and my father, a way past the dispute that neither of my parents acknowledged, not with words. Billy could get my father talking with that sweet way of his, tricking him with his grin and self-effacement into believing that nothing was really that bad, nothing was worth getting all steamed up about, and for Billy, after all he'd been through, truly there was nothing worth worrying about. Life was good.

"We were late planting last year," said my father. "Then that storm last spring cleared out the flax crop, nearly wiped us out. I don't want that happening again."

"We're already on it," said Billy. "Got the oats planted. Dennis harrowed the cornfield before he left. I'll get at the flax today. It's going to be a good year. I can feel it."

I was listening in, putting together a tray of tea and cakes for my father, as he and Billy talked in the parlor. Billy said something I didn't quite catch and then laughed his high sweet laugh that made me smile and shake my head. Then he was in the kitchen with me, tugging at my apron strings. He glanced to make sure my father wasn't looking and ran his hand down my cheek before leaving the house.

But my father must have seen or sensed something because as I put down a tray of tea and oatcakes beside him three days after his arrival — three days of him not so much as saying hello — my father ran his hand up the back of my legs under my skirt. I spun around and stepped back and held my lightning arm in check, though it wanted to slap him. Instead I pointed at him, stuck my finger right in his face so he sat back in surprise.

"You never touch me again," I said. "Keep your goddamned hands off me. You're my father, for Christ's sake."

I surprised myself with my cussing and expected him to yell me down, or throw off his weakness and push me against the wall. But I held my ground and kept my eyes on him, and he did nothing of the kind. He began to cry, hard, as Coyote Jack had sobbed the day he'd hung himself. A man crying was no small thing. It confused me. I didn't know what to do. I removed the record my father had been playing night and day for the past three days, but that had no effect. I offered him a cup of tea, but he refused, didn't once look at it. When I put my hand on his shoulder, my father went on sobbing and that made me angry just as Coyote Jack had made me angry. I yelled at him to stop. I kicked the table beside him and when that only made him cry harder, I slammed out of the house.

My mother was crossing the yard. She said, "What's the matter?"

I threw up my hands, and said, "I don't know," and my mother rushed into the house and that began another harried three days because it took that long for my father to stop crying.

My mother talked to him, pleaded with him, paged through her scrapbook, looking for some cure to comfort him with and, finding none, she paged through it again. She took the cream into town and bought Dr. Chase's Nerve Food and fed him that. She baked him a pound cake that he wouldn't eat, poured him cups of tea he wouldn't drink, and made him poultices for his chest which he wouldn't allow her to apply. When his nose grew dry from blowing, he pushed her hand away when she tried to dab petroleum jelly around his nostrils. He yelled at her to leave him alone and that only made her fuss around him more. Exhausted by three days of frantic caring, my mother finally exploded. When my father slapped the oatcakes my mother offered from her hand, she slapped him back, hard, across the face.

"Enough of this foolishness," she said. "Quit acting like a child."

My father held his cheek, sobbed once, and that was the last of his crying. He withdrew again and wouldn't talk to anyone, not even Billy. When another three days of his silence had passed and the parlor was taking on the foul smell of a sick room, my mother rubbed her forehead, and said, "He needs some air."

Together my mother, Billy, and I coerced, carried, and pushed my father into the democrat. We didn't go far, just to the first slough past our driveway where the turtles crossed in such numbers that there seemed to be a moving, living blanket crossing the road. My mother brought the horses up and we all sat in the buggy for a while, watching the turtles swarm around us. After a time Billy and I jumped off the wagon and started helping turtles up to the red sand bank, where they would lay their eggs.

It's funny how a place will stir memories. A certain hill, the smell of red dirt, the wind of a road through swamplands, will bring a time tumbling back on you. While I picked turtles off that stretch of Blood

Road with my bracelet jingling on my arm, I watched Nora leave all over again. She was walking away from me, down the stretch of road. A trail of blood chased her. As she turned to wave, her necklace jingled, catching the light and catching the eye of crows that came swooping over her head. I got lost in the sight of Nora, the remembrance of her. Then she was gone and Billy was standing behind me, holding my shoulders.

"What you seeing?" he said.

"Nora."

"She coming?"

"No, no, just remembering."

"You glad you stayed?" he said.

"I'm glad I didn't go with her."

I turned to look at my mother and father sitting there in the democrat, watching Billy holding on to my shoulders. My father huddled into himself. My mother had seen Billy and me all right, but she wasn't going to say anything, I could see that. She lifted her chin and breathed out. What could she say? I was sixteen now; my birthday had passed in February with only a slice of cake and a cup of tea for hullabaloo. Still watching her, I reached over and held Billy's hand and he held it right back. My mother looked away, at the turtles, and got down from the buggy. She went around to my father's side to help him down from the democrat. They stood there in the middle of Blood Road watching the turtles with their backs to Billy and me. After a time my mother reached over to my father, and he took her hand in his fist and held on to it for dear life.

Index to Recipes and Remedies